THE BRITISH GOVERNMENT AND
THE SPANISH CIVIL WAR, 1936–1939

THE BRITISH GOVERNMENT AND THE SPANISH CIVIL WAR, 1936–1939

Jill Edwards

Foreword by
Hugh Thomas

For my Family

First published 1979 by
THE MACMILLAN PRESS LTD
London and Basingstoke
Associated companies in Delhi
Dublin Hong Kong Johannesburg Lagos
Melbourne New York Singapore Tokyo

Printed and bound in Great Britan by
Redwood Burn Limited
Trowbridge & Esher

British Library Cataloguing in Publication Data

Edwards, Jill
    The British government and the Spanish civil war,
    1936–1939
    1. Great Britain – Politics and government –
    1936–1945   2. Spain – History – Civil War,
    1936–1939 – Foreign public opinion, British
    I. Title
    946.081   DA586

    ISBN   0–333–24260–2

Contents

List of Tables

Foreword

People began to try and write in a serious historical manner about the Spanish civil war in the late 1950s and early 1960s. At that time, a great deal of good historical writing had already appeared on the subject of nazi Germany and other regimes which had foundered in 1945. Indeed, ever since 1945, the 1930s had in most countries seemed reasonably good territory for the reflective historian. Spain was rather behind the rest of the world in this respect: the people who had won the civil war in 1939 were still in power in Madrid, and Spain itself seemed a hidden land where enquiry into the recent past was impossible. Then a few histories began to appear, some of them doing what they could to chart out the problems. By the end of the 1960s, archives began to be generally open, particularly those of foreign governments, and including the British ones for the period of the war. Jill Edwards, who went to Reading as a student in 1970, is the first person, I think, to have been systematically through the rich hoard of material in the Public Record Office on this theme.

Now the Spanish civil war was in origin a Spanish conflict. The bulk of the fighting was done by Spaniards. When the cloud of war passed away, to other countries, the Spaniards were left alone facing the memory of the tragedy and its legacy, and it has been Spaniards who, in the years since General Franco died in 1975, have been so adept at reconstructing a new political life for themselves. Nevertheless, the actual course of the Spanish civil war was largely affected by what outside powers thought and did. Or did not do. For while Germany, Italy and Russia, with France and Portugal not very far behind them, were positively concerned, Britain's role was largely an important negative one. Yet she was then the paramount power in the Atlantic and Mediterranean, her strength depending on a reserve of naval capacity which was then more formidable than that of any other nation of the region, and her interests sharpened by military and economic concern for the future of Spain and Portugal. How were these interests defined? How were they articulated? Who did the business of articulation?

All these and other interesting problems could only be partially answered, if at all, until the archives were open to researchers. Dr Edwards' patient and methodical study shows where polemical journalists and even polemical historians have left the right track and careered off on their own into a bush, colourful at times, of their own making. Of the different themes treated in this book this is especially true of Dr Edwards' consideration of the origins of non-intervention, about which more rubbish has probably been written than (I must choose my words carefully, since it is a wide field) on any other matter connected with the Spanish civil war.

In many respects, this book represents a victory for the idea that diplomatic history counts. I daresay that, in the generation after 1914, too much attention was paid to the details of diplomatic affairs, as if they alone could give an answer to the shattering breakdown between states that the wars of 1914 and 1939 meant, and in whose shadow we still live. Now, diplomatic history is rather unfashionable. The history of parties and of social conditions, of ideas and of technology, seem more fruitful fields, explaining the course of human events, than the history of how states interreact. Yet the unpalatable truth must be faced: foreign offices and diplomats, industrialists and bankers do affect events more than either dukes or dustmen. The mechanism whereby foreign policies are evolved needs careful study. For it is as a result of their decisions that thousands of people live or die. This is particularly the case in respect of countries such as Spain, which had, by the 20th century, come to realise that their internal politics is often determined by events beyond the Pyrenees.

Admittedly, Dr Edwards has not written a diplomatic monograph of the old sort which simply related what one chancellor said to another in one foreign ministry or another. She has been careful enough to investigate, where she can, the influence that powerful pressure groups, such as the City, had on policy. She is perfectly aware of the role of propaganda in modern war and the part played by the press and by foreign correspondents. She has been equally adept at distentangling the complicated matters raised for international law by this war, especially the matters affecting the law at sea. The significance of Spain to the British chiefs of staff, and their own concerns for British security, are also well covered. It is obvious, therefore, that in the future, students of the part played by Britain in the Spanish war will have to begin with Dr Edwards' book. Doubtless, like all good students, reading any good book, they will find a good deal with which to disagree and from which to continue their work. But, if they are honest, they will be grateful, I think, to Dr Edwards for starting them off on a subject which does not permit of easy or simple conclusions.

Acknowledgements

It would not have been possible to complete this study without the help and co-operation of many people, and to all those who were in any way involved in this project I wish to express my deep appreciation. For their kindness in answering my enquiries or allowing me access to private papers I am especially grateful to Lady Vansittart, the late Sir Laurence Collier, Sir Walter St. C. Roberts, Sir Evelyn Shuckburgh, the Rt. Hon. George Strauss, M.P., Mr Stephen Spender and Mr Donald Maclean. For permission to read or quote from the private collections listed in the bibliography my thanks are due to the University of Birmingham, Cambridge University Library, Churchill College, Cambridge, Corpus Christi College, Oxford, the BBC Written Archives Centre, the Royal Institute of International Affairs, and to the Controller of H.M. Stationery Office by whose permission quotations from the papers in the Public Record Office appear.

In particular I wish to thank Professor Hugh Thomas for suggesting the need for research into this subject, and for his helpful guidance and kind encouragement. I am also much indebted to Dr Paul Preston for reading my manuscript and offering constructive criticism. For advice on specific topics I should like to thank Admiral Sir Peter Gretton, Professor David Williams, Mr Philip Knightly, Dr Neville Waites, Mr Charles Harvey and Miss Teresa Lawlor. Finally my thanks are owed to Mrs Mava Quinlan whose typing brought order from chaos, and to Mrs Pamela Payne who designed the map on p. 55.

Note on Sources

Research for this study has been conducted primarily into the documents available in the Public Record Office, including Cabinet, Foreign Office, Admiralty and Non-Intervention Committee papers. Regarding these, several points should be made. First, the Cabinet Conclusions give at best only a brief summary of what has passed at a Cabinet meeting. In contrast the General Correspondence of the Foreign Office can often provide invaluable background material which clarifies ministerial attitudes and decisions. But here, too, caution is needed, since some volumes of documents are not complete, many folios remaining unreleased. As it is not always possible to establish the reason for the retention of the material, its relevance cannot be assessed.

Some reference has been made to published foreign documents, but this is essentially a study of British Government attitudes as revealed from official British documents. However, besides these, three other main groups of archival material have been studied. These are the private papers of ministers and diplomats, the comprehensive collection of foreign and British newspaper items housed until recently in the Press Library of the Royal Institute of International Affairs, and the Parliamentary debates of the House of Commons.

Regrettably less fruitful than those sources are the leading memoirs of the period. Certainly the Spanish Civil War dominated the international and domestic scene for Britain between July 1936 and February 1939 to a far greater extent than might be supposed from the memoirs of Cabinet Ministers. Those of Lord Avon are the most notable exception, and some diplomats are more forthcoming on this issue, although posthumously published diaries of men such as Sir Alexander Cadogan and Lord Harvey remain the most informative records from that source. Notable for their disregard of the Spanish question, and aptly entitled *Old Men Forget*, are the memoirs of Duff Cooper, First Lord of the Admiralty from May 1937 to 27 October 1938, whose Department was one of those most closely concerned with events in Spain.

Yet neglect of this subject, which extends also to secondary sources, does not accord with the prominent position occupied by the Spanish Civil War in the deliberations of the Cabinet during that period. Between July 1936 and March 1938 Spain was discussed at no less than seventy-five per cent of Cabinet meetings. Even during the last year of the Civil War when attention was focused on the plight of Czechoslovakia and the growing German threat, the Spanish question could not be put aside and occupied attention during at least half the Cabinet meetings in those months. A similar point can be made concerning the Foreign Office documents for the period. The documents for Spain in 1935, for example, have been bound in 14 files, but for 1936 there are approximately 77 files, for 1937 126 files and for 1938 96 files. However much official memoirs may appear to belie the fact, Spain was therefore a matter of major concern to the British Government during the three vital years leading up to World War II.

The reader should note that in speaking of the anti-Republican forces, the terms rebel, insurgent or Nationalist have been used as thought appropriate. In accordance with international law, the British Government and the more serious sections of the Press used the term 'rebel' during the first three to four months of the war. After November 1936 those forces were designated 'the insurgents' until the summer of 1937, when it was felt more politic to refer to General Franco's forces as 'the Nationalists'.

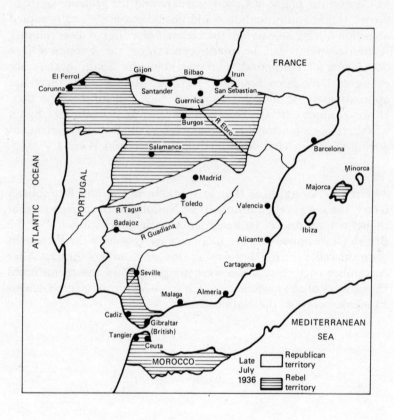

FRANCE

El Ferrol
Corunna
Gijon
Bilbao
Irun
Santander
San Sebastian
Guernica
Burgos
R Ebro
Barcelona
Salamanca
Madrid
Majorca
Minorca
PORTUGAL
ATLANTIC OCEAN
R Tagus
Toledo
Valencia
Badajoz
R Guadiana
Ibiza
Alicante
Cartagena
Seville
Malaga
Almeria
Cadiz
Gibraltar (British)
Tangier
Ceuta
MOROCCO
MEDITERRANEAN SEA

Late July 1936

Republican territory

Rebel territory

1 Britain and the Origins of Non-Intervention

Advising the Foreign Secretary, Mr Anthony Eden, as to British interests in the Spanish Civil War just six weeks after the military revolt of July 1936, a senior official in the Foreign Office presented the following clear alternatives:

> ... an extreme right victory is likely to be embarrassing in respect of our foreign policy and interests, while an extreme left victory might be equally embarrassing, though in a different way, to any country which desires the maintenance of ordinary democratic government in those countries in which it still survives.[1]

For the Conservative-dominated National Government of 1936 the choice was obvious. Sympathy lay with the rebels who, supported by landowners, Church and Army, were pledged to stem the extreme radicalism which the Popular Front Government, supported by industrial workers, landless peasants and left-wing intellectuals, was held to represent. Thus, despite adherence in August 1936 to a multilateral policy of non-intervention in Spain, the British Government's unilateral policy was to work increasingly to the advantage of the Spanish Nationalist cause, with profound significance for her own position in Europe.

For on the broader stage of Europe the scene was no less disturbed, and while the conflict which had erupted was a bitter tragedy for Spain, it was also to prove a major test for European stability. The Great War, as it was fearfully remembered, had exhausted the victors without improving the lot of lesser powers, and had not noticeably soothed the still ardent passions of nationalism. Above all, two powerful ideologies, communism and fascism, competed for the support of nations, cutting across traditional groupings and exacerbating both internal and external tensions. Indeed, far from securing the settlement of Europe, the series of treaties which followed the Versailles Treaty of 1919 seemed more often to provoke than to control. Moreover, the League of Nations, set up as a supreme council of democratic arbitration and peacekeeping, was soon recognised to be as insubstantial as the treaties it purported to uphold. By late 1935 it had already been sorely tested – notably by the Japanese invasion of Manchuria in 1931, and by the Italian invasion of Abyssinia in 1935 – and had, in both instances, failed.

But nor had the powers sufficiently recouped their strength to enable them to act unilaterally, as was demonstrated when the once-great martial power of France failed to resist Hitler's reoccupation of the Rhineland in March 1936. Equally, groupings such as those formed by Britain, Italy and France at Stresa in 1935, which had appeared to patch over the flimsiness of the Locarno Treaties,[2] were soon revealed to be inadequate in the current spirit of unrest.

Therefore, despite the decidedly unsettled internal situation which prevailed in Britain in 1936, the continuing stress on Anglo-Italian relations following the Abyssinian affair, together with the acute crisis engendered by the German reoccupation of the Rhineland on 7 March that year, ensured that foreign affairs remained the prime concern of the British Government.[3] Since the German *démarche* the focus of attention had once more turned northwards, and thus, on 16 July, the day before the military coup of the Spanish generals began in Morocco,[4] the British Cabinet was engaged in discussion of the arrangements for a five-power conference aimed at producing a revision of the Locarno Treaty. Such a conference was, as the Cabinet had agreed earlier that month, essential in view of the generally recognised weakness of France and of 'some important lesser Powers, especially Spain'.[5]

Reference in this context to Spain was far from gratuitous, for 'weakness' here referred not only to military unpreparedness of potential allies, but also to the increasing division of both France and Spain into extremes of political ideology, conveniently though loosely covered by the blanket terms of 'fascism' and 'communism'. Both countries had recently acquired Popular Front governments, and, although in neither case was communist participation of any numerical consequence,[6] fear of the spread of communism was an important factor in British foreign-policy formulation in regard to both countries. This was partly the instinctive reaction of the

Nationalist Government, predominantly Conservative in composition, but reflected also the appreciation that the dictators used reaction to communism as a rallying point for their cause. While fascism and communism were regarded in the Foreign Office as the 'mumps and measles' of world society, the former was believed to be an urgent but short-term problem; the latter a longer-term one, which in consequence was never quite out of view, and especially in regard to policy towards France or Spain. Ultimately Britain's non-intervention policy was to be woven from many different strands, but in the first weeks of the rebellion it was the thread of anti-communism which formed the warp of British Government attitudes. Not until six weeks later did the Cabinet take fully into account the strategic implications of the Civil War, by which time the Non-Intervention Agreement was already in being, and the Non-Intervention Committee in preparation.

It is clear from the conclusions of the Cabinet meeting of 16 July that Spain had already engaged the attention of the British Government, and the generals' coup did not appear entirely unheralded upon the international scene. It is proposed, therefore, to look first at Anglo-Spanish relations in the months preceding the military rebellion, before examining the origins of the non-intervention policy and the setting up of the Non-Intervention Committee.

THE BACKGROUND TO ATTITUDES

Certainly the possibility of a coup from either right or left was well appreciated by the British Foreign Office from the early months of 1936, but the major preoccupation in January that year regarding Spain was the setting in motion of the Anglo-Spanish Payments Agreement of December 1935,[7] and consideration as to how the Agreement might be affected by the results of the coming elections fixed for February 1936. Hinting at communist intervention, Señor Angel Herrera, a member of *Acción Popular*, editor of *El Debate*, and close associate of Gil Robles,[8] leader of the Catholic CEDA party, warned the British Ambassador, Sir Henry Chilton, that a victory for the left in the coming elections would have grave repercussions for foreign interests such as Rio Tinto and other British mining companies. He also suggested that while the army was 95 per cent loyal to Gil Robles for the present, it could not count on so large a number were the extreme left to attain power. However, with only 2,000 regular troops and 1,400 Civil Guards in the city against the Government's 5,000 assault troops, he did not believe a military coup to be a possibility before the elections. Although the warning had been repeated to the United States Ambassador, Mr Claude Bowers, Herrera did not intend to repeat it to the French Ambassador, M. Jean Herbette, whom he described as a socialist and a freemason.[9]

During this tense period British representatives took soundings from other quarters in Spain: from the press, newly released from censorship laws; from the Jesuits – of whom the younger, more socially aware ones were described as 'indifferent to the monarchy', and from other foreign representatives. The German Ambassador, Count Johannes von Welczeck, for example, believed the left to be 'ominously quiet', adding perspicaciously that 'the men would follow the officers if the NCOs were killed first and vice versa'.[10]

During January the danger from the left was felt to have receded, and it appears to have been with some astonishment that Chilton recorded the victory of the Popular Front Government in February: 'Spain is a country where the unexpected often happens . . . It is difficult to account for such an emphatic defeat of the right', he wrote, ascribing it to the last-minute Jesuit backing for Gil Robles which in turn had brought a left-wing backlash. Even so, he believed it possible that the newly-elected premier, Azaña, might have an easy time for the first six months to a year, but that sooner or later Largo Caballero, 'the Lenin of Spain', would begin to give trouble.[11]

At this stage, Chilton's reports do not, on the whole, substantiate accusations of bias later brought against him by colleagues, notably Claude Bowers, who wrote of him: 'My British colleague, Sir Henry Chilton, was violently against the loyalists from the first day, and he habitually called them "reds"';[12] although it must be said that this view is amply attested by Sir Henry's later dispatches. In view of his later prejudice, his first impressions of members of the new Popular Front Government are of interest. 'The new Government', he reported, 'appears to consist of men of moderate views . . . intellectuals rather than practising socialists – some men with considerable fortunes.' He could himself, he declared, bear out the embassy porter's description of Señor Barcia, the new Minister of State, as '*un hombre muy fino*', and one who was, in addition, 'cultivated and intelligent'.[13] Initially, then, the attitude of the

British Ambassador was cautiously sympathetic, despite earlier misgivings about the future of British economic interests in Spain under a left-wing government.

In this respect, however, Herrera's warning proved right, for the Foreign Office soon became the clearing-house for an increasing number of complaints from all sectors of the British community in Spain, backed by consular reports describing incidents relating to, or hardship suffered under, what was widely regarded as a 'communistic' régime. Typical of such reports was one received by Baldwin, then Prime Minister, from the seemingly authoritative pen of Arthur Bryant in April 1936:

> In Spain things are far worse than is realised here. In the big towns and show places it is hidden away, but everywhere else revolution is beginning. I travelled 5,000 miles in Spain and except in Catalonia saw on the walls of every village I visited the symbols of the hammer and sickle, and in the streets the undisguised signs of bitter class hatred fomented by increasing agitation of Soviet agents.[14]

Certainly, many commercial concerns were fearful of the effect of the various economic decrees of the new Popular Front Government, although as the British Counsellor in Madrid, George Ogilvie Forbes, pointed out, there were no grounds for intervention on behalf of British firms affected, so long as the decrees were imposed universally and impartially.[15] Most hated of all was the labour decree promulgated immediately after the February election, requiring all firms to reinstate and compensate strikers dismissed after the uprising of 1934. This was resented by those who had been forced to streamline their staffs and had no wish to re-employ men regarded as troublemakers trying to reorganise firms on so-called 'soviet' lines. The raising of customs and tariffs, the imposition of surcharges, and in some cases the expropriation of land were all regarded as outrageous, while, for mining companies, the final blow was the announcement in June of a bill to be presented to the Cortes providing for state control of mines. Tracts such as *¿ España de Quién?*[16] written by an ex-official of the Ministry of the Interior, and felt to represent new Spanish attitudes to foreign investors, abounded, and chauvinism manifested itself in strikes, sabotage and bomb outrages. The reported discovery of bales of 'communist' uniforms in Madrid left no doubt in many British minds as to the political complexion of the culprits, and an even more melodramatic report from the British consul at Vigo, W. H. Oxley, that '10,000 communists' were in control[17] confirmed the impression of anarchy.

While the Foreign Office in London maintained a detached view of these reports, others did not. For instance, the Royal Automobile Club of Great Britain warned its members that no guarantee could be given for any motor car entering Spanish territory. Expressing his sense of shame that such a circular should have been issued, Ogilvie Forbes assured the Foreign Secretary, Anthony Eden, that the Commercial Secretary to the Embassy had just returned from a tour of southern Spain in a car not carrying diplomatic plates and had suffered no inconvenience.[18] Sir George Mounsey, Assistant Under-Secretary at the Foreign Office[19] and no admirer of communism, made the same tour and hearing on his return to London of the warning to tourists minuted 'I can't think why'.[20]

Such detachment was difficult to maintain, however, after an incident on 2 July in which the British manager of a Barcelona lace factory, Mr Joseph Mitchell Hood, was murdered, deepening the fears of the British colony there.[21] So grave were fears that assurances were sought from the Spanish Government, and on 13 July Lord Cranborne, Parliamentary Under-Secretary at the Foreign Office, informed the House of Commons that these had been given by the Spanish Government for the prompt protection of British lives and property.[22] On that very day, however, José Calvo Sotelo, right-wing monarchist politician, was assassinated in Madrid and the Republican Government was brought one pace nearer direct confrontation with militant right-wing forces in Spain.

Rumours of such a confrontation had long been rife, although Chilton had informed Eden towards the end of March that the right was 'strangely quiet'.[23] But far from indicating an imminent coup, doubts as to the likelihood of such a coup had, for a while, grown. 'Those who pinned their hopes on the appearance of a dictator from the army are beginning to despair,' wrote Norman King, British Consul General in Barcelona.[24] There is much evidence that the Popular Front Government was itself taken off guard by the events of 17 and 18 July.[25] 'In spite of the atmosphere of civil war which prevailed in Spain,' wrote José Giral, the Republican Premier in an interview reported in *La Petite Gironde* on 8 August 1936, 'I admit that the military *coup d'état* took us by surprise. We knew there was a great deal of fascist propaganda in the Army but we had no grounds for thinking that the majority of officers were involved.'[26]

As to the Foreign Office in London, Arthur Loveday claimed in his book *Spain, 1923–1948* (Boswell, London 1949) that documents pertaining to a communist uprising were handed to the Foreign Office who, curiously, rejected it.[27] Indeed, such rumours were generally treated with considerable scepticism. For example, in May the Foreign Office received information that there was to be a *coup* within the next two weeks, and that the organisers were anxious that the British Government should know it was not a fascist movment but merely intended to restore order and bring in a right-wing civilian government. The warning was dismissed as 'vague and perhaps far-fetched'.[28] Probably the situation had been volatile for so long that there was no reason to give credence to this particular rumour.

It was inevitable that official reports from Spain should have been concerned mainly with the disruption to business experienced by British residents and investors in Spain, for it is a primary function of the Diplomatic Corps to represent their fellow nationals abroad, to secure, when possible, their interests and, if need be, their protection. But in their more important functions as impartial observers and intermediaries,[29] Britain was increasingly ill-served in Spain by her representatives, who, with some important exceptions, became openly antagonistic towards the Republican Government. In particular, the continuing disintegration of Spanish society seems to have had a profound effect upon Sir Henry Chilton. At fifty-nine he would have expected his current post, which he had held for less than one year when the rebellion broke out, to be his last.[30] His initial cautious optimism after the February election doubtless reflected the bad record of the previous government in social stability. Following the lifting of the censorship laws at Christmas 1935, it was reported that there had been 9,000 strikes and 200 churches destroyed during the previous period of government.[31] The change to a Popular Front government did not, therefore, necessarily, at least at first, augur a change for the worse.

By summer, however, Chilton's frail hopes had given way to impatience which crystallised into an unquestionably anti-government view. This was partly a result of the treatment he received at the outbreak of the rebellion which found him, as was the custom for the Diplomatic Corps during the Summer months, at the northern resort of San Sebastian. Against his will he was escorted from there to the small village of Zarauz by 'two armed communists', or, as he described it, *'force majeure'*, an incident which imbued him with a deep antipathy towards 'the Reds'. On 1 August he was taken by HMS *Kempenfelt* to St. Jean-de-Luz[32] where he remained until the autumn of 1937, working from a small office by the International Bridge at Hendaye, just inside the French border.[33] He became increasingly intolerant, and in contrast to his earlier reports was writing, by August, unreservedly, that in his view the issue had resolved itself into a struggle of 'rebel versus rabble'.[34] 'The situation', he continued, 'is beginning to resemble that of the French Revolution, except that the rifle and revolver have taken the place of the guillotine. The Scarlet Pimpernel is badly needed in Spain.' It should be noted, however, that his, and other partisan reports were treated with considerable scepticism at the Foreign Office.[35] He declined to return to Madrid, suggesting that if a member of the Embassy staff were required in the capital then Mr George Ogilvie Forbes should be sent back from leave in Britain.[36]

In Ogilvie Forbes Britain had a quite exceptionally able representative, for this Catholic, bagpipe-playing Scot seems to have been universally admired. He was described by the distinguished socialist Julio Alvarez del Vayo as a man 'of charming manners, intelligent and broadminded, endowed with great quickness of perception and a strong human kindliness';[37] while a colleague, Geoffrey Thompson, wrote of his 'personal courage and kindness'.[38] He was recalled to Spain on 10 August to restore order to the British Embassy, which, left in the charge of the Acting Consul, Milanes, in the absence of both Ambassador and Counsellor, was disturbed by internal friction. Travelling to Valencia by British destroyer, Forbes arrived in Madrid on 16 August.[39] Throughout that month and often thereafter, the embassy was in very real danger from daily bombing raids, but although, when the extremity of danger was recognised, the Foreign Office gave Forbes every encouragement to leave, he declined to do so.[40] His ability was fully appreciated in London and his success in establishing friendly relations with Alvarez del Vayo – 'chief lieutenant' to Largo Caballero and as such widely tipped as Minister of State in the 'Socialist' Government[41] – was highly praised. An outstandingly able man, Forbes not only refused to leave Madrid, but rejected the suggestion that Henry Chilton should be sent back to aid him, for as he tactfully explained, 'with patience and calm, we will pull through all right'.[42]

In contrast to amiable reports of Ogilvie Forbes, Stephen Spender's portrait of Norman King, Consul-General at Barcelona, provides a devastating indictment of the attitude adopted by many British in Spain at this time. Spender, who dined with King in Barcelona, was appalled by the mandarin attitude of the British with whom he spoke, who appeared to regard themselves almost as an occupying élite. The Consul-General's guests, wrote Spender later in an article in the *News Chronicle* on 1 September 1936, had spoken disparagingly of Spaniards and Spanish culture, and King himself had given it as his opinion that Luis Companys, then President of the Catalan Generalidad, should have been shot after the 1934 uprising.[43] There was undoubtedly much in Spender's story, although, as King pointed out, the article could have jeopardised the lives of all diplomats in Spain, since people were being shot for lesser offences than those described in Spender's account. 'Diehard Tory', as by his own description he was, King remained in Barcelona when he might quite honourably have left, visiting the morgue and witnessing the results of grotesque atrocities, graphically reported to the Foreign Office and later described by Eden as rivalling 'the most harrowing of Goya's drawings'.[44]

King's attitudes to Spaniards were reflected among many British in Spain, who, although they deplored to the chaos of war, welcomed the military uprising, which where successful, had apparently brought stability to local affairs and order to everyday life in such matters as communications and other services.[45] For some there was actual advantage. Lord Bute, for example, had for the past three months been storing in the British Consulate at Algeciras a collection of Spanish paintings the export of which had been prohibited by the Spanish Government, and it was now suggested that the opportunity should be taken to 'smuggle' the pictures to Gibraltar.[46] Many refugees, too, were aided by various embassies during the first weeks of the uprising, and old friendships were often invoked in the rush of members of the Spanish upper classes seeking protection in the British and other embassies. For, although the Foreign Office advised strongly against the giving of asylum, an absolute veto was not imposed and it was left to the representative to decide the issue on grounds of humanity.[47] Thus by 9 November 1936 there were in the British Embassy 125 refugees, of whom some fifty were British subjects, the rest being described as Embassy staff.[48]

It is true, however, that at the outbreak of war in Spain, relations between the Republican and British Governments were less than cordial, and perhaps the Spanish Government should bear some blame for this, being too occupied with a difficult internal situation to develop external relations as fully as desirable. But there seems to have been little effort on the part of Britain's official representatives – with the important exception of Ogilvie Forbes – to forge strong links with the Popular Front Government before the outbreak of hostilities. No member of the Government was then a communist, although Chilton plainly came to regard all its members as tainted by that ideology. Some idea of what this could mean in British diplomatic circles at that time may be gleaned from Ivan Maisky's description of his chilling reception in London as Russian Ambassador in 1932.[49]

With so great a chasm in outlook between the Spanish Republican Government and British residents in Spain, small wonder that, when the holocaust began on 18 July, signals were sent from the Rio Tinto mining company and other British enclaves requesting British naval support or evacuation.[50] For although, throughout the war, the British community in Republican Spain received every consideration possible in the circumstances, they had little reason to hope for such courtesy.[51] It is against this background of ill-will in Spain itself that the initial reactions of the British Government and Foreign Office were formed.

FIRST REACTIONS

It will be recalled that the major preoccupation of the Foreign Office throughout the summer of 1936 was the hope of an early conclusion of a new Locarno Pact, preferably in the autumn. Meanwhile Eden's most pressing concern was to finalise arrangements for the Anglo-Egyptian Treaty, which was signed on 26 August,[52] and Spain was at first no more than a minor issue which, it was hoped, might quickly resolve itself. As for Baldwin, he was not much interested in foreign affairs, and by midsummer 1936 was, in any case, showing signs of exhaustion, longing to be rid of the responsibility of office.[53] He was therefore content to leave matters very much to his Foreign Secretary, although this was a burden Eden was thought then to resent.[54]

Yet Eden's task was not made easier by the proliferation of would-be foreign policy advisers in the Cabinet at this time. He recalled that there were, following Sir Samuel Hoare's reinstatement as First Lord of the Admiralty (and consequent membership of the Cabinet Committee on Foreign Policy), three former Foreign Secretaries in the Cabinet,[55] all eager to advise. Baldwin, who sympathised with Eden's position in this, commented that out of twenty of the Foreign Secretary's colleagues there was probably not more than one who thought he ought to be Minister of Labour and nineteen who thought they should be Foreign Secretary. 'I was aware', wrote Eden, 'that my appointment was not welcome to all my elders in the Cabinet, where there was already no lack of former Foreign Secretaries and other aspirants to office'.[56] Besides the three former Secretaries of State, chief rival at this time to Eden's authority as Foreign Secretary was Viscount Halifax, Lord Privy Seal and Minister without Portfolio. A devout Anglo-Catholic, noted for his indolence,[57] he deputised for Eden in August, during the period when non-intervention was finally adopted, when Eden was on holiday. The desire of these men to participate actively in formulation of foreign policy made conclusion of all decisions in Cabinet laborious and the creation of coherent policy difficult, especially in view of the antagonism between Eden and certain of his colleagues, notably Sir Samuel Hoare, Eden's ex-chief at the Foreign Office whom he had replaced at the end of 1935.

Eden, like Baldwin, had had a particularly fatiguing parliamentary session, retaining his responsibility for League affairs which had previously been a post separate from the main stream of foreign affairs although remaining under the overall authority of the Foreign Secretary. An additional factor important to decision-making during the first phase of the Spanish Civil War was the long parliamentary recess, which meant not only that there would be no Cabinet meetings between 29 July and 2 September,[58] but that ministers were widely dispersed during this period. For all these reasons the rôle of the Foreign Office officials during the early weeks of the Spanish crisis was even more important than it might otherwise have been, and in consequence their minutes and memoranda take on especial significance. Here too, however, seasonal absence played a part. Sir Robert Vansittart, Permanent Under-Secretary at the Foreign Office, who believed firmly in the need for rapprochement with the USSR[59] while sharing Eden's antipathy to the dictator powers, was spending what he described as a 'busman's holiday' in Berlin.[60]

Despite some affinity of outlook, Eden hoped to replace Vansittart with Sir Alexander Cadogan, recently recalled from Peking for that purpose[61] and now Deputy Under-Secretary at the Foreign

Office.[62] So far Vansittart had declined to abdicate and take the position of Ambassador in Paris. However, it was Cadogan, 'patient, quiet in his manner, more of a civil servant than was Sir Robert',[63] who worked closely with Halifax in the formulation of British policy towards Spain during August, and indeed during the first week of that month appears to have been in overall charge. Halifax's presence was not sought until 5 August, although all policy decisions concerning Spain were authorised by him until Eden's return. Important, too, was Sir George Mounsey, one of four Assistant Under-Secretaries of State and sharing with Cadogan the supervision of the Western and League Department. Others who later took part in decision-making on Spain were Sir Orme Sargent, Superintending Under-Secretary of the Central Department, under whose aegis came all matters concerning France; Walter Roberts, Head of the Western and League Department; Owen St. Clair O'Malley of the Southern Department, among whose concerns was Italy and the Mediterranean; and finally Charles Howard Smith, Principal Establishment Officer. In addition to these men, four clerks were chiefly responsible for Spanish affairs, C. A. E. Shuckburgh, W. H. Montagu Pollock, R. M. Makins and Donald Maclean, and of these the first, Evelyn Shuckburgh, came to bear the brunt of the immense increase in the material concerning Spain which arrived in the department after 18 July.[64]

At first, as was to be expected following the suddenness of the *coup*, there was no clear pattern to this material. First impressions were of a high degree of confusion, and failure of normal channels of communications. Use of the telephone, for example, was forbidden between rebel Vigo and Republican Madrid.[65] However, British diplomats were quickly able to overcome any disruption to their usual channels of information by means of telegrams relayed by HM ships in Spanish waters or at Gibraltar. Thus Eden's statement to the House on 22 July to the effect that it was difficult to obtain accurate information was reasonable though somewhat misleading.[66] By then, it was known in the Foreign Office that Gen. Franco had arrived in Tetuan on 19 July and had left for Ceuta; that the Foreign Legion in Morocco had revolted against the Republic; that the Spanish Zone of Tangier was in the hands of the military; that there had also been a military rising in Burgos, the ancient Castilian capital; and, most significant from the point of view of policy-making in Britain, that the crisis in Spain was so severe as to have brought about a reconstruction of the Republican Government in

Madrid.[67] All this information immediately preceded the first major decisions of the British Government.

Of necessity the first response of the British Government to the crisis of 17–18 July was to secure the safety of all British nationals in Spain. Within days, thirteen British warships were stationed around the coast of Spain, and by the 27th of the month some 785 evacuees had been ferried from Barcelona and other Catalan ports in the cramped quarters of British naval vessels.[68] Of these, 544 were British subjects and the remainder included citizens of seventeen different nations of whom many were right-wing Spaniards fleeing for their lives with whatever jewels or valuables they were able to conceal.[69] The decision to send ships to Spain was an entirely British concern, and even the question of evacuation of Spanish nationals, although rather more delicate, could be justified on grounds of humanity. However, the situation which soon arose at Tangier (then under control of an international committee) involved broader considerations. Since these preceded any firm decision on Britain's part to adopt a policy of non-intervention, this early international complication deserves some attention.

At the outbreak of hostilities, destroyers were sent by the Republican Government to quell the rebellion in Morocco. The officers, hearing Franco broadcast from Las Palmas, determined to join him but were foiled by a counter-mutiny from the junior officers and crews, who overpowered their superiors, imprisoning or killing them. The movement spread quickly and soon the major part of the Spanish navy was being reorganised by the men.[70] Two ships, followed later by others, made quickly for the safety of the international port of Tangier and two more for Gibraltar, where they lay immobilised for lack of fuel and provisions, their normal sources of oil now being in rebel hands.

For Franco, loss of most of the navy was a severe blow, and temporarily thwarted in his plans to ferry his troops to the mainland, he immediately threatened to bomb both Tangier and Gibraltar if the Spanish vessels in the ports were refuelled. On the evening of 20 July he also urged the British Consul-General, E. F. Gye, not to allow ships to obtain fuel supplies at Tetuan.[71] The following day, the Spanish Ambassador in London, Señor López Oliván, called on Viscount Cranborne to ask if Britain would sell oil from Gibraltar to the Spanish fleet, and after reference to the Secretary of State, was told he was at liberty to purchase privately owned oil.[72] Private companies, however, were less than happy to comply, and the Asiatic Petroleum Company sought government authorisation (which was later given) before they would agree to sell to 'ships in the hands of sailors' soviets'.

On 22 July, the rebels, apparently by accident, bombed two British ships, the SS *Fabian* and the SS *Mahratta*. Although Franco immediately apologised, the Governor at Gibraltar, Sir Charles Harington, was most alarmed, the more so since the ships which Franco was assumed to have been aiming at were commanded by 'junior officers with no uniforms, who gave the communist salute'.[73] On the other hand, the Vice-Admiral at Gibraltar advised against selling fuel to the Republican navy, since he believed that if the Spanish warships remained immobile from lack of oil there would be less chance of any further bombardment of towns where British life and property might be endangered.[74]

That day, Wednesday 22 July, the Cabinet discussed the sale of oil, but the outcome, though not clear, seems to have been unfavourable.[75] It is regrettable that the Cabinet Conclusion for the meeting that day gives so little detail, for it is likely that some discussion of the situation in Spain took place, although none is recorded.[76]

Franco's warning of the 20th was followed by telegrams to the International Control Committee of Tangier, urging the committee to place the Spanish 'pirate' ships in a 'state of neutrality', i.e. neither to fuel nor victual them, and suggesting that one of the ships was planning to bring arms to 'revolutionary elements' in Morocco in order to foment counter-revolution. But already the International Committee of Control had called an urgent meeting of its members, realising that in Tangier lay the 'elements of a dangerous situation which might involve the Powers'.[77] As a result of this meeting, the French, who (according to the British Ambassador in Paris, Sir George Clerk) were particularly perturbed by the presence of Spanish men-of-war at Tangier, instructed their Ambassador on 21 July to draw the attention of the Spanish Government to the danger of retaliatory measures being used by aviation and other units of the rebel army and to persuade the Spanish against using Tangier as a base. The British and Italian Ambassadors received similar instructions.[78] What is important, here, is that at so early a stage the French, albeit in conjunction with their colleagues of the Control Committee, were prepared to take the lead in a move clearly contrary to the interests of the Republican Government, and did so, it seems, as a result of their own appreciation of the difficulties, both strategic and external, which might arise from the situation rather than from any pressure from their co-controllers at Tangier.

THE FORMULATION OF POLICY

Evidence of French caution at so early a stage is of interest because, although the question of pressure by the British Government on France to adopt a policy of non-intervention has been the subject of continuing controversy and close scrutiny,[79] it is necessary at this point to reconsider the issue. It is not possible to recapitulate in detail the theories expounded by those who have argued for or against the belief that the French Government wished to give practical aid to the Spanish Government in its struggle against the rebels, and came to promote the policy of non-intervention only under pressure from Britain. Three main occasions when such pressure may have been applied are commonly instanced. The first is generally suggested to have occurred during the Three-Power Conference in London on 23–24 July, and is said to have contributed to the reversal on 25 July of the French Premier, Léon Blum's decision to send arms to Spain in response to a plea received from the new Spanish Prime Minister, José Giral, on the 20th of that month.[80] The second episode cited concerns the rebuff delivered to service chief Admiral Darlan by the British Admiralty when he was sent to London to persuade his naval counterpart of the vital strategic implications of the Spanish affair. The third occasion to prompt rumours was the announcement on 7 August of France's firm decision to adopt a policy of non-intervention. The decision was believed to follow the application of considerable diplomatic pressure from Britain.

The key to these events lies in two factors: the international situation and in particular Anglo-French relations; and secondly, in the internal politics of both countries, but especially of France. As regards Anglo-French relations these had grown distinctly chilly following not only the failure of the Hoare-Laval pact of late 1935, but also the signing of the Franco-Russian Alliance of 2 May 1935 and the Anglo-German Naval Agreement of 18 June 1935. By the latter treaties both great democracies appeared to have chosen diametrically opposed futures. For although the Franco-Russian Alliance forged during Flandin's premiership, against the wishes of

Laval,[81] demonstrated only the politics of necessity, it came to be regarded in London as an extension of the internal politics of France under the Popular Front Government; just as the Anglo-German Agreement similarly was viewed in French circles as reflecting political attitudes of the Conservative-dominated National Government of Stanley Baldwin.

France, like Spain, was deeply riven by industrial, financial and political unrest, with both extreme left and right in a state of nascent rebellion. Thus while it was considered highly desirable to support a friendly, socialist, Popular Front government on France's south-western frontier for ideological as well as strategic motives, it was also imperative that internal pressures be balanced most carefully if France were to retain her own socialist government at all.

On 20 July, and shortly before the hastily arranged Three-Power Conference, the French Premier had received an urgent message from José Giral: 'Are surprised by dangerous military *coup*, we ask your immediate support with arms and aircraft. Fraternally yours, Giral'.[82] Blum, in consideration of the terms of a secret supply-of-arms clause of the Franco-Spanish commerce treaty of 1935,[83] and with the support of his Minister of War, Edouard Daladier, and Minister for Air, Pierre Cot, decided to comply with the request. Herein, according to rumour, lay the reason for Blum's apparent last-minute invitation to London: that the British Government might have the opportunity to impress upon him the necessity for caution in Spain. There is, however, no great mystery about Blum's invitation, for the Cabinet Conclusions of 16 July, two days before the rebellion in peninsular Spain and one week before the conference, show that Blum himself had suggested that he should go to London and the British Government favoured the move as an opportunity for Blum to meet the Prime Minister'.[84]

This is not to argue that no warnings were given to the French Premier while in London, for he appears to have received at least three. First, Blum is reported to have been warned by Baldwin himself, that if French intervention in Spain provoked conflict with Italy, Britain would remain neutral.[85] The Premier was also visited in his hotel room by the journalist Pertinax (André Géraud), who suggested that the sale of arms to Spain was viewed with disfavour by Britain. To this Blum replied that he intended to go ahead nonetheless. Finally, Anthony Eden, bidding Blum farewell, added what has been called a 'casual reference to Spain',[86] although it is surely difficult to construe any parting remark made by the British

Foreign Secretary to a French premier on his first official and very brief visit to London, as casual:

> 'Are you going to send arms to the Spanish Republic?' asked Eden.
> I replied, 'Yes, that's right.'
> 'That is your affair,' said Eden. 'But I ask one thing. Be careful.'[87]

In his memoirs, however, Eden denies that Spain was discussed, although he makes no comment on Blum's account of this exchange.

Returning to Paris from London on 25 July, Blum found a serious deterioration in the situation in France. The Spanish Chargé d'Affaires, Señor Castillo, and the Spanish Military Attaché had resigned, on the grounds that they did not wish to be a channel through which weapons would be purchased to kill their fellow-Spaniards.[88] Both the French Government and the French press, to whom the details of the arms deal had been released by the Spanish Attaché, were now more deeply divided on this issue than before. So much so that the situation seemed insupportable to Blum, and he seriously considered resignation.[89]

Indeed, the power of the press in France was considerable, and writers such as Pertinax of the right-wing *Echo de Paris* and Mme Geneviève Tabouis, foreign editor of the left-wing *L'Oeuvre* wielded immense influence.[90] Rumours abounded. The extreme right-wing royalist *Action Française* group claimed that the military attaché 'of a certain Great Power' had visited the French Foreign Ministry to warn that if France did not respect the principles of non-interference in Spanish internal affairs, his country would consider herself free to furnish war materials to the rebels.[91] In a sense the veracity of such stories was less important than the vehemence with which they were expressed.

So controversial had the issue become that Blum called an emergency meeting of the Cabinet late on 25 July and, after what was described to Sir George Clerk by M. de St. Quentin, Director of African Affairs, as a 'sharp clash of opinion in which the President, M. Lebrun, played a significant rôle', it was decided not to furnish the Spanish Government with aeroplanes or munitions. Later that evening a semi-official communiqué to the effect that France intended to abstain from all intervention was issued, although this declaration was not entirely what it seemed for arms were dispatched via Mexico.[92] At roughly the same time it became known to the British Government that 19 million francs in gold, intended as a *quid pro quo* for arms, had been landed from a Spanish Government aircraft at Le Bourget,[93] strengthening the feeling of obligation to Spain on the left in the French Cabinet.

Up to this point the British Government had not been approached by the Spanish Republic for arms, only for fuel oil, but negotiations on behalf of the rebels and conducted by Señor Delgado, manager of the Ibarrola Oil Company at Ceuta, were under way for the purchase of four old Fokker aeroplanes belonging to Imperial Airways.[94] Protesting at the sale of aircraft to the rebels, the Spanish Ambassador repeated to Eden on 28 July that as yet he had no instructions from his government to ask for any supply of munitions, but he asked tentatively what the attitude of the British Government would be were he to receive such instructions.

Baldwin, however, influenced perhaps by reports from Spain such as he had received from Arthur Bryant, and by the very recent horror of the Mitchell Hood affair, had already given his Foreign Secretary explicit, though informal, instructions that in the Spanish affair: ' . . . on no account, French or other, must he bring us into the fight on the side of the Russians.'[95] Given Baldwin's normal reticence on foreign affairs, the direction was certainly emphatic. Now, following the visit from López Oliván, the Ambassador's plea was duly considered at the Cabinet meeting the next day, although it had not been listed in the original agenda. Again, there is no record of the discussion of the implications for Britain of the rebellion, although this must surely have taken place.[96] Eden informed the Cabinet that the Spanish Ambassador had given warning of his soon asking to purchase arms for his country. The Spanish Government was a recognised government, Eden reminded his colleagues, and could not be refused arms, but if it were a question of purchasing new weapons the defence departments might wish to stop supply on the grounds that the whole of Britain's productive resources were required. The Cabinet agreed that, if appealed to, ordinary procedure should be followed and no exceptional step need be taken.[97] Even so, it seemed likely that it would be only a short time before British arms manufacturers were approached, and for ready gold would be willing to conduct deals with the Republican Government. Indeed it was shortly announced that Vickers Armstrong were negotiating to sell the Spanish Government 4,000 shells.[98]

Clearly the danger of intervention of any kind was in Eden's mind

as the parliamentary summer recess began, for in a hasty minute of
31 July he gave precise instructions for the conduct, in his absence,
of policy towards Spain. Noting that the French Government had
informed the Spanish Government that the export of war material
was now forbidden, Eden expressed the hope that His Majesty's
Government would 'be able to avoid supplying [arms] *by some means
or other*' (my italics).[99] Thus although Baldwin and Eden both
temporarily left London and the running of the Foreign Office was
left to Halifax, the chain of direction from Baldwin through Eden to
the Foreign Office staff is firmly established.

The broad aim of policy – not to be drawn into the war on the
Republican side – was plain enough. The means by which it was to
be achieved and by which the parliamentary position of the
Government, defined by Eden on 27 July as one of non-
intervention,[100] was to be upheld, were left for the Foreign Office to
devise.[101] This was somewhat difficult in view of the various
transactions already under way between both Spanish parties and
British firms. Only where aid of a non-commercial kind was
involved and the co-operation of the British Government was
required, was the Foreign Office adamantly against any collaboration. Thus a request by the Spanish Ambassador on 4 August
for permission for the Republican Government to send a Spanish
destroyer to fetch a Spanish Savoia seaplane from Gibraltar was
rejected as constituting 'intervention' on the part of Britain.
However, it soon became evident that even private commercial
transactions would become sources of international friction when
the Fokker aircraft destined for the rebels were grounded at
Bordeaux, having been refused permission to take off after a brief
landing to refuel.[102]

Action against the Fokkers had been taken independently by the
port authorities at Bordeaux, but was in line with the general
French policy of non-intervention announced on 25 July and
maintained by the French Government despite their awareness that
communications between the Balearics and Tetuan, in North
Africa, were being kept open by German aeroplanes.[103] But when,
as shortly happened, foreign intervention became public knowledge, it was no longer possible for the French Government to
blink the fact. On 30 July three Italian Savoias bound for Spanish
Morocco and carrying arms made a forced landing in French
Morocco, and once again the press lunged into battle. Still more
heat was generated by the announcement from the Portuguese

radio to the effect that because the French Assembly had passed a resolution to aid the Popular Front Government in Spain, England and Germany had decided to help the military rebels. This line was taken up by Mme Tabouis, who also pointed to the intimacy between 'fascist' Portugal and Conservative Britain.[104] Meanwhile, news that Portuguese troops were being moved to the Spanish border only served to underline the growing isolation of the Spanish Republic, and the danger of the division of Europe into two opposing blocs.[105]

Wide publicity given to the intervention by Italy helped Blum, despite opposition, to carry a declaration at the next meeting of the Senate Foreign Affairs Committee on 31 July, that if Italy and Germany were going to contribute arms openly, his government would consider itself free to act in a similar fashion.[106] As the British Ambassador, Sir George Clerk, warned the British Foreign Office later that afternoon, this latest announcement would ' . . . not only make things more difficult for those members of the French Government who have hitherto successfully stopped the President of the Council and the Air Ministry from supplying bombing aeroplanes and arms to the Spanish Government, but may have wider repercussions in Franco-Italian relations',[107] and, by implication, for the proposed five-power conference so central to British policy.

On the same day M. Roger Cambon, Minister at the French Embassy in London, told Sir George Mounsey of his country's concern at the open intervention of Italy in the Spanish Civil War. The French Government were greatly perturbed by this development, he said, and were considering the idea of an international conference, perhaps composed of the Tangier powers, which would come to an agreement to refrain from giving any military assistance to Spain. He, however, regarded this as a cumbersome process and thought that agreement might more easily be reached by semi-official diplomatic talks such as they were already having. Mounsey agreed, for as yet he did not favour any move which would tend to cast Britain irrevocably into the French camp, one which according to a report by Clerk received two days earlier, was dominated by communist influence.[108]

Later that day, 31 July, a meeting was held in the Foreign Office between Sir Horace Seymour, Sir William Malkin, Legal Adviser to the Foreign Office, Lord Cranborne, Parliamentary Under-Secretary of State, and Mr Ormsby-Gore of the Colonial Office.[109]

The meeting was called primarily to discuss the plight of the Fokker aircraft, but the presence of the minister from the Colonial Office, a quite separate entity, with responsibility for Gibraltar, suggests that the discussion may have ranged over wider issues than that of four antiquated machines. At any rate, in view of Lord Cranborne's words earlier that day in the House of Commons to the effect that the Government had 'taken no improper action in regard to this dispute',[110] and also doubtless with regard to Eden's own directive, it was decided to ask for the return of the planes, and instructions were telephoned to the Paris Embassy on the evening of 31 July. Some form of contact between the British representatives and the Quai d'Orsay would therefore have taken place, probably late on 31 July, the evening preceding the next major crisis for Blum, which broke during the cabinet meeting on the afternoon of 1 August. At the same time the French Ambassador in London, M. Charles Corbin, expressed his government's hope that as many governments as possible would adopt a similar attitude of grave concern at the situation.[111] At this stage, however, although there was naturally close communication between the Quai d'Orsay and the Foreign Office, there is no direct evidence extant of pressure on the French Government by the British.

As a result of Blum's declaration to the Foreign Affairs Committee, the Premier faced what he termed an even more violent campaign in both government and press circles, and was particularly aware that the majority of the foreign press sympathised with the rebel coup.[112] The stormy cabinet meeting of 1 August was survived only by a masterly compromise, the essence of which was an appeal by the French Government to Italy and Britain, as Mediterranean powers, to join with them in adopting a policy of non-intervention which might be extended to other interested powers. The French Government meanwhile, in deference to its left wing, reserved the right to depart from their previously declared policy and to assist the Spanish Government. The note informing the British of this decision was examined on Sunday 2 August, and Mounsey, not wishing to send a flat refusal but preferring to maintain the unilateral stance adopted by the British Government, advised Halifax thus:

> I think we must be careful about our answer. The French Government would no doubt like to draw us into some commitment to support, even if only morally, the present Spanish

Government, and deter other foreign governments from sending arms to the rebels in face of Anglo-French opposition. We are as anxious as they can be to hold the ring, but our main object should, I think, be to be completely impartial and free to pursue the policy of non-intervention in Spain. An Anglo-Franco-Italian Agreement would not be of the slightest use (and might be more dangerous) unless other important countries, such as Germany and also Soviet Russia came into line, and I do not think we should tie our hands to any agreement which is not practically universal.

Mounsey, concerned for the future of the five-power talks, therefore proposed a fairly noncommital reply which would not commit Britain too definitely to the list of powers from whom guarantees of non-intervention would initially be obtained.[113]

Temporarily released from non-intervention by the decision of 1 August, it appears that Cot hastily dispatched a number of French military aircraft. The gesture raised the fury of the French right and notably of M. Xavier Vallat, a deputy who challenged Cot in the Chamber on 4 August, with the sending of fifty-two military aircraft.[114] Cot denied the charges but it was evident that a new crisis was imminent, one in which once again British pressure has been said to have played a great part. Indeed, the next steps in the development of non-intervention as a multilateral policy are important, because it can be shown from archival evidence that the Popular Front Government of France was impelled for reasons of internal dissension to appeal most earnestly to the Conservative-dominated National Government of Britain for support, which it would receive despite the incongruity of the situation.

Though Mounsey had written to Halifax on 2 August, so far no reply had been sent to the French note of that date. On the day of Cot's 'grilling' in the Chamber, Cambon called on Mounsey to press for an immediate reply. Only by an exhibition of Anglo-French solidarity, Cambon emphasised, could M. Blum resist those elements in France determined to support the Spanish Government, adding that it might already be too late to do so. The British reply was therefore dispatched later that day. While cautiously conceding the need for agreement, it was suggested that no agreement would be of any use unless accepted simultaneously by France, Germany, Italy, Portugal and Great Britain.[115] Yet Cambon called again in the evening to renew his pleas. He accepted that the British had

done what they could to help his government, but doubted if it would
be enough to them to resist the increasing pressure to depart from a
neutral attitude. To stress the strategic danger, Cambon informed
Mounsey that two French naval officers were travelling to London
to see their counterparts in the British Admiralty in order to discuss
the situation in the Mediterranean.[116]

Talks took place the next day between the British First Sea Lord,
Sir Ernle Chatfield, Admiral Darlan, Chef de Cabinet Militaire,
and Rear-Admiral Decoux of the French Ministry of Marine, who
represented those in the French Government who believed there
existed a real threat in the Mediterranean from Italian expan-
sionism which would seek to draw the Balearics into Italian thrall.
From the French point of view the talks were a failure, and can have
served only to alienate the two services. Darlan expressed his fears
regarding the Mediterranean in view of the 'Predatory natures of
Italy and Germany', but also his desire to follow whatever course
was decided upon by the British Admiralty: 'If you intend to leave
ships on the coast of Spain, we will do so, if you intend to withdraw
them we shall also withdraw ours.' He particularly wished to see Sir
Maurice Hankey, who he was convinced would listen to his
appeal.[117] Although his plea eventually reached Hankey it did so
only after it had been categorically dismissed by the First Lord of the
Admiralty, Sir Samuel Hoare, who noted:

> I should [however] be astonished if either Government con-
> templates action of this kind at the moment when both have
> agreed to take part in the new Locarno conversations and when
> Italy seems anxious to resume friendly relations with France and
> ourselves.

This was followed by a revealing outburst from Hoare, which is
important because it indicates the degree of anti-communism which
was so important a factor in the formulation of British policy
towards Spain in the vital early days of the rebellion:

> When I speak of 'neutrality' I mean strict neutrality, that is to
> say, a situation in which the Russians neither officially or
> unofficially give help to the Communists. On no account must we
> do anything to bolster up Communism in Spain, particularly
> when it is remembered that Communism in Portugal to which it
> would probably spread and particularly Lisbon, would be a
> grave danger to the British Empire.[118]

These words are surely what Blum referred to when he later claimed that Darlan returned to Paris, his mission unfulfilled and convinced of the pro-Franco attitude of the British.[119] Moreover, Chatfield – who later declared Franco's cause to have been 'much nobler than the Reds' '[120] – for instance expressed the view that once in power, Franco would be quite able to defend himself against Italian aspirations concerning the Balearics. This was akin to the view very widely held in the Foreign Office as a whole, and certainly by Mounsey and Seymour, that it was 'not a Spanish characteristic to bargain away his property'.[121]

Meanwhile, somewhat less phlegmatic as to the outcome of the war, the Foreign Office was more responsive to the urgency with which the French regarded the situation. Precisely what happened following Cambon's appeals and the visit of the French naval officers is not clear, but from the diplomatic papers available it cannot now be ruled out that instructions were telephoned on the 6th or 7th to the British Embassy in Paris authorising Sir George Clerk to approach the French Foreign Minister Yvon Delbos, and unofficially 'strengthen his hand'. Indeed, the exact means of so doing may have been left to the Ambassador's discretion as certainly happened on subsequent similar occasions.[122]

Records of discussions preceding the Three-Power Conference in July show that on the whole the Cabinet had then wished to support the Blum Government, though it was doubted whether it would outlast the autumn.[123] As reported, events in Spain itself had so far tended to confirm and justify Baldwin's and Hoare's worst apprehensions. 'The anarchists and communists are still *de facto* masters of Barcelona and the surrounding countryside,' wrote King, adding, 'In some towns I hear that practically all the property-owning class has been exterminated.'[124] Now the French had openly declared themselves free to help the Spanish Republic. The Cabinet as such was not available to advise, but clear instructions had been given by Baldwin and Eden and were now reinforced by Hoare, to the effect that Britain should steer clear of all entanglements which might align her with Russia. Yet Britain's major ally was pleading either for active intervention in the Mediterranean on strategic grounds, or at very least, for support for the establishment of multilateral non-intervention. No response had as yet been made to Cambon's appeals.

Up to this point constant contact had been maintained with the Embassy in Paris on the progress of the Spanish affair. So delicate was the situation deemed, however, that the Ambassador and his staff had clear instructions from the Foreign Office that on Spain they were to ' . . . do nothing at all, even in this direction [the Fokker aircraft] without hearing from us'.[125] It is therefore inconceivable that the interview between the British Ambassador and the French Foreign Secretary on 7 August, could have taken place—as Clerk in his report insisted it did-without instructions from the Foreign Office, although it is true that none appear to have been recorded. Indeed, in that interview Clerk actually referred to the question of British aircraft detained in France, before concluding the exchange with Delbos by expressing the hope,

> that the French Government, even though, pending an agreement of non-intervention, they might feel themselves precluded from stopping private commercial transactions with Spain, would do what it could to limit and retard such transactions with Spain as much as possible. I asked M. Delbos to forgive me for speaking so frankly and I repeated that all I had said was entirely personal and on my own responsibility but I felt that in so critical a situation I must put before him the danger of any action which might definitely commit the French Government to one side of the conflict and make more difficult the close co-operation between our two countries which was called for by this crisis. M. Delbos said that, on the contrary, he thanked me for speaking so openly and that he and his colleagues wished for nothing more than that the two Governments should act together as closely as possible. He viewed the situation with the gravest anxiety. He had every reason to fear that General Franco had offered the bait of the Balearic Islands to Italy and the Canaries to Germany, and if that materialised, goodbye to French independence.
>
> I realise my responsibility in speaking to the Minister for Foreign Affairs as I did without instructions, but I had reason to believe that the extremists in the Government were putting pressure on M. Blum and I felt sure what I said might strengthen the hands of the moderate and sober elements.[126]

The events leading up to this important meeting can be partially reconstructed from correspondence between Sir Alexander Cadogan and Mr Hugh Lloyd Thomas, Minister at the British Embassy in Paris, who wrote privately to Cadogan on the 5th, 11th and 25th

August.[127] On the 11th Thomas sent a confidential report to Cadogan, giving his version of the origins of Clerk's démarche and his assessment of its efficacy. On the morning of Friday, 7 August, Bargeton, an official at the Quai d'Orsay, had called at the British Embassy in Paris, and according to Thomas had told him that the 'position of Delbos, Chautemps and other more reasonable members of the Government was very shaky and that anything we [Britain] could do to strengthen Delbos' hand would be most welcome'. Following Bargeton's visit to Thomas, Sir George Clerk called on Delbos that afternoon and reproached the Foreign Minister for sending Dewoitine aircraft to Spain when four British Fokkers had been held up in France. He asked the Foreign Minister if 'he were sure that the Government in Madrid was the real Government and not the screen behind which the most extreme anarchist elements in Spain were directing events'. His final point concerned the difficulty of future close co-operation between Britain and France, although he twice stressed that what he said was 'entirely personal and on my own responsibility'.[128]

However, in view of Bargeton's visit to Lloyd Thomas, it seems probable that the latter informed the Foreign Office by telephone of the French appeal, and that Sir George Clerk was then instructed to call on Delbos. Since the appeal came through Bargeton from 'the more reasonable members of the Government' and not necessarily from Blum himself, it is also likely that the Ambassador was instructed, as happened on subsequent occasions,[129] to emphasise that the visit was personal. How far Delbos was able to interpret Clerk's words so as to achieve the absolute ban on aid to Spain which was the outcome of the Cabinet meeting of 7 August is not known, but the French Foreign Minister's own account of the conversation is rather different. He claimed that Clerk spoke 'unequivocally of his Government's concern at the Spanish affair', and emphasised the need to push through an agreement on non-intervention, while observing a strict embargo on arms to Spain. Delbos also indicated that although the British Admiralty received Darlan coolly, the Foreign Office may have placed more importance on his visit, since he claims Clerk referred to the Italian threat to the Balearics and also to the relative insecurity of Gibraltar.[130] At all events, Viénot, the French Under-Secretary for Foreign Affairs, who had attended the French Cabinet meeting of 7th, told the British Minister that 'the Ambassador's timely words had been most useful'. Certainly the Foreign Office believed Clerk's *démarche* to have served its purpose and its mode of delivery to have been appropriate, for he was told, 'Your language is approved and appears to have had good results.'[131] It may be that in response to Delbos' urgent appeal Clerk's action, as opposed to his language, had had prior sanction.

Approval did not mean that all those concerned with French or Spanish affairs at the Foreign Office were aware, at the time, of the Bargeton-Thomas talk: it was almost certainly known to Cadogan, probably not to Mounsey nor to Seymour, who was most emphatic that 'H.M.G. did not make any *démarche* of the kind suggested'.[132] But it can be seen that there was indeed discreet pressure brought by the British upon the French Government, though only at the request of certain members of that government. The factionalism within the precariously balanced Popular Front Government, which spanned quite wide extremes of political opinion, is important here. As Geoffrey Warner has commented, 'Rarely has any government pursued two completely opposite policies with such tenacity at one and the same time.'[133] Right-wing members such as Delbos and Chautemps had on their side in this the considerable talents of Alexis Léger, civil head of the French Foreign Ministry, who was able to use contacts in the British Embassy to tap the sympathy of those in the Foreign Office of similar views. It has been suggested that some rumours of British pressure may have been 'clandestinely inspired by members of the French Cabinet',[134] and this is supported by a letter from Lloyd Thomas to Sir Orme Sargent, Superintending Under-Secretary of the Central Department, in which he wrote, 'In the meantime, the Quai d'Orsay and the more reasonable members of the Government seem to have got the upper hand as far as Spain is concerned, and since last Friday they have been much more confident of being able to keep out of trouble.' He then continued with apparent complete disregard for the explanation he had sent to Cadogan a fortnight earlier:

> I do not know how they have dealt with the 'interventionist' members within the Government and the extreme elements outside, but Citrine and Gillies,[135] who came to see me on Saturday, told me that the representatives of the Confédération Générale du Travail and other Labour leaders, whom they had met, were convinced that H.M.G. had told the French Government that, if the latter intervened actively on behalf of the Madrid Government, they would no longer be able to count on

the support of H.M.G. in the event of trouble with Germany. The result was that Jouhaux and Co. had decided to put water in their wine and to slacken their pressure on M. Blum.[136]

There are several interesting points here. First, it seems very likely that Blum would have had little difficulty in accepting whatever interpretation Delbos put upon Clerk's *démarche*, which would in any case have been very much in line with his own experience of British attitudes towards Spain. Forced to capitulate, the theory of British pressure was much the most acceptable explanation to offer his extreme left wing and the trades unions, and it was, after all, in a sense true. The second point raised by Thomas's letter is that the labour and trades-union leaders were quite explicit that the threat was the withdrawal of British support 'in event of trouble with Germany'. Yet Clerk's words, as reported, made no direct reference to Germany or the Locarno Pact. In relation to this point it is of interest to note that within days of Clerk's *démarche* similar pressure was brought to bear in Lisbon, although in this case specific allusion was made to the Anglo-Portuguese Alliance.

If Mounsey had seemed unenthusiastic at first about the French proposal, by the end of the first week of August he was compelled to appreciate the advantages that a multilateral agreement might bring, for the Portuguese, whom the British had agreed to approach on behalf of France, were proving unexpectedly recalcitrant and seemed set on intervening. 'I think,' he minuted, 'we should bring pressure at once at Lisbon where there is evidently going to be great obstruction – if we can without having to make definite commitments.' Cadogan agreed, and a telegram was drafted by him the following day authorising an oral *démarche* to cover several points of which the last read:

H.M.G. have always admitted the validity of the treaties between themselves and Portugal though they have of necessity retained the right of judging the circumstances under which these treaties should come into play. . . . H.M.G. have themselves welcomed the French proposal and trust that it will also commend itself to the Portuguese Government.

The circumstances of this *démarche* at Lisbon were different from those obtaining in France. The Portuguese Government was particularly anxious for assurance that in the event of the

'. . . march on Lisbon if the Spanish Government win, British soldiers [would] be on Portugal's frontier and British aeroplanes be above Portugal within twenty-four hours.'[137] It was to be expected, therefore, that the British approach would mention the Anglo-Portuguese alliance, but it does indicate that during the second week of August the British Government was prepared to call in question a long-standing treaty as a means of applying pressure in relation to their Anglo-Spanish policy.

Finally, why did Lloyd Thomas purport not to know 'how they have dealt with the "interventionist" members'? The explanation for this would appear to lie in the return to the Foreign Office of Eden on 16 August,[138] and the growing anger of the left in Britain at rumours now freely circulating of British pressure on France in the adoption of non-intervention, a policy to which Blum was ideologically opposed. Indeed, the French Premier declared himself to be 'in torture' at the course he had been forced to adopt, and was in such a nervous state he was unable to eat or sleep properly.[139]

Eden's part until mid-August had been extremely limited. When he left for Yorkshire on 31 July it is doubtful whether the Spanish affair was foremost among his concerns. But the press was now vocal and divided: on the one hand Britain was felt to be dragging her feet in response to Blum's appeal for multilateral non-intervention, while on the other, there were growing protest at what Lord Strabolgi, the Labour peer, had called the 'malevolent neutrality' of British policy.[140] Since opposition from the left was likely to increase, it may be that Eden was given only the briefest outline of the events which had taken place in his absence. For the same reason Lloyd Thomas may have chosen to tone down his account of the development of the French position in his letter to Orme Sargent.

The need to do so was accentuated when on his return to the Foreign Office on 16 August the Secretary of State was asked to receive a deputation of Labour leaders headed by Mr Arthur Greenwood, Deputy-Leader of the Labour Party – Clement Attlee being in Russia. He was accompanied by Sir Walter Citrine and William Gillies, who repeated the information they had received in Paris concerning British pressure on the French Government. Paradoxically the deputation, like Eden himself, was also concerned at press reports of Foreign Office equivocation in coming to a swift acceptance of the French proposal for a non-intervention agreement. Eden explained first that the initiative was entirely French;

that a division of Europe into blocs just before entering on the five-power conversations would be a 'real calamity', and also that far from following the French lead quietly, the Foreign Office had given strong support in Berlin, Rome and Lisbon.[141] The same deputation called again a week later, and the Secretary of State again categorically denied, as indeed was true, that the initiative for non-intervention had come from the British Government.[142]

So firm was he in his belief that no pressure had been applied that when Mr George Strauss, Labour M.P. for North Lambeth, gave notice of his intention to put two questions in Parliament concerning the Spanish situation and the question of British pressure on France, the Secretary of State insisted on answering in the House, although he was strongly advised by Hankey not to do so. It seems highly unlikely that Eden would have insisted on answering the question, when his advisers suggested Strauss be asked quietly to drop his questions, if he had been aware at that time of the existence of Hugh Lloyd Thomas's letter to Cadogan of 11 August.

In order to prepare an answer for him, the files were searched for any representations of the kind Strauss referred to, but in vain. Lloyd Thomas's letter to Cadogan appears to have been overlooked. Finally, as regards recent research, it must be added that several folios which may eventually offer further evidence have been extracted from the files. Meanwhile, perhaps the last word on the issue of British pressure should be left with the clerk, who having conducted the search of the files commented cryptically that: 'The connexion between Sir G. Clerk's question and the French Government's decision is a matter of which there can be no proof.'[143]

THE CONSOLIDATION OF BRITISH ATTITUDES

Although the Foreign Office had been most eager for France to adopt a policy of non-intervention, there was considerable reluctance to give an outright committal on the part of Britain, at least until such time as Germany and Italy had shown more than mere 'agreement in principle' to the French proposals. Neither of those countries at the beginning of August found any advantage in a speedy conclusion of an agreement; both were now backing the military rebellion, and both therefore raised peripheral questions as being essential to any agreement. Italy emphasised the need for moral as well as material disarmament, mentioning in particular the problems of volunteers now pouring into Republican Spain, mainly from France, and also the question of funds; again, a form of intervention mainly favouring the Republic and raised in, among other countries, France, Britain, but also – especially abhorrent to Italy – in Russia. Germany suggested naval control of Spanish imports and was shortly presented with an excellent excuse for delaying full agreement when, on 19 August, the Spanish Republic impounded a German aircraft. Suspicion in the Foreign Office that this was a tactic employed by the Republic in order to postpone an agreement regarded as contrary to their interests was strengthened when, two days later, the German ship *Kamerun* was forcibly detained by a Spanish warship as it attempted to enter Cadiz in contravention of the Republican blockade.[144]

In addition to Italian and German reluctance to join in an agreement, British hesitancy also owed much to events in Spain, where the outcome of the conflict was far from predictable. Despite initial obstacles facing the rebels, which should have given the Republic a decisive advantage, reports from Spain appeared to indicate a total collapse of civil order and the onset of the long anticipated left-wing counter-revolution. From Barcelona came reports that Madrid was expected to fall at any moment, and that the 'Madrid Government' was about to withdraw to Valencia.[145] In contrast to the disarray reported from Republican Spain, the *Junta de Defensa Nacional*, the rebel authority newly established at Burgos, appeared to be consolidating its initial victory, albeit slowly, and was confidently inviting the return to the army of all officers retired under the premiership of Azaña.[146] By 7 August, so the Foreign Office was informed, thirty-four cities from Tetuan in North Africa to El Ferrol on the north coast of Spain had fallen to the rebels.[147] Even where the military rebellion was unsuccessful, as in Barcelona, the ruthless putting down of the rising was repugnant to many in Britain. The prospect of the execution of the rebel generals Goded and Burriel appalled Halifax, and only with difficulty was he dissuaded from intervening on their behalf.[148]

However, both Mounsey and his chief assistant in Spanish matters, Evelyn Shuckburgh, were alert to the partisanship of reports from Spain and the undecided nature of the situation. 'The Spanish Government', minuted Shuckburgh, 'have popular support and are represented as freeing the public from the previously existing tyranny. Nor', he continued, 'after a month is there any sign of a leader (on the Right) who is likely to capture the public mind.'[149] But generally in the Foreign Office there was little sympathy for the Republic. Even Mounsey was quick to point out to Eden, when drafting a reply to the formal letter presented by the Labour delegation, that:

> . . . though it might appear on the surface that the present Government of Spain is the constitutionally appointed Government of which Mr Greenwood spoke there is reason to fear that the Government is itself at the mercy of extremist elements whose object in the event of its obtaining the upper hand of the rebels, is to overturn it and establish in its place a reign of anarchy which would be out of harmony with all English ideas of constitutional democracy. But perhaps [he added sagely] if this letter may be published, the latter argument is not one to be included.[150]

Certainly at the end of the second week of August fear of the division of Europe into two ideological blocs was the motivating force behind British policy. On 12 August, Delbos approached Clerk, saying that just as he had listened to Clerk's appeal the previous Friday he hoped Clerk would listen now to his appeal. This appeal, which resulted in the signing of British and French notes in Paris on 15 August,[151] set off a flurry of discussion and analysis of the British position regarding Spain.

The emergence of ideological blocs would, argued Sargent, be detrimental to the negotiation of a five-power pact, and would moreover be

> a very different and far more horrible development than the creation of national and imperialistic blocs of satisfied versus dissatisfied Powers which we have hitherto foreseen and feared, for the creation of ideological blocs would not merely divide Governments from one another far more deeply than any political dispute, but would also cut across the domestic politics of each individual country.

Britain, he said, should take the initiative to prevent this from happening; and

> we ought to be able to strengthen the French Government in its

efforts – or indeed bring pressure to bear to force it – to free itself from Communist domination, both domestic and Muscovite.

He believed Italy and Germany were drawn together by their isolation in Europe rather than by fear of communism, but in so far as the latter was a motivating force, that anxiety was focused on the future of France rather than on the outcome of the civil war in Spain. He therefore stressed the importance of:

  (i) our preventing France by hook or by crook from 'going Bolshevik' under the influence of the Spanish civil war; and
  (ii) our freeing Italy from the feeling of isolation and vulnerability which the Abyssinian affair has left her with.

Cadogan agreed, although both he and Mounsey, doubtless from recent experience, felt the need for caution in influencing France lest 'any false step on our part might be misinterpreted and produce exactly the opposite result to what we intended'. Mounsey, however, shrewdly saw in non-intervention an opportunity for a dress rehearsal for the five-power conference:

Is it not something [he asked] if by our energetic support, we can get the French to invite and bring round a table both Germany and Italy on one side, and Russia on the other? That was one of our objectives when we insisted that France must widen the circle of non-arms-supplying Powers, rather than confine it to an initial Anglo-Franco-Italian agreement. And won't it be something still more if once round a table, all those Powers can seriously be got to agree publicly to the principle of non-intervention? Whether they observe it or not, that is the first step surely in any effectual effort to stem the outbreak of further Fascism v. Communism in Spain.[152]

Yet despite the signing of the Agreement on 15 August, British policy was still far from settled. Following Delbos' appeal on the 12th, policy discussion now turned to broader aspects of the problem presented by the conflict, and Cadogan asked Major-General Ismay, newly appointed Deputy Secretary to the Committee of Imperial Defence, to have drafted a paper setting out the strategic implications of the situation in Spain for Britain. Mr Owen St. Clair O'Malley, Counsellor and Head of the Southern Department, which covered Italian affairs, pointed out to his colleagues that there had been several recent Cabinet papers on the British position in the Mediterranean which made it clear that any question of Italian expansion or extension of her power in that area ought to give rise to the 'gravest misgivings'.[153] In the light of the recognised importance of the Mediterranean and efforts recently expended in strengthening Britain's position in the eastern Mediterranean, (the Montreux Conference, and the Anglo-Egyptian Treaty) it seems strange that strategic questions raised by the civil war in Spain were not discussed until one month after the military rebellion.

Meanwhile, the dilatoriness of Italy and Germany in the formal signing of agreements on non-intervention[154] prompted the Foreign Office to examine British policy towards Spain in the event of a complete breakdown of the negotiations and failure of the French initiative. Ruling out any assistance to the rebels as 'contrary to all our principles of correctness and justice', Mounsey set out the alternatives facing the Government in what appears to be the first really detailed analysis of the British position on Spain. These were:

1. To continue to maintain our previous policy of impartiality, discouraging the supply of arms and munitions to either side and finding reasons for issuing no licences for export of arms destined for the Spanish Government when applications are presented, without actually refusing on principle to consider applications from the Spanish Government;

2. To adopt a policy of conformity with that observed towards other Governments in normal times: viz. to allow licences to be issued only when the arms etc. are guaranteed to be for the use of the Spanish Government themselves for defence purposes;

3. To allow arms to be exported to any destination in Spain.

But Mounsey felt there were objections to all these:

1. will become increasingly difficult to maintain and justify when the Spanish Government press us to allow the exportation of arms for their own use. The delays and difficulties that we can interpose will gradually be taken to be discriminatory action against the existing Government in Spain and will affect their attitude towards HMG in the event of their recovering their control of the country;

2. will lay us open to less justifiable charge on the part of the rebels of favouring the rival party. It will also align us with France as against Germany, Italy and Portugal. . . . It will deprive us of the impartial attitude which must in the future be our strongest hand in renewing good relations with whatever party emerges on top as a result of the present struggle;

3. . . . implies we do not recognise the Spanish Government at all.

He therefore considered (1) to be preferable, although recognising that it would give the Opposition press great opportunity for abusing the Government's policy. Cadogan agreed broadly but went further in acknowledging real opposition to the Spanish Government:

> In normal circumstances – i.e. if the 'existing Government' exercised real control and had any chance of surviving – I should say that, failing international agreement, we should most scrupulously observe our regular and normal policy of allowing, or licensing shipments to the established Government and not to the rebels;
> In the present state of Spain, or in the situation that is likely rapidly to develop, the ordinary rule cannot be blindly followed. What is the existing Government? How far do those in power in Barcelona recognise the Madrid authorities? How far in effect have the latter control of Madrid itself?
> I should have thought it would be better, probably to maintain our present attitude. Apart from the international aspect of the matter and our desire to avoid alignments, it may well be that in the near future it will become clearer, even to our Labour people, that the existing Government is becoming less and less deserving of their sympathy.

However, he believed that it was difficult 'to lay down here and now' what should be done. Eden, too, endorsed Mounsey's first proposal, and thus it was agreed that British policy in the event of failure of the Non-Intervention Agreement would be to continue to place obstacles in the way of any attempt of the Spanish Government to obtain aid from Britain.[155] Here too was recognition for the first time of the need to maintain 'good relations with whatever party emerges on top', a theme soon to be reinforced by the Chiefs of

Staff. So far political considerations had outweighed all else in
Britain. In France, however, the danger to vital French interests of a
hostile power athwart France's main sea route to North Africa from
whence her vast African army would have to be transported in time
of European war, was recognised by both left and right, although as
to which would present the greater peril, a Russian- or an Italian-
dominated Spain, there was naturally no consensus of opinion.[156] In
Russia the strategic issue was proclaimed to be of the first
importance to the democracies, according to the official news
organs *Izvestia* and *Pravda* which formed the major source of
information from that most secretive of countries.[157]

The report issued by the Chiefs of Staff[158] on 24 August
concluded:

1. Our interests in the present Spanish crisis are the
   maintenance:
   (a) of the territorial integrity of Spain and her possessions; and
   (b) of such relations with any Spanish Government which
   may emerge from this conflict as will ensure benevolent
   neutrality in the event of our being engaged in a European
   war;
2. Open intervention by Italy in support of the insurgents in
   Spain would precipitate a major international crisis;
3. The occupation by Italy of any territory in Spain itself would
   be detrimental to British interests;
4. The Italian occupation of any part of Spanish Morocco, and
   particularly of Ceuta, would be a threat to vital British
   interests;
5. The Italian occupation of any of the Balearic Islands, Canary
   Islands, and/or Rio de Oro, is highly undesirable from the
   point of view of British interests, but cannot be regarded as a
   vital menace;
6. Any of the contingencies specified in (2) to (5) above would be
   injurious in greater or lesser degree to French interests;
7. The conclusion of any Italo-Spanish alliance would constitute
   a threat to vital British interests;
8. The threat of effective action, other than action in a
   diplomatic sphere, to thwart Italian designs would involve a
   grave risk of war;
9. Italy is the only Power whose forces are mobilised and ready
   for immediate action. Her preparedness for the initial phase of

hostilities, *vis-à-vis* Great Britain, is greater than it was nine
months ago.

The Chiefs of Staff recommended that:

1. The principle that should govern any action on the part of His
   Majesty's Government should be that it is most important to
   avoid any measures which, while failing to achieve our object,
   merely tend further to alienate Italy;
2. We should press for the earliest possible conclusion of a non-
   intervention pact in Spain, embracing France, Russia, Portugal, Germany, Italy and the United Kingdom;
3. If no general agreement can be reached, we should impress on
   the French the desirability of giving no cause for intervention
   by Italy;
4. We should maintain sufficient naval forces on the Western
   Mediterranean and Spanish Atlantic coasts to ensure that we
   have at least one ship at every port where the Italians have
   one, and that at important ports the British SNO is, if possible,
   senior to the Italian;
5. We should, if possible, get an agreement with the other Powers
   that any landing or other action by armed forces to preserve
   order should be not only international in character, but also,
   wherever this is possible, preconcerted between the Powers
   affected;
6. Failing such agreement, every endeavour should be made
   locally for concerted action to be taken when the occasion
   arises;
7. We should make it known to Signor Mussolini that, in the
   words of F.P. (36)10, 'any alteration of the *status quo* in the
   Western Mediterranean must be a matter of the closest
   concern to His Majesty's Government', in order that he may
   be under no misapprehension as to the consequences of any
   action that he may take to disturb the existing balance.[159]

Whether the Chiefs of Staff need have been quite so timorous
before the military might of Mussolini appears, in retrospect, open
to question,[160] but certainly the options open to the British
Government in the light of the report were very limited: they must
pick a very careful course between offending Italy on the one hand,
and offending either of the warring parties in Spain on the other.

Since the Spanish rebels and Italy were already firmly linked, policy tended inevitably to be weighted in their favour, but continuing support for non-intervention fulfilled in some measure the obligation not to offend the Spanish Republic.

The meeting of the Foreign Policy Committee on 25 August was used by Eden to outline to his colleagues events and decisions of the past weeks. He informed the Committee that the French did not wish Paris to be the clearing-house for further action, and that he had agreed, subject to the Committee's approval, that London should perform this function. An international committee, mooted since 12 August, would be set up, and would supervise arrangements and reach agreement on questions such as categories of arms to be included in the general embargo. Summarising, the Secretary of State said that '. . . in the opinion of those best competent to judge, the situation in Spain would almost certainly result in a stalemate, provided that there was no foreign intervention on one side or the other.' Thus it is clear at this point that opinion in the Foreign Office, at the Committee of Imperial Defence, and after 2 September in the Cabinet, found consensus in the need to pursue rigorously a policy of non-intervention.[161]

In political circles first reactions of the British Government had been emphatic. 'We English', Baldwin is reputed to have told a colleague, 'hate fascism but we loathe bolshevism as much. So, if there is somewhere where fascists and bolsheviks can kill each other off, so much the better.'[162] Certainly, from the first, restrictions had been placed on the Republican Government in the matter of fuel purchases and movement of shipping and aircraft, occasioning grave disadvantage for the Republic. Reluctant to join in a multilateral agreement, but also wishing to hold France back from decisive involvement in the Spanish affair, the Foreign Office agreed, somewhat grudgingly, to support a formal declaration of non-intervention. At the same time, by emphasising the isolation in which France would find herself by acting unilaterally, considerable support had been given to those elements within the French Government and at the Quai d'Orsay who hoped to restrain their more tempestuous colleagues from direct intervention in Spain. Nevertheless, it was the French who had pressed for and concerted action to protest at the use of Tangier by the Spanish Government, who had first proposed a conference of Tangier powers and later a three-power meeting to solve the problem of intervention. By the second half of August, the intense interest which the rebellion had provoked, both in Britain and internationally, together with the delicate balance of French politics and increasing awareness of the strategic aspects of the situation, contrived to make a multinational agreement the most satisfactory solution for the immediate crisis, although reservations were held for the future. 'We shall have to watch', minuted Cadogan, 'how things develop.'[163]

2 Non-Intervention

Britain had now, although somewhat tentatively, committed herself to non-intervention both in the Agreement and in the setting up of a committee of co-ordination. Over the next two years many efforts were made to bolster this commitment. Ever since then contradictory criticisms of these efforts have been made. It has been argued on the one hand that non-intervention was farcical and unable to prevent massive intervention by Italy, Russia and Germany. On the other hand it is claimed that non-intervention prevented France from aiding the Republic. If either of these views is true, then clearly the role of the British Government in supporting non-intervention was crucial to the outcome of the Spanish Civil War. Here it is proposed to examine the efficacy of the actual machinery of non-intervention: its powers and limitations as imposed by the agreement, the Committee, and later by the Control Scheme.

THE AGREEMENT

The first step towards a broadly-based European agreement on the Spanish question was taken by the British in their reply of 4 August to the French note of 1 August. In response to that reply, and after taking soundings as to its likely reception,[1] a formal text was circulated to a further fourteen countries on 15 August, and ultimately twenty-seven countries made declarations of acceptance.[2] The most notable European exception was Switzerland, which, although agreeing in principle, wished to retain her traditional neutrality. The United States, after early consultation by France, wisely, perhaps, took a similar line.[3]

Although the replies from governments acquiescing in the general precepts of the French Declaration were subsequently referred to as the Non-Intervention Agreement (hereafter NIA), because they were received sporadically over a period of some weeks and differed one from another in textual details they cannot be regarded as constituting a treaty in the formal sense but were rather a series of unilateral accords.[4]

The Declaration fell into two parts. The first, the preamble, spoke of abstention from all interference, direct and indirect. There followed three specific points covering the proscription of export, re-export or transit to Spain or her possessions of all war materials, aircraft and ships, including current contracts. Governments would keep each other informed of measures taken to enforce the Declaration.[5]

However, although most governments followed the wording of the three enumerated points, there were many deviations from the original text, and some countries – Germany, Hungary, Italy, Latvia, Poland and Turkey – entirely omitted from their reply the preamble of the original note and did not therefore agree to abstain vigorously from 'all interference direct or indirect', only from that which they individually specified. In addition, five replies were further hedged about with various conditions of acceptance. Only fifteen countries followed verbatim both the preamble and the three main policy clauses. Such discrepancies severely weakened the Non-Intervention Agreement and account for much subsequent equivocation on the part of the signatories.[6]

Thus the NIA was no more than a series of slightly differing accords which had, as the Foreign Office noted from the first, no force in law,[7] and which formed a most unstable foundation on which to build the Non-Intervention Committee. Since no agreement was formed which was legally binding on all, any country could withdraw from the Agreement at any time without violating international law, and threat of withdrawal could be, and was, as with the League of Nations used on several occasions to manipulate Committee decisions.

There were many anomalies, too, in the specific listing of the arms embargoes.[8] The relevant clause in the original declaration spoke only of ' . . . all arms, munitions and military equipment, as well as aircraft, assembled or otherwise, and all warships'. Although this was obviously intended to give good umbrella cover, and given a general wish to conform might have worked, in the acutely belligerent atmosphere of Europe in 1936 it could not work because it was insufficiently specific.

Many countries had existing legislation concerning the export of war material, which covered in part the lists submitted by the NIA,

and while it could have been effective, perhaps, if one comprehensive agreement had been drawn up to cover the duration of the
Spanish war, this was not done. Each country composed its own
arms 'embargo list – true, with close reference to the schedules
proposed by the NIA (which were based on work done by the US
Government for the Conference for the Reduction and Limitation
of Armaments) and which enumerated various categories of
arms – [9] but these were followed with individual differences which
created from the beginning the possibility of breaches of the policy
of non-intervention.

Britain drew on existing legislation, the Arms Export Prohibition
Order, 1931, as did some other countries, but about half those
concerned had to pass new legislation of some kind, a decree, order
in council, etc., although Yugoslavia needed no new legislation,
having no private manufacture of arms. Most had to make at least
some supplementary edict to bring existing legislation into line with
the schedules of prohibited arms and war material.[10] All countries
included in the list rifles and carbines, but Germany did not list the
fourth category, which included revolvers and pistols. Tanks and
armoured vehicles were not banned by the Irish Free State, nor
were gas, aircraft and certain chemicals such as nitrates. Indeed the
Irish Free State was prominent among some other countries for the
number of things it did not prohibit. Other articles or implements of
war not covered were vessels (Category 13), range-finders (Category 15), searchlights, signals and wireless apparatus. The significance of this was not that it would leave Ireland free to engage in her
own trade in these items, but that Ireland could, if agreeable, be
used as an entrepôt by other European states wishing to export such
restricted items to Spain.

The blatant abuse of such loopholes was to offer an excuse to
other states who later wished to exploit the situation and revoke part
of their own agreement. For example, since neither France,
Germany, nor Britain had included Item 17, Category E (vehicles)
in their list of prohibited items, Italy informed the NIC in March
1937 that she, too, would no longer include this item.[11]

An even more striking example both of the discrepancies among
embargoes and of bad faith was the early discovery that the German
arms embargo regulations were applicable only within the sphere of
the German internal customs area and not, as the German delegate
and Ambassador to Britain, Ribbentrop, later pointed out, 'in those
parts of Germany which, as areas excluded from customs or as free

zones, i.e. outside the internal customs area, are consequently treated as external territory for customs purposes'. Thus, while still obeying to the letter its arms embargo, Germany could lawfully contravene the intention of the NIA, since its largest port, Hamburg, lay outside the customs restrictions as did Bremen and several other ports. This loophole was not only to the advantage of Germany if she should choose to use it, but also attracted independent gun-runners of all nationalities including British.[12]

The general lack of sincerity with which governments approached the arms embargo can also be gauged by the advantage that was taken of the gap between the agreement and the actual date and implementation of the legislation to cover it. Both Germany and Italy used this time-lag to explain breaches on non-intervention brought before the Committee in its early stages. The Italian reply to the Spanish Government's accusation of a delivery to the Nationalists of Caproni aircraft was that the aircraft 'if that they exist' had left before the embargo had actually come into force.[13] In view of the duplicity of the signatories to the Agreement, the lapse of nearly seven weeks between the date when the first prohibition was made effective (that of France on 9 August) and the date of the last (Estonia on 10 September)[14] could have made a vital difference, and in any case provided a plausible answer to subsequent questioning of any infringement during that period. Thus the initial Agreement was full of holes and there was clearly a need for reinforcement of some kind if non-intervention was to be sustained.

THE COMMITTEE

The need for some kind of joint scrutiny of the NIA had been anticipated in the third clause of the declaration and France had urged the signatories to consider the creation of a committee. Unwilling to act as host to the Committee, the French Government suggested that delegates should meet in London, although this was not at first welcomed by the British Government which had hoped to play a less conspicuous rôle in the proceedings.[15] The matter was first raised on 12 and again on 24 August, when it was proposed that London should become the clearing-house for any further action on Spain.[16] However, the idea of a committee was, not unnaturally, greeted in some quarters with great caution, particularly among the dictators who feared – even as. Mounsey had, on the contrary, hoped – that this was a device to 'get them round the table' as a prelude to the new Locarno talks before they themselves were ready for them. The Germans were assured, therefore, that the function of the Committee would be confined to matters directly concerned with the arms embargo and that the British Government was fully aware of the danger in 'ventilating delicate questions in the Committee, or in entrusting to it tasks which fall outside the immediate problem of arms embargo'.[17] Accepting these assurances, Germany then agreed to join the Committee,[18] preparations for which went ahead at speed.

The responsibility for the Committee now lay fully with the British Foreign Office, and so great was the haste to begin that W. S. Morrison, Financial Secretary at the Treasury, was chosen to chair the first meetings, although it was known he would shortly be leaving for Geneva.[19] From 20 September he was replaced by Lord Plymouth,[20] representing the Foreign Secretary, who himself chaired some of the more difficult meetings, notably in the summer of 1937. As Secretary, the Foreign Office selected Mr Francis Hemming of the Economic Advisory Council, a body not at that time over-employed. Hemming, a lepidopterist of repute, appears to have entered into this work with ingenuous enthusiasm, apparently maintained throughout the course of the Committee's existence despite the burden of his new task, attested by the forty official volumes of the NIC and the equal number of boxes now in the Public Record Office.[21]

At the Foreign Office much of the real burden of work was done by Evelyn Shuckburgh until he was succeeded by John Coulson in September 1937. The Legal Department of the Foreign Office was also closely involved in Spanish affairs from July 1936 onwards, mainly with the twin problems of belligerent rights and recognition. Shipping problems were at first dealt with by Mr Gerald Fitzmaurice, the Third Legal Adviser, and later by Mr W. E. Beckett, Second Legal Adviser.[22] The First Legal Adviser, Sir William Malkin, attended the NIC as required and chaired the Committee or Jurists (see below).

Initially twenty-six countries sent representatives, usually the ambassador or head of mission, although attendance was often delegated to the next in command. These were joined by the twenty-seventh representative, Senhor Armindo Monteiro of Portugal, at the fourth meeting of the Committee on 28 September. It had been foreseen that the size of the plenary Committee would be too cumbersome to promote efficiency, and on the morning after the first meeting of the Committee in the Locarno Room at the Foreign Office on 9 September, a small group met in Lord Cranborne's room to discuss future organisation. The Foreign Secretary proposed that the bulk of the work should be conducted by sub-committees, two such to be proposed at the next meeting to aid the Chairman in settling the work of the Committee. The first of these was to be composed of the representatives from those countries adjacent to Spain: France and Portugal, together with representatives of arms-producing countries: the United Kingdom, Germany, Italy, Belgium, Sweden, Czechoslovakia and Russia, again with Morrison as chairman. This committee was known as the Chairman's Sub-Committee (hereafter CSC) and become the real power-house of non-intervention.[23]

Recognition of the need for sub-committees suggests that the Foreign Office foresaw in non-intervention the possibility of a long and complex struggle, and so it was to prove. In all there would be thirty meetings of the plenary Committee and ninety-three of the Chairman's Sub-Committee, while seven further sub-committees dealt with technical problems as they arose.[24] Yet despite the meticulous organisation of the Committee it was clear from the beginning that genuine non-intervention was no more than a chimera.

PROCEDURE

The hope was expressed that once formed, the NIC would act solely to alert governments to 'inadvertent' breaches of the NIA and that steps would then be taken to avoid any repetition. That blatant intervention might continue had certainly been envisaged in the Foreign Office, but the disadvantages had seemed outweighed by the value of such an opportunity for close communication with the dictators and by the need to support the French. The former, however, saw in the NIC an unrivalled public rostrum from which to address Europe while continuing in their selected policy towards Spain. In fact, from the autumn of 1936 Italy, and to a lesser extent Germany, stepped up aid to Spain and were, if anything, even less circumspect than before as to their involvement. The USSR acted similarly.

The first meetings of the Committee were taken up with the constitution of the Chairman's Sub-committee; the lack of authority of the Committee; and the absence of Portugal. The question of procedure was examined, and the Soviet representative presented detailed accusations of breaches of the NIA against Italy and Germany. But far from facilitating the presentation of complaints, the procedure of the Committee actively discouraged them.[25] This was in part due to the rapidity with which the rules for dealing with accusations had been hurried through, both in order to deal with Soviet allegations of breaches of the NIA and to enable Portugal to attend the Committee. This was necessary since that country declined to do so until assured of the Committee's competence to deal with so large a number of delegates and of its authority and impartiality. Furthermore, Portugal insisted on approving the rules of procedure, which were therefore finalised at the fourth meeting of the Committee on 28 September.[26] In the last moments of euphoria accompanying the setting of the Committee in motion, the hope was expressed that few complaints would be received. If they were, the Committee would examine them and endeavour to verify the facts. Astonishingly this was the full extent of the Committee's powers, and even these were curbed by conditions. The Committee would only consider complaints emanating from a responsible source, of a magnitude to demand attention, and based on reliable evidence. The final provision was ambivalent in the extreme and made inculpation of offenders virtually impossible.

Moreover, complaints would be considered only if they were put forward by one of the nations participating in the Agreement, a point which effectively ensured that the Committee would not be pestered by either of the belligerents themselves nor by journalists or other private citizens on the spot. Such obvious sources of information would only be heard through a participating government willing to sponsor them, thus losing the impact of a direct claim. Even then, since the Committee was not provided with means by which accusations could be verified at local level there was little hope of redress. The procedure demanded only that on the submission of a complaint, the Chairman should request from the representative of the government charged 'such explanations as are necessary to determine the facts in the case', and only then would the NIC endeavour to verify the accusation if that was considered necessary.[27] To be more specific would have been to court the very danger of overt declarations of intent towards Spain which the

Committee still hoped to avoid. The only way out of the dilemma was to examine the huge and increasing volume of evidence which poured in on every side and then solemnly to reject it as 'unsubstantiated'.[28]

A further aspect of the procedure of the Committee was the clause demanding written replies to accusations. Since delegates had little real power and were obliged to refer back to their governments, this had the effect of greatly protracting the proceedings. At the fifth meeting both the Italian and Soviet representatives expressed themselves willing to exchange verbal replies to their mutual accusations, but this the Chairman would not allow as it would, he ruled, contravene procedure. By insisting on written replies Lord Plymouth gained a further fortnight before the next plenary session of the Committee on 23 October, and postponed the need at that point for a political decision on his part as Chairman of the Committee.

Most of the evidence of intervention could be easily dismissed as unreliable. Accusations were countered with flat denials or counter-accusations, lapsing frequently into petty squabbling. Indeed it was deliberate policy of the protagonists that this should be so,[29] and the overt antagonism between the Soviet delegate and the delgates of Germany, Italy and Portugal made each meeting a minefield through which Lord Plymouth picked his way with increasing difficulty.

The first major crisis at the NIC came just one month after its inception when Russia, fearing that the dictators had gained the ascendancy at the Committee, withdrew support from the NIA. No less culpable in intent than Italy or Germany, but facing far greater difficulties in trans-shipment, the Soviet delegate, frustrated through reasons of protocol by rejection of patently reliable reports of Italian and German intervention, pleaded for control of Portuguese ports at least, and threatened withdrawal from the NIA if violation of it were not immediately halted.[30] Both these demands were rejected but Russian defiance was continued, with the delivery at the Foreign Office on 12 October of a note which called for the control of Portuguese ports by Britain and France, for although material aid came chiefly from Italy and Germany, its point of ingress in the early stages of the war had undoubtedly often been Portugal, a fact made much of at the plenary sessions by the Russians.[31] Further, the Soviet delegate demanded that his proposal be discussed at the next NIC meeting, to be called immediately.[32] The British Cabinet dismissed a Russian demand that they should accept joint responsibility with the French for a naval patrol of Spanish waters[33] as, indeed, the Russians must have known they would. On 23 October, having failed to galvanise the Committee to action, and failed to spur Britain and France to accept responsibility for the waywardness of Portugal, the Soviet Union openly returned to the Spanish Republic the right to purchase arms.[34]

Given the new situation created by the Russian *démarche* and by increasing fear of Russian intervention in Spain, the British Government had once more to reassess its position *vis-à-vis* non-intervention, a position tied, it seemed, inextricably to that of France. For the latter, however, this was a peculiarly testing time in view of the existing Franco-Soviet pact.

What the British Cabinet had until this point believed was that the Spanish Republic was very close to capitulation. Indeed, as Eden had admitted to Corbin, the French Ambassador, on 23 October, Britain would most probably have afforded a degree of recognition (belligerent rights) to Franco on the fall of Madrid, which was then believed to be imminent. Russia's willingness to dictate terms to the NIC, following shortly on news of the first arrival in Spain of Russian tanks and munitions, changed the situation in the Committee almost overnight.[35] No doubt to retain the equilibrium in the Committee so essential to internal French stability, Corbin was willing to support Russia to the extent that he felt the Committee should at least consider a proposal for supervisors on the spot, although he admitted it was doubtful whether the Spanish Government would be persuaded to agree such a proposal. It was, however, agreed to put the proposal to the Committee when it reconvened that afternoon.[36]

Faced with total disintegration of the Committee and the NIA, the Chairman's Sub-committee met the next day and delegates agreed to sound out their respective governments on a proposal for supervision of the principal ports of entry into Spain. The delay entailed meant that not until 9 November was a draft statement for submission to both parties in Spain ready for the approval of the Committee, and it was not sent until December. This was the beginning, however, of the ambitious and largely impracticable series of solutions for the control of Spanish imports of arms which was to engage so much of the Committee's time over the coming months.

That it should have been the Russian Government which demanded control just as their first consignments of military aid were beginning to arrive may appear paradoxical, but was in fact quite logical. First, it established Russia as a force to be reckoned with in an international committee in which all the success so far appeared to belong to the dictators, and especially to Portugal which had deigned to attend only on its own terms. Second, discussion of control represented informal acknowledgement of Italo-German intervention, which had already taken place, even though it seemed unlikely that it would gain approval of either party in Spain. And finally, in the unlikely event that control were accepted and imposed, Russia would be able to withdraw honourably from what otherwise threatened to become a Herculean task.

CONTROL

Over the next twelve months the sub-committees were to formulate a succession of plans controlling intervention, each one differing from its predecessor by amendments or complete revision, but each proving ineffectual as new problems arose. Such an undertaking, as was constantly stressed, was a venture new to diplomacy, and the Committee throughout its duration was constantly aware of this aspect of its function.[37]

The scheme first mooted on 2 November had envisaged the stationing in Spain and the Spanish dependencies of impartial bodies at forty principal points of entry by land and sea. Apart from Portugal, which abstained, the detailed proposals were approved at the twelfth plenary session of the Committee on 2 December and an approach was then made to the respective parties.

It was not for one moment expected that either would agree to the proposals, and there were some misgivings lest it should be taken too seriously or even be accepted. 'It must be admitted', minuted Shuckburgh, 'that this scheme is not being put forward because anyone thinks it is a good scheme, or even because anyone thinks that it is likely to lead to any practical result, effective or ineffective.' Rather, it was advanced simply to save the NIC. There was therefore some disquiet in the Foreign Office at approaching the Cabinet for approval of the funds required to pay for Britain's share in a scheme on a 'tacit understanding that the money will never be wanted'. ('If we have £160,000 to spare', commented

Vansittart, 'I want it for cultural propaganda, not a scheme that no one believes in.')[38] Fortunately, then, from the British point of view, the response from Spain was sufficiently negative for this first attempt at control to be shelved. The Republic's reply reproached the NIC for not verifying its reports of violations of non-intervention, and stressed that as the legitimate government it had every right to procure arms openly and would be fully justified in rejecting the proposals, but would accept them in principle, reserving the right to reject them in part or in whole. The observation was added that the first thing to do would be to control the Portuguese harbours. The rebel – or Nationalist government, as Hitler now decided it be called[39] – replied in far less accommodating fashion, laying down a list of precise conditions for their acceptance of the kind of control suggested in the proposals. In view of the antipathy expressed in both these replies, it was decided to reorganise the control scheme. The forty points of entry were to be exchanged for offshore zones, which would not require Spanish approval.

The technical information required for the necessary amendments, as for the original and subsequent plans, was provided by a series of technical advisory sub-committees, some seven in all.[40] The first was set up to examine the possibility of the 'supervision of aircraft entering Spain by air' and was short-lived. After seven meetings between 14 November and 18 December 1936 it was reluctantly concluded that air control was not practicable. Like the first proposals for control, it had, said Shuckburgh, 'been conceived in a mood of fantasy'. The scheme proposed the sending of twenty agents into all countries within 1,500 miles of Spain, six being allotted to Germany. Quite apart from the absurdity of attempting to scan every German airport with so small a number of agents, no access would be made to German military airfields.[41] Thus one of the most important forms of intervention remained beyond control.

Technical Advisory Sub-Committee No. 2 was created on 14 December to prepare schedules for supervision of various Spanish ports and crossings by rail and road, and to consider any other technical aspects of supervision by land and sea. This was attended by diplomatic and Service representatives from Germany, France, Italy, Sweden and the USSR. But it, too, was eventually superseded by Technical Advisory Sub-Committee No. 3, when the first plan was rejected.

New problems seemed to mushroom daily. How was the scheme

to be financed? Should the scheme cover the problems of indirect aid such as subscriptions to either side: and what of the many bona fide and other 'volunteers' now pouring into Spain? For each of these problems a separate sub-committee was set up. Technical Advisory Sub-Committee No. 3 examined and reported on 'the methods by which the NIA could be extended to cover the question of entry into Spain of foreign nationals', whilst Technical Advisory Sub-Committee No. 4 was to cover the 'shipping to either party in Spain of financial aid'.[42] The recommendations of these committees were considered by the plenary Committee and proposals which were adopted were eventually incorporated into each new draft of the scheme.

When it became clear that these had failed, two new attempts were made in the autumn of 1937 to tighten non-intervention. Technical Advisory Sub-Committee No. 5 was created to examine the possibility of 'the grant in certain circumstances of belligerent rights to the two parties in Spain'; and No. 6 to examine a scheme for the extension of the Non-Intervention Agreement to include a plan for the withdrawal of volunteers. There was, in addition, a Committee of Jurists, lawyers drawn from several countries including Britain, who were to investigate the use outside Spain of capital assets including Spanish gold – a point of great controversy not only with Germany and Italy but with Franco's adminstration.[43] A draft formula was drawn up asking for information from governments regarding the import into their respective countries of Spanish capital assets. Since this, if taken to its logical conclusion, involved close scrutiny of all governments' finances, the idea was not surprisingly quietly dropped, and the Committee disbanded after some five meetings.[44] This was a rare victory for the Republican Government, which had warned the Foreign Office in January 1937 that any interference in the matter of the gold would be regarded as a 'signal intervention'.[45]

With the rejection in December 1936 of the first draft of the control scheme by the two Spanish belligerents,[46] the responsibility for technical advice devolved to Technical Advisory Sub-Committee No. 3, which drew up a new scheme following the lines of the former but much cheaper. By February 15 all powers had also agreed to a proposal to control entry into Spain of their nationals, and this became law at midnight on 20–21 February 1937, covering recruitment of, the transit through, or the departure from the countries of the respective signatories, or any person of non-Spanish origin for the purpose of service in the Spanish war.[47]

Although it had been originally hoped that the control plan would be in operation by 6 March 1937, delays were caused not only by the many genuine hitches which occurred, but by the deliberate delaying tactics of the delegates and the especial obduracy of both Russia and Portugal.

One of the most intractable problems which faced the constructors of the control scheme was the absolute necessity of enlisting the support of Portugal, since early reports indicated that the Portuguese-Spanish border was the point of entry of large quantities of aid of all kinds. Portugal was in an especially difficult position in many ways. Her sympathies were wholly with the military rebels,[48] yet she could ill afford to make any move which might irrevocably mortgage her future as the smaller partner in the Iberian Peninsula, nor could she easily offend the two democracies with whom she had close ties.[49] Portugal had been reluctant to join the NIC and had done so only belatedly and then on special terms. She was immediately co-opted on to the Chairman's Sub-Committee, where her participation was considered essential. But lack of diplomatic relations between Portugal and Russia made agreement on any topic extremely difficult between these countries.[50] No workable plan could be found without the close co-operation of Portugal, but the Portuguese Government remained adamantly opposed to any proposal for foreign troops to patrol its border. Finally an acceptable plan was put before the Chairman's Sub-Committee on 15 February 1937, to entrust the supervision of the Portuguese-Spanish border to the British Government. This would be done by 130 special officers attached to the British Embassy in Lisbon, who were promised 'every facility and freedom necessary to their task'.[51]

However, as the Soviet representative, Cahan, pointed out, the original draft had referred to the 'control' of borders. That term had been superseded by the word 'supervision', which now the Portuguese insisted be replaced by the much weaker 'observation'.[52] The proposals were in fact agreed simply to get some form of supervision under way, although it again placed the Portuguese, outspoken insurgent sympathisers, in a very privileged position since both France and the Spanish Republic had agreed only very reluctantly to international supervision of their borders. Even so, Portuguese commitment to the supervision scheme remained arbitrary, and its support was withdrawn after the crisis which halted the scheme in the early summer, further exacerbating the situation which then arose.[53]

To administer the Observation Scheme, as it was now officially known, an International Board for Non-Intervention was created on 6 March 1937. Its function was to be purely administrative, and it had no juridical authority. Funds were to be paid into a limited liability company registered under UK company law.[54] It was at first intended that the Board should have five members: Britain, France, Germany, Italy and Russia, but to these were added a Mediterranean representative from Greece, a Scandinavian from Norway, and for the Baltic a delegate was chosen from Poland; Czechoslovakia, as a major arms producer, was also included. The Board's administrative officers were: Chairman, Vice-Admiral van Dulm of the Netherlands; Secretary, Mr Francis Hemming; Chief Administrator Sea, Rear-Admiral Olivier of the Netherlands; Chief Administrator France, Colonel Lunn of Denmark; and Chief Administrator Gibraltar, Land and Sea Observation, was Captain Dagada of Turkey. The Scheme as a whole was adopted by the NIC at its seventeenth meeting on 8 March 1937.

Control was to be divided into three main parts: a Naval Patrol Scheme, Sea Observation, and Land Observation. The Sea Observation Scheme – to be distinguished from the Naval Patrol – drew on neutral countries for staff: Estonia, Norway, Latvia, the Netherlands, Denmark, Turkey, Yugoslavia, Finland, the Irish Free State and Sweden. Similarly the Land Observation Scheme drew its officers from Sweden, Norway, Finland, Latvia and the Netherlands. The division of labour was to be as follows:

For the *Sea Observation Scheme* 550 observation officers were to be appointed to observation ports whence they would escort and scrutinise merchant ships of non-intervention countries. All such shipping would call at one of the seven principal points of embarkation to pick up officers.[55] These were:

1. The Downs	5. Palermo
2. Cherbourg	6. Marseilles
3. Gibraltar	7. Madeira
4. Lisbon	

Officers would supervise the unloading of cargoes in ports but would not land, thus obviating the need for permission from either party in Spain. In conjunction with this scheme ran the *Naval Patrol Scheme*, which was entirely under the auspices of Britain, France, Germany, and Italy – Russia reluctantly having waived her claim to a share in the patrol[56] – who were to check that merchant ships complied with the NIS rules and who shared supervision of the waters around Spain and her dependencies in the following manner:

Naval Observation Zones[57]	*Power entrusted with observation duties*
A. North coast of Spain from French frontier to Cape Busto	United Kingdom
B. North-west coast of Spain from Cape Busto to the Portuguese frontier	France
C. South coast of Spain from the Portuguese frontier to Cape de Gata	United Kingdom
D. South-east coast of Spain from Cape de Gata to Cape Oropesa	Germany
E. East coast of Spain from Cape Oropesa to the French frontier	Italy
F. Spanish Moroccan coast	France
G. Ibiza and Majorca	France
H. Minorca	Italy

All ships of participating countries were to fly the non-intervention pennant – two black balls on a white background – when within ten miles of the Spanish coast. Patrol ships would operate from ten miles to within three miles of the coast. Although observers had the right to stop participant ships if they could, they had no right to take the ship to the nearest observation port for examination. Ships not flying the pennant could not be approached although reports of breaches of the scheme, or suspicious activities of ships were to be reported. By mid-April all countries had promulgated the decrees necessary to ensure their merchant shipping complied with the provisions of the scheme, and the Sea Observation Plan finally creaked into life at midnight on 19–20 April 1937. Even then, it was begun with a restricted complement of officers, for by 15 April only 300 of the 550 men required had been recruited for the Sea Observation Plan and posted to their duty ports.

Much the same was true of the Land Observation Scheme, which by the same date had only 35 officers in position, although in all 80

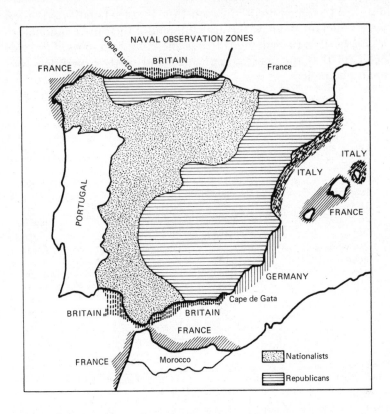

had been recruited and it was believed that this would constitute a sufficiently large skeleton force to begin the scheme. It was also hoped that there would be no need to recruit the full 130 allowed for by the final draft of the scheme if it proved possible to do the work with a smaller number and at a lower cost.[58] Such penny-scrimping attitudes served only to underline with what little faith the scheme was started, for there was in fact no question of performing land observation efficiently with so few men.

Not surprisingly, the cost of the operation met with resistance from representatives far from convinced of either the efficacy or the sincerity of the scheme. But the need to keep to as low a budget as possible further weakened the scheme. Thus, although it had been hoped that it would be fully operational by mid-May, numbers of officers were still below target.[59] Several countries had initially declined to contribute to the Non-Intervention Fund[60] and others were reluctant to allow the appointment of their own nationals to higher posts in the scheme.[61] It was, therefore, in a spirit of extreme cynicism that this most complicated and costly experiment was finally launched.

Table 1   Total income assured to the Non-Intervention Board
for first year: 1 March 1937 – 28 February 1938

	£		£
Albania	500	Italy	143,680
Austria	4,960	Latvia	1,796
Belgium	13,470	Lithuania	2,694
Bulgaria	200	Luxemburg	898
Czechoslovakia	17,960	Netherlands	17,062
Denmark	8,082	Norway	6,286
Eire	7,184	Poland	22,450
Estonia	1,796	Portugal	3,408
Finland	7,184	Roumania	7,000
France	143,680	Sweden	13,470
Germany	143,680	Turkey	7,184
Greece	5,388	USSR	143,680
Hungary	5,388	United Kingdom	79,680
		Yugoslavia	11,674
			820,434

Note: Britain paid £64,000 towards the cost of supervising the Portuguese border, in addition to her contribution towards the main fund. See above, p. 52.

WEAKNESSES AND BREAKDOWN OF THE SCHEME

Faults were evident in the development and structure of the scheme from beginning. First, it was quite simply too late. Although a plan had been discussed and initiated in the autumn of 1936, it was five more months before the scheme was brought into operation in its final form, by which time foreign intervention by all interested parties in the shape of both arms and volunteers was so well established that any pretence of neutrality had long been abandoned in all quarters except, officially, the NIC and the British Government. Germany, Italy and the Soviet Union were all fully committed and the attitude of France was at best equivocal. The scheme could not lessen or control one iota the tension between the countries, although this, it should be remembered, was the declared purpose of non-intervention. Whether practical measures taken in the initial stages to put into execution the principle of non-intervention could have saved the Spanish Government remains open to dispute, but such an objective could not, by definition, have been part of any non-intervention policy.

In the period between the signing of the accords and the setting up of the Observation Scheme, not only had the pattern of external interference been fixed at certain governmental levels, but amongst private shipowners and gun-runners a wide variety of means of evasion had already been created, and far from being now easily detected by the control system, these were simply elaborated as necessary. Many ships had re-registered with another company belonging to a country not participating in the NIA, and many others had transferred to British companies in order to profit from the protection of the British navy. Count Grandi, Italian Ambassador to London claimed that in the first six months of 1937 forty-seven foreign ships had transferred to the British register and were shipping cargoes to Bilbao in this way.[62] Some ships sailed under false colours and others transfered illicit cargoes in mid-ocean to non-participant shipping. Yet others hid arms beneath legitimate cargoes of food, some openly risking detection, others painting out their registration marks. More deviously, some foreign munition-carrying ships allowed themselves to be seized by the rebel fleet and conducted into Nationalist ports under the pretext that they were transporting war materials for the Government forces. Thus arms were obtained under the pretext of impounding them, and at the same time false evidence of gun-running with its attendant propaganda value could be fed to the NIC which was not equipped to check such reports.

The second great weakness of the Observation Scheme lay in the sharing of responsibility of the Naval Patrol between those powers most committed to one side or another; although Russia did not participate, France, Italy and Germany were all at one time or another actively partisan and of course Britain had no intention of offending the latter couple. This was a sure recipe for the disaster which so shortly followed the setting in motion of the scheme. Inevitably the Spanish Government viewed the patrolling of its coastal waters with great hostility.[63] On 24 May 1937 five Martin bombers of the Republican forces bombarded Palma, Majorca, which was then a Nationalist stronghold under Italian command,[64] apparently with the intention of attacking Italian vessels which were flying the non-intervention pennant and lying just outside the port. In a second raid on 26 May the Italian ship *Barletta* was severely damaged and three others slightly so – the *Quarlo*, *Nevona* and the *Mirabello*. Several officers were wounded and six were killed. All four ships, claimed Grandi, had been engaged in the Naval Patrol, although as the Soviet delegate at the NIC quickly pointed out, Majorca was not within any zone allotted to the Italians but was a supply base for the Italian navy in general. The Italian ships could not, then, claim the protection of the NIC. Cahan protested most strongly that the NIC had no right to demand 'explanations' from the Republican Government; Italian ships should not have been flying non-intervention pennants outside their zone; the raid was clearly aimed at an enemy base and was not a matter for the NIC.

Indeed, this latter point was precisely the Italian case, as Grandi had made clear, when he proclaimed Italy's right to take unilateral action.[65] Germany, too, as soon became apparent, felt equally free to act independently of the NIC. For, three days later the German battleship *Deutschland*, which after the attack on Palma had removed to Ibiza, was bombed at its anchorage. Eighty-three men were wounded and twenty-two killed. Enraged by this humiliation, Hitler cancelled the projected visit to Britain of his Foreign Minister, von Neurath. Retaliation against the Republic, however, was swift, more direct, and openly defiant of non-intervention. The Committee was presented with a letter from Ribbentrop, German Ambassador and representative, in which he started that this was simply the last in a series of attacks which had begun in April on the armoured ship *Graf Spee* and followed on 8 May with the attack on the *Leipzig*. The German Government would discontinue participation in both the Control Scheme, as well as the discussions at the NIC, until guarantees against the recurrence of such events were given. Orders had been given to their battleships to repel by force any approaching aircraft. As a warning, moreover, that very morning German forces had shelled the fortified port of Almeria with the intention of destroying the harbour works and batteries.[66]

The Italians wrote in similar vein withdrawing from the supervision scheme as well as, temporarily, from the meetings of the NIC, both of which were plainly no longer tenable. The Portuguese wrote reserving their attitude towards agents entrusted with naval observation, and shortly withdrew their permission for the border patrols. Later the French, always sensible of Portuguese privilege, threatened to do the same, and suspended facilities accorded to observers from noon 13 July 1937.[67] Thus in just seven days between 24 May and 31 May 1937, the six months of hard work which had gone into the construction of the Observation Schemes was undone.

How effective had the control scheme proved during its brief existence? On 25 August 1937 a *Joint Report on the Operation of the Observation Scheme* was issued by Admiral Van Dulm and Mr Francis Hemming, Chairman and Secretary respectively of the Non-Intervention Board. It was a survey of the information received by the Board covering the period 19 April – 31 May 1937. During this time 323 ships of participating countries had been observed entering Spanish territorial waters. Of these, 44 had been reported by the naval patrol as having failed to comply with the procedure of the Observation Scheme, but only 8 of these had in fact failed to comply, and of these 6 had already been detected by the Board of Trade's own Shipping Intelligence division. The Observation Scheme had, therefore, revealed only two new names of culprits. In the same period 79 ships were known to have passed unidentified and a further 415 ships in the same period did not submit to the provisions of the Observation Scheme, i.e. were registered with non-member countries. The report stressed the futility of a scheme in which patrol vessels were not entitled to employ force to compel ships to stop and submit to identification and could take no action when ships ignorged signals made to them. The Sea Observation Plan, it concluded, had been of extremely limited value.

In contrast, the Land Observation Scheme was believed to have been more successful. Such breaches as had occurred contravened, it was said, the spirit of non-intervention rather than its law, since many articles clearly for use in the war, such as unarmoured vehicles and chemicals used in the manufacture of munitions, fell beyond the scope of the list already drawn up. No assessment was made of the plan as regards the Portuguese Spanish border since it came under the special Anglo-Portuguese Agreement.[68]

In its conclusions on the efficacy of the Sea Scheme, undoubtedly the report was right to pronounce failure. No control was exercised over movement by air or in foreign vessels not belonging to the scheme, or to Portuguese ports. The War Office report for April therefore rightly concluded that it was 'not surprising to find, since 20 April, aircraft flown to Spain, normal arms traffic continuing in Spanish and "Panamanian" ships, and an apparent increase in the

movement of disguised consignments to Lisbon'. In this period
Germany and Italy were slightly more circumspect than before in
direct shipments of aid, but arms from Russia appear to have
actually been stepped up at this time, with reported deliveries of at
least 11,450 tons of war material, 40 lorries, and a number of
aircraft. Gun-runners of no political conviction continued as usual.
For example, one ship, the *Axpe Mendi* from Antwerp, having
delivered half its cargo, 5,500 rifles and 13,000 revolvers, to Oporto,
continued its voyage to Spanish Government territory to discharge
the remainder.

It is more difficult to comment on the Land Observation Plan and
on Hemming's assessment of it. Since it began with a limited
number of officers, this alone might well account for the failure of
the observers to detect infringements of the control scheme. But
certainly shipments of material from France continued in the last
week of April after control had begun, and, later, arms appear to
have been sent fairly freely by rail.[69] As to observation of the
Portuguese-Spanish border where a similar deficiency in staffing
existed, a report to the Foreign Office from Sir Charles Wingfield
stated:

> I am of the opinion that no prohibited articles have crossed the
> frontier into Spain at any of the posts and sub-posts where our
> Observers are stationed, during the period since observation has
> commenced. I do not, however, exclude the possibility that large
> quantities of munitions or other prohibited goods may be crossing
> the frontier unperceived by the frontier guards . . . at night it
> would be an easy matter for pack mules to pass, as there are
> numerous mule tracks available.[70]

In view of this report, of War Office reports, and of the Hemming-
Van Dulm report, it seems reasonable to state that non-intervention
in any practical sense was a failure, both as regards land and sea,
and by mid-1937 was known to be so by all concerned.

Procrastination on all sides had meant that the creation of the
scheme had been long delayed, and it lacked from the beginning
any real authority or power to execute its intended function. After
the withdrawal of Germany and Italy from the Naval Patrol both
the scheme and the Committee had lost all credibility, but
amazingly the British Government, supported by the French,

endeavoured to maintain the myth of non-intervention. For only through the NIC, as will later be demonstrated, could Britain co-ordinate the conflicting elements of her policy: obey the Chiefs of Staff dictum by remaining on good terms with whichever side emerged victorious in Spain; prevent France 'going bolshevick'; maintain a veneer of impartiality which would quieten, if not wholly satisfy, the left in Britain; and, above all, impede the growing alienation of Italy and Germany from the rest of Europe. Other adherents to non-intervention also saw profit in continuing to support the Committee, for after a token absence from the Chairman's Sub-Committee of 31 May, Germany and Italy resumed attendance at both these and plenary sessions.

In order to maintain some semblance of activity during this threat to non-intervention, a proposal was made by the British and French that they should take over the working of the Naval Patrol Scheme, between them patrolling the entire Spanish coast.[71] It was a proposal which, not unexpectedly, brought protests from the Italian and German representatives that this would upset the balance of 'impartiality', since Britain and France were purportedly 'friendly to the Valencia Government', and, unlike the dictators, refused to grant the Nationalist Government juridical status.[72] They offered counter-proposals for reconstructing the scheme, the essence of which was the recognition of the Nationalist Government and subsequent granting of belligerent rights to both sides. To escape from the impasse, a proposal by the Dutch delegate, Marees van Swinderen, proposed that Britain should find some compromise solution was adopted. Maisky supported the proposal, but em-phasised the anomaly which would remain with an open Portuguese border and a closed French one.[73]

The new proposals arrived at by the British Government were duly presented at the next plenary session of the Committee.[74] The first report of the International Board which would reveal the futility of the Sea Patrol had not yet appeared, and so it was proposed to re-establish supervision on similar lines to those set up before the withdrawal of Germany and Italy. In addition, officers would be placed in Spanish ports to ascertain that ships entering ports had complied with the requirements, that is, they had taken an observer on board at one of the designated observation ports. These practical measures would be reinforced by recognition of the belligerency, (i.e. rights of search),[75] of both sides subject to two conditions:

1. When arrangements for the withdrawal of volunteers were satisfactory;
2. When withdrawal had made satisfactory progress.

The British proposals were indeed a compromise, but far from drawing the two sides together they proposed the two principles on which neither side could, or would, give way, thus guaranteeing continued argument with no prospect of definite conclusion. By proposing the stationing of officers in Spanish ports, the scheme had come full cycle, for it was, if anything, less likely than in the previous December that either party in Spain would agree, and both had now to be approached for permission to proceed with the new proposals if the NIC itself could first agree them. But since the object was to keep the ball in court rather than to finish the game, this obstacle was not regarded as a hindrance. Indeed the British Government's attitude to non-intervention was admirably expressed by the new First Lord of the Admiralty, Alfred Duff Cooper, at a meeting of the Foreign Policy Committee on 1 July, when he described the Anglo-French proposals as 'useful to gain time'. Furthermore,

> he did not see that the continuance of the non-intervention scheme without control was impossible. After all, non-intervention had been carried on for a long time before the Naval Patrol had been instituted. Even the patrol scheme had not made non-intervention effective, but there was no essential reason why the scheme should be effective, or should be useless if it was not fully effective.[76]

While this might be seen as cynicism writ large, the British Government had hoped to justify 'control' as an experiment in diplomacy, a test, as it were, of the dictators' sincerity. For it had been wishfully believed at the beginning of the year that interventionists might welcome the scheme as an excuse for withdrawing from Spain without loss of prestige.[77]

From the summer of 1937 any such hope had been proved false. By then, however, the British position had become increasingly complex and cannot be considered further solely in relation to the formal organisation of non-intervention. As to the Committee itself, the Chairman's Sub-Committee and Advisory Sub-Committees continued to meet in pursuit of two major projects, the withdrawal of volunteers and the strengthening of control.[78] But after the twenty-seventh meeting of the plenary Committee on 16 July 1937, only three more such meetings were held, and non-intervention in any practical sense may be said to have ceased, if indeed, despite such elaborate planning, it had ever truly begun.

3 Economic Aspects of British Policy

It has been suggested in preceding chapters that Britain's chief interest in the Spanish conflict was seen by her policy-makers to lie in the political position which would ensue at the close of hostilities, and that they recognised that Britain must remain on good terms with whichever power emerged victorious at the end of the war. This did not mean, however, that the Cabinet and Foreign Office were able to ignore the economic difficulties presented by the war. On the contrary, a large portion of the work of the Foreign Office in connection with Spain during these years was concerned with economic questions. But it does mean that rather less emphasis than has sometimes been suggested was given to such aspects, which were viewed from an almost wholly political perspective. For, as in other areas of British policy towards Spain, the delicate balance of British impartiality had to be seen to be upheld at all costs – even if these proved to be very great indeed.

In fact, there was a widely held assumption in government circles that in the long term Britain's economic future in Spain was probably assured, since Britain alone in Europe would be able to provide the necessary funds for Spain's post-war reconstruction, whichever side should win.[1] Yet despite this, the serious nature of the Spanish conflict, its likely protraction, and increasing fear of a second great international conflict meant that such confidence was at all times backed by a high degree of diplomatic caution in every sphere of economic activity, including the reorganisation of Anglo-Spanish trade, settlement of claims for compensation, or negotiations on the requisitions of ores from British-owned mines. In each of these areas it can be demonstrated that while everything possible was done to protect trade and commerce, or to ameliorate conditions in which these were carried out with both Spanish parties, immediate, specific economic interests were always subordinated to the higher demands of Britain's overall policy towards Spain.

BRITISH ECONOMIC INTERESTS IN SPAIN

1. Investment

Before examining these problems in more detail it is essential to assess the extent of Britain's economic interests in Spain at that time. For the purposes of this study these may most conveniently be divided into two major spheres: investment and trade. The former is difficult to quantify and the British Government itself appears to have experienced some delay in obtaining an accurate assessment. The Government requested an estimate of British capital invested in Spain[2] in the autumn of 1936. However, not until January the following year was Lazards, the firm of City bankers appointed to compile the figures, able to present their 'very tentative estimate'. Overall, British capital investment in Spain was given as £40,000,000, showing an increase of over 50 per cent on an estimate of £26,000,000 given by the same firm a few years before. This rapid growth was tempered to some extent, however, by the fact that the figures given were taken from nominal stock values only, at a time when market values of Spanish shares had fallen dramatically. For example, the report pointed out, the nominal stock value of the Rio Tinto Company, a major British investor, was given as £5,550,000, although its market value stood at only £3,790,000.[3]

By themselves such figures mean little, and, it is important to place them in the context of British investment as a whole. A useful comparison might be made, for example, with British investment in China at the outbreak of hostilities in the Far East in 1937, when it was estimated that between £273,000,000 and £300,000,000 were invested, mainly in Kowloon and Peking.[4] At a conservative estimate British world investment in 1936 amounted to £3,364,000,000.[5] Investment in Spain, therefore, whilst not negligible (and from the Spanish point of view most important, constituting perhaps as much as 40 per cent of total foreign investment in Spain) was not in itself sufficiently large to have been the main consideration in such critical times, although naturally the Government would do all within its power to offer protection to investors.

Actually, the very pattern of investment in Spain would have tended to reinforce government determination to remain on good

terms with both sides, for investments were almost equally distributed between the two rival territories in Spain, but with slightly
over half located within the Republican zone. The largest single
investor in that area was the Barcelona Traction Company with
£6,000,000 out of the total investment in Republican Spain of
£25,000,000. Since the estimate did not include the Spanish

Table 2 Distribution of British investment in Spain, January 1937

	Government Territory	Insurgent Territory
	(£000)	
Government loans	300	
Alcoy and Gandia Railway	530	
Bilbao and Cantabria Railway	50	
Great Southern of Spain	1,600	
Anglo-Spanish Construction	1,590	
Bacares Iron Ore	110	
Hispano-Americana	1,250	
Barcelona Traction	6,000	
Fuerzas Motrices	1,500	
Asfaltos	100	
Olives	1,000	
Anglo-South American Bank	750	250
Aporama Land and Minerals		200
Huelva Copper and Sulphur		750
Pena Copper		180
Rio Tinto		5,550
Seville Sulphur		120
Tharsis Sulphur		1,250
Tigon Mining		160
Other lead mines		2,000
Sherry industry		2,000
Total:	14,580	12,460

A further £7–12 million was invested in the following companies, the majority of
which were situated in Republican territory:

Courtaulds	Shell Transport
Dunlop Rubber	Anglo-Persian oil
General Electric	Babcock & Wilcox
Imperical Chemical Industries	Gust, Keen & Nettlefold
African and Eastern	Ford Motor Company.

All these with additional unspecified investment brought the total to roughly
£40,000,000[8].

dependencies, which lay mainly in Nationalist hands, it might be supposed that an inclusive assessment would have raised total British investment in Nationalist territory at the beginning of January 1937 to roughly equal that of the Republic. Clearly with such an equal division of investment, the British Government had no reason *vis-à-vis* individual shareholders to favour either side in the conflict. Nor should it be assumed that at a higher level, all major companies were pro-Franco, although it is true that the most vociferous tended to be so. For example, although the pro-Nazi chairman of the Texaco Oil Company directed that Franco should receive oil deliveries on credit,[6] Shell Oil refused to take up a rebel order for oil without payment in advance;[7] and the Orconera Iron Company at first, together with many others, expressed itself well satisfied with conditions in Republican territory. Even the underlying Foreign Office belief that 'a communist Spain would mean the loss of the whole of the British capital in Spain and the end of British capitalist enterprise in the Peninsula and also lead to communism in France'[9] was curbed by the acceptance of the dogma: 'Neither side must bear a grudge.'

Investment in Spain was also of very different types in the respective territories of the opposing parties, and this has sometimes been thought to have influenced British Government attitudes. Behind the Republican lines the bulk of British investment lay in service industries: railways, electric power companies, etc., as well as banking and insurance, but with the important exception until mid-1937 of the iron mines of north-eastern Spain. In Nationalist Spain, on the other hand, investment was primarily in the rich mines of the south, which accounted for some 83 per cent of British investment, the rest being made up from companies dealing in sherry, cork, olives, etc. Not included in the original survey were the mines of the Riff, or the market gardens and plantations of the island dependencies. Here the question of investment begins to shade into that of Britain's trade with Spain, which is to be discussed later. But first let us examine the way in which the British Government responded to the innumerable claims and petitions for help from British interests in Spain.

2. *Requisitions and Compensation*

Insofar as the British Government was under pressure, this came ostensibly in the form of a flood of complaints from British interests in Spain. Throughout the war the Board of Trade and the Foreign Office were inundated with petitions from those who had suffered requisitions or damage by one side or the other in the conflict. Inevitably, the impression is given of a greater number of complaints from those whose interests lay on the Republican side, since it was here that the greater number of small firms or properties lay. Whereas these were generally of a disparate nature, the weight of investment behind Nationalist lines was more homogeneous and mine-owners were able to band together to press their case more forcefully.

From the earliest days of the rebellion, and particularly from the industrial centres, came reports of requisitions of property, vehicles, currency, jewellery, anything which would oil the vast machinery of war. Initially the Legal Department of the Foreign Office advised that Britain had the right to object to such requisitions under the terms of the commercial treaty with Spain (1922), although if the rebels were recognised as belligerents different rules would then obtain. Following the example of his German colleague, Ogilvie Forbes therefore extracted a promise from the Spanish Government on 20 August that all British goods acquired under the new emergency measures would be paid for in cash. The autonomous Catalan government was also informed of this undertaking, but as the British Chargé reported, scant attention was paid to the Madrid directive and many goods were seized at pistol point while others said to be 'anarcho-syndicalists' were reported to demand goods in exchange for IOUs presumed to be worthless.[10]

The immediate need for both parties in the conflict to obtain ready cash led to a prompt proliferation, on both sides, of decrees governing commerce and trade. In Nationalist Spain decrees were passed concerning the sherry exporters and the mining companies of southern Spain. However, on the Republican side the picture was greatly complicated by the autonomous nature of the Basque, and more especially the Catalan, provinces. Between the end of July and the beginning of September, thirty-eight decrees affecting banking alone had been passed by the Catalan *Generalidad*. Under the new decrees a company was obliged to place its pesetas in a current account to which workers' committees would have access. Although it was admitted, King reported, that a fair rate of exchange had been agreed – 227 paper pesetas to 100 gold pesetas – it was doubted whether the paper notes offered anything more tangible than a receipt.[11]

On 20 July a decree was issued suspending operations of the Spanish Commercial Exchange, forbidding withdrawal of sums exceeding 2,000 pesetas from any bank account and proclaiming a moratorium, initially for two days but later extending for many months. Actions such as these did nothing to promote the confidence of British investors, nor, more significantly from the Republican point of view, of the British Foreign Office, where developments of this nature confirmed the belief that separatist movements were one of the weakest aspects of the Popular Front Government.[12]

Equally vulnerable were the insurance companies, when on 31 May 1937 three decrees were published requiring deposits to be made with the Spanish Government of 30 per cent of the annual premiums collected, or a minimum of 3 million pesetas. Recognising the impotence of the British Government to act in the prevailing circumstances and concerned at the problems facing them, members of the British Chamber of Commerce for Spain established in London, on 21 October 1936, a centre which would operate for the duration of the war and assist its members as far as possible in pressing claims for damage or loss as soon as the war was ended.[13]

As to the result of any claims which might be made by the British Government, the Foreign Office held out no hopes, despite the creation by the Negrín Government in August 1937 of a Commission of Foreign ·Claims to examine and report on all claims and petitions for loss incurred after 18 July 1936. The Spanish Government denied in a *note verbale* of 31 March 1938 that any undertaking in which British interests were involved had been appropriated by the state, and claimed that where intervention had taken place it had been precisely to protect the legitimate personnel and technical and economic interests. Dr Negrín also affirmed that the Spanish Government would honour all obligations to foreign holders of Spanish 4 per cent bonds, but these were a fairly limited issue.[14]

It is scarcely surprising that in the middle of a full-scale war neither side had much time to devote to the question of compensation, but the Republic loath, to alienate potential allies, endeavoured to act within the framework of international law, something the Nationalists did not find necessary. However, it was believed in Britain that the commission set up in Spain was purely advisory and not in a position to give any decision regarding the claims submitted to it. On 25 February 1938 Mr John Leche,

Chargé d'Affaires in Spain after the departure of Ogilvie Forbes,[15] advising the Foreign Office that it was not an opportune moment to press claims, noted:

> Moral arguments are of no value in order to get blood out of a stone . . . It seems to me perfectly clear that the Spanish Government has no intention of meeting them [the claims]. I do not believe that they have any money whatever, especially to meet foreign debts.

Reluctantly, the Foreign Office, too, agreed that no pressure could be put on the Spanish Government in the matter.[16]

Once again the Spanish Government had the worst of all worlds. To be acknowledged as the legitimate government of Spain – for they did not admit the legitimate belligerency of the rebels – they were obliged to accept responsibility, not only for their own debts of compensation but, in the event of victory, for those of the rebels. The latter on the other hand had nothing to lose by openly repudiating all responsibility for loss or damage, and were, besides, believed to be in a very strong position to retaliate effectively against any measures Britain might take, by seizing British-owned mines and other property. It therefore became Foreign Office policy not to present claims to General Franco's administration, only to reserve the right to submit them in due course.[17]

Even towards the end of the war when shipping claims were estimated at £8 million,[18] Britain was in no position to dictate to Franco, and Germany, too, experienced comparative failure in attempts to gain appropriate payment in any form in return for very considerable expenditure in Spain.[19] The most that had been achieved was recognition of responsibility by the Republican Government for foreign economic interests in Spain; from Franco not even this was forthcoming. British investors remained vociferous throughout the war,[20] but their plight was regarded as largely peripheral to British Government attitudes to non-intervention.

ANGLO-SPANISH TRADE

It was said that to be a merchant in Spain during these years required as much courage 'as to go to the battle front'.[21] While this may have been a rather picaresque exaggeration, it does convey the

Table 3 *Decline in British trade and comparative increase in German trade with Spain during the first quarter of the years 1934–6*[22] *(in gold pesetas)*

Country	Imports into Spain			Exports from Spain		
	1934	1935	1936	1934	1935	1936
Germany	33,617,316	37,955,448	35,408,871	23,488,942	26,594,320	39,006,488
Britain	29,357,588	28,861,667	26,177,585	48,851,106	45,306,518	44,547,440
USA	48,986,877	46,522,456	50,092,203	17,974,513	19,883,017	18,929,858
France	22,449,920	15,387,344	19,680,864	32,960,289	24,524,479	31,831,171

extent and diversity of the problems confronting those engaged in trade with Spain at this time. Yet it should not be thought that the war alone was responsible for the decline in Anglo-Spanish trade at this time, for figures for pre-war trade show that this trend had already begun by 1936, and that at a time when British trade in general was expanding her trade with Spain was diminishing. It is possible that this factor contributed to the apparent complacency of the British Government in dealing with economic factors during the first six months of the war.

In broader terms Anglo-Spanish trade could be viewed only as part of world trade, and policy had to be formulated with regard to Mediterranean and Empire trade. Yet any such consideration immediately focused attention on strategic and political questions for both the British Government and British traders. Many of those trading with Spain also had interests beyond Suez (e.g. Rio Tinto), and although in the extreme case of war closing the Mediterranean it would have been possible to adopt the Cape route for Empire trade this would have added considerably to transport costs.[23] There was, therefore, every reason to view even questions of Anglo-Spanish trade from a predominantly political viewpoint which favoured non-intervention. Nevertheless, as much as was consistent with British policy and compatible with war conditions was done to overcome individual problems as they arose. Indeed, the Foreign Office never failed to quote economic factors in support of policy even when they were only marginally relevant, nor the Government to cite them in the House of Commons, since then as now economic necessity was an argument to which all parties responded.

1. The Anglo-Spanish Payments Agreement

One of the first manifestations of this ambivalence of attitude towards economic aspects of the war in Spain was demonstrated in the discussions leading up to the suspension of the Anglo-Spanish Payments Agreement in December 1936. British trade with Spain was steadily declining in the years immediately prior to the rebellion in 1936, a decline exacerbated by the increasing difficulty experienced by Spain in foreign exchange. Debts owed by Spanish importers mounted, reaching £6 million in 1935, and British firms became increasingly reluctant to export without guarantee of payment. In line, therefore, with many similar arrangements already made between Spain and other trading partners,[24] the

British Government negotiated, and in December 1935 concluded, the Anglo-Spanish Payments Agreement whereby all payments due from Spain to the United Kingdom were paid, in pesetas, into the *Centro de Contracion* in Madrid, while all payments due from the United Kingdom to Spain were paid into the Anglo-Spanish Clearing Office in London. The money was paid out, not necessarily to the exporter to whom it was directly owed, but to whomever stood first on the debtors list. In this way, although payment was slow it was at least more sure than previously. The system worked in exactly the same way in both Madrid and London, but since the balance of trade lay in Spain's favour the debt outstanding to British exporters had been reduced by mid-1936 to £5 million.

The efficient working of the agreement, however, depended upon the relative stability of the peseta and free communication with all creditors throughout Spain. By undermining both these requirements, the Civil War rendered the agreement totally impracticable. Both sides in Spain experienced severe monetary crises,[25] and by the autumn of 1936 insurgent fronts effectively cut Spain in two, making strict chronological payment of debts impossible. From the beginning of August, therefore, the agreement had in practice ceased to exist causing complete chaos for Anglo-Spanish trade. As in every other aspect of economic and social life, both sides in Spain introduced new measures to tackle their problems. In Nationalist Spain, decrees were passed requiring prior payment for exports and these affected British sherry importers and mining companies of southern Spain, although Rio Tinto was able to take advantage of a legal loophole in order to maintain exports of pyrites indispensable to the British rearmament programme.[26]

Faced with total breakdown of the commercial agreement, it was agreed at an interdepartmental meeting in October that the clearing agreement ought to be suspended, leaving Britain free to trade with either side in Spain. However, although initially mooted in September by the Board of Trade and the Foreign Office merely as a pragmatic remedy for the problems of trade and commerce,[27] motives for suspension had become less clearly defined only one month later. For the move to suspend the agreement coincided now with Foreign Office attempts to reach a degree of recognition of Franco's position in Spain at a time when it seemed likely that Madrid would soon fall to the rebels. Indeed, even before the main advance on Madrid, it had been proposed to send a commercial mission to the rebel leaders, rather on the lines of the mission to

Moscow in 1921 which had helped establish communications there with the new regime.

It was fully appreciated that the Spanish Government would resent the degree of recognition of the rebels implicit in the suspension of the clearing agreement, and that public opinion in Britain would be adversely aroused by the decision. Yet it was believed that the fact that the move was ostensibly dictated by the needs of British commerce would satisfy the latter, and that appreciation of Britain's desire to protect her considerable volume of trade with both sides, in the interests of post-war trade, would help mollify the former. It was also argued, with some justice, that suspension would be of as much benefit to the Republican Government as to Franco, since the agreement had long since ceased to operate, and trade could be resumed on a new basis. For example, it was thought that it would be of especial benefit at Valencia where the large seasonal orange crop – representing some 21 per cent of total Spanish exports[28] – normally marketed in Britain, awaited export and was in danger, meanwhile, of rotting.[29] Under the terms of the new agreement, the crop was to form one side of a barter exchange in coal.

The balance of pressure between economic and political factors on this issue can best be gauged by Treasury objections to the Foreign Office proposal, on the grounds that the proposals were not economically favourable to Britain. Certainly by late October, political considerations were foremost at the Foreign Office. The decision to suspend the agreement, would, it was suggested, have an immediate effect upon Britain's relations with the two parties in Spain, and would ultimately affect the part which Britain would be able to play in the final settlement. Germany and Italy already had close relations with Franco, who, if he won, would be under an obligation to them for the assistance received. From then on it would not be so far a step to a policy which took 'no account of British interest in the Western Mediterranean'. Eden, although he did not yet take so serious a view of the situation, was most anxious that the decision to suspend the agreement should be taken immediately, there being, he suggested, 'advantage in taking action within forty-eight hours'.[30] It is not clear whether this haste was intended to secure a firm decision before the new parliamentary year began on 5 November, or whether, as seems more likely, it was prompted by information which had reached Eden from secret sources, that the dictators were considering recognition of the insurgents. Despite the Foreign Secretary's declared intention to recognise the insurgents when and if Madrid should fall, the Legal Department of the Foreign Office had expressed strong reservations on this.[31] The opportunity of forging more direct links with Franco, with whom negotiations of even a commercial nature were impossible while the clearing agreement remained in force, was therefore promoted energetically by the Foreign Office.

Not until 10 November, however, did the Chancellor, Neville Chamberlain, agree to suspension of the agreement, and then only on two fairly stringent conditions. First, sterling proceeds obtained from the import of Spanish goods to Britain were to be used wholly or mainly for the purchase of British goods. Second, past debts whether to traders or bankers were to be recognised. Moreover, the Chancellor insisted that the clearing agreement be kept until the conclusion of the discussions.[32]

After some difficulty the deputation was at last received by a Nationalist delegation from the Commission of Industry and Commerce, headed by Señor Juan de la Cierva, the autogyro manufacturer.[33] Unofficial discussions continued up to 4 December and were concluded by a formal agreement that nothing in the conversations or in the initialled record of them should be interpreted as implying in any way recognition of General Franco's administration. This, however, was only one side of the new agreement. Not until 16 and 17 December did discussions take place in the Foreign Office with Republican representatives, Señor Fernando Shaw and Señor de Torres, Director of Economics from the Board of Finance at Valencia; who expressed regret that Britain had found it necessary to hold conversations with Burgos as well. The French, it was pointed out, had not taken such a step.[34] This was not strictly correct, however, for the French Government had opened negotiations with the insurgent authorities earlier that month.

The Clearing Office (Spain) Amendment No. 2 was issued following the talks of 17 December, and despite denials of British officials which deceived no one and stirred even the House of Lords to protest at the 'back door recognition',[35] it marked a high degree of recognition of the Franco régime. Henceforward, trade would be conducted as between two separate countries in Spain. As to the insurgents, the arrangement had more political than economic impact. From Seville, where a stream of anti-British propaganda had been broadcast by the 'radio' general Queipo de Llano, local broadcasts when referring to British policy were now reported to be at least courteous even if not well informed.[36] On the other hand, the new agreement brought little direct economic advantage to Britain, and Franco renegued both conditions laid down by Chamberlain, so that by early 1938 the exercise was generally admitted to have been a failure.[37] Further evidence of the political emphasis of the gesture lies in the British Government's attitude to a similar approach from the Basque authorities, who also asked to be released from the clearing agreement and proposed sending a commercial mission to Britain.[38] Their request was merely acknowledged without comment, although economically the Basque region was one of the most important areas of Spain. In truth, a tempting opportunity for rapprochement with Franco without any formal recognition had weighed heavily in favour of suspension of the clearing agreement. Trade with all parts of Spain would remain precarious, but by this manœuvre Britain established early links with the insurgent forces essential to her policy in Spain.

2. *Wartime Trade*

Britain had, from the beginning of the decade, been Spain's foremost importer, and this was to remain true of the Republic throughout the duration of the war.[39] As official channels of trade and commerce broke down in Spain, makeshift patterns emerged on both sides. A large proportion of shipping entering Spanish ports was British, although fewer cargoes carried were from the United Kingdom, partly as a result of the various prohibitions of the NIA. As already indicated, both the Board of Trade and the Foreign Office were, from the first, acutely conscious of the threat to Britain's future trade with Spain. It should be noted, however, that attention focused initially at least as much on the falling-off of coal exports to Spain as on the better-publicised question of imports of minerals to Britain, for the Abyssinian war had cut off an important British market in Italy, opening up the way for German exports of coal.

In March 1936 at a meeting of the Mines Department it had been announced that the United Kingdom was to provide 98 per cent of total Spanish coal imports from all sources – a figure which was to include coal supplied to the Balearic Islands and the floating fuel depot, though not to North Africa and the Canary Islands. Although described as a maximum target, the amount was not to fall short of $1\frac{1}{4}$ million tons per annum, although it would vary

Table 4 *Share of major participants in total Spanish trade, 1929–38 (%)*[40]

	1929	1935	1936*	1937	1938*
Imports into Spain from:					
Argentine	5.6	2.5	5.7	6.1	8.0
Belgium	3.0	3.4	3.3	10.5	7.5
Germany	10.5	13.7	13.2	0.5	–
Italy	3.4	3.0	0.2	0.2	–
Netherlands	1.8	3.6	2.7	6.7	5.3
United Kingdom	13.0	10.4	9.3	9.3	11.1
USA	15.9	16.8	17.9	11.8	10.5
USSR	2.6	1.3	0.9	11.3	30.2
Exports from Spain into:					
Argentine	6.0	5.4	3.4	2.2	1.1
Belgium	3.4	5.0	5.8	7.3	6.7
Germany	7.4	12.7	13.3	0.1	–
Italy	4.5	3.3	1.2	–	–
Netherlands	4.9	5.1	5.3	3.5	0.2
United Kingdom	18.9	21.7	25.1	35.8	34.6
USA	12.2	9.5	7.9	4.1	2.6
USSR	0.7	0.1	–	6.2	24.7

Figures apply to Spanish Government territory only.
* First quarter only.

according to production in Spain itself. (On average, Spanish production equalled 18–20 per cent of total Spanish consumption.[41] The new estimate testified to Spain's increasing demand for coal:

Table 5 *Imports of coal into Spain, 1932–5 (in long tons)*[41]

	Total imports	From United Kingdom
1932	736,952	735,614
1933	680,420	679,403
1934	946,650	924,258
1935	997,788	964,309

At the time of the revision of the Anglo-Spanish Payments Agreement, the question of coal was again raised. It was then estimated that at least 50 per cent of the coal-consuming areas of Spain (including, rather prematurely, the Madrid area) were under the Burgos authorities. A further 1 million tons each were consumed in areas under the control of the Valencian and Catalan governments, and the remainder in disputed areas. It was proposed that as part of the re-negotiation of the clearing agreement, the Burgos Government should obtain from the United Kingdom all the coal requirements to which they were not already committed. Again this was a maximum request, and the Department agreed that it would be an achievement if as much as 75 per cent could be assured.[42] Increased exports of coal were therefore made an integral part of the new agreement signed at Burgos in December 1936.

In the conditions prevailing during the Civil War, however, no agreement could be regarded as secure and the concessions gained at Burgos were treated in cavalier fashion by the Nationalist authorities. At the time of the signing of the agreement, coal exports to Spain were substantially down on the previous year, and remained low for 1937. The following year saw some increase, but in 1939 imports were again dramatically reduced:

Table 6 Exports of UK coal to Spain, 1935–9 (in long tons)[43]

1936	1937	1938	1939
731,603	757,496	1,003,898	40,504

Nor was the agreement kept more faithfully in other spheres, although there seems to have been some confusion in the Foreign Office as to whether Franco had in fact kept his part of the bargain. Opinion was to change from belief that the revision of the payments agreement was working well (Cranborne used this as an argument in favour of granting some degree of recognition to Franco in August 1937),[44] to acknowledgement six months later that, far from spending an agreed 30 per cent of sterling gained from Spanish exports in England, a considerable proportion of this money was being spent on goods from Germany, Argentine and other countries. Indeed, from 1937 exports from Britain to Spain dropped generally, with those areas clearly under Nationalist control showing the most dramatic decline,[45] thus supporting Chamberlain's doubts of November 1936 as to the worthiness of the re-negotiation of the payments agreement so eagerly pursued by the Foreign Office and Board of Trade.

Table 7 Anglo-Spanish trade 1935–9 (£.)[46]

	1935	1936	1937	1938	1939
Imports into Britain from Spain					
Spain	11,119,060	10,515,485	8,509,910	5,675,604	5,830,913
Canary Islands	1,874,361	1,884,670	2,209,875	2,266,994	2,023,576
Spanish ports in North Africa	260,140	173,173	240,489	268,440	193,190
Spanish West Africa*	37	122	4,364	2,149	232
Exports from Britain to Spain					
Spain	5,758,323	3,217,413	3,410,535	4,154,863	1,603,955
Canary Islands	1,041,911	708,428	414,801	314,067	279,658
Spanish ports in North africa	324,586	145,629	93,746	38,231	22,828
Spanish West Africa*	51,068	39,613	7,475	5,443	1,826

* Including Fernado Po.

A particularly alarming aspect of this trend for Britain was the opening to German competition of all areas of trade, a problem exacerbated by the foreign-exchange difficulties faced by both Hitler and Franco. Although both sides in Spain experienced considerable frustration in monetary matters, the Spanish Government in this respect had an initial advantage in having in their possession the greater portion of the bullion wealth of the country. Estimates vary,[47] but in 1937 the British Government believed that Spanish gold on 1 August 1936 had equalled 2,200,000,000 gold pesetas. Of this it was thought that up to November 1936 gold pesetas to the value of £20 million sterling had been exported to France.[48] Later it became clear that the bulk of Spanish gold had gone to Russia where it was held in exchange for goods and military equipment, especially armaments denied the Spanish Government from any other quarter. The Nationalists, on the other hand, were forced to depend to a large extent on barter trade, a system already carried on extensively by Germany with certain South American and European countries. Lacking at first the mining or industrial centres, the chief products available to Franco were agricultural, above all the market-garden produce of the Canaries. By September he had gained the mining areas of Huelva, and one year later the mineral wealth of the north was also entirely under his sway.

When the British Commercial Secretary, A. J. Pack, visited the insurgent territory in the autumn of 1936, he reported that the authorities there were most eager to extend their barter system to Britain. This Pack recommended, although he advised the Foreign Office not to follow the German and Italian practice of letting the insurgents have what they wanted on credit. Many countries practising barter trade with the insurgents were also signatories of the Non-Intervention Agreement, among them Belgium, Holland, Czechoslovakia, Norway and Sweden, but although such compensation transactions were frowned on by the Foreign Office there was little that could be done, since the arrangements involved comparatively small sums and usually were made by private individuals, not by government agreement. This type of arrangement was not in any case particularly favoured, except by Germany which obtained special concessionary prices. For example, fruit purchased by Germany in April 1938 at £9 per ton cost Denmark £16.05 per ton in the same month. Indeed, the Civil War years saw an astonishing growth in trade between Germany and Spain under the Nationalists:

Table 8 *Increase in Spanish exports*
to Germany in 1937 (in '000,000 RM)[49]

1934	approx.	99.7
1935	,,	118.3
1936	,,	97.7
1937	,,	135.9 (Nationalist Spain)

The figures for 1937, representing as they did exports from Nationalist Spain only, were remarkable, surpassing, as the eulogistic report prepared by the 'Official Spanish Chamber of Commerce' put it, 'the exports of the last years before the beginning of the glorious movement of the Saviour of Spain'.[50] Such developments were regarded by the Foreign Office with misgiving, since any expansion by Germany in Spain was a threat to British influence not only in the economic, but also in the political sphere. All vagaries of Spanish trade were therefore followed with concern whether they involved the falling off of coal exports or interruption to imports of tomatoes and bananas. Over all else, however, hung the question of the future of Spain's mineral wealth.

SPANISH MINERALS

Spain is a country rich in minerals of great variety. For the purposes of this study they may be divided into two main commercial groups, the iron ores of the northern provinces, in particular Vizcaya, and the pyrites of the south, especially those of the Huelva district. Both were tempting prizes to Germany, whose rearmament programme was essential both economically and politically to the emergent Reich, since mineral ores formed an indispensable link in the chain which would enable Hitler to barter arms for essential foodstuffs and commodities, for which Germany could offer no other viable exchange. In turn, the rearmament programme provided employment and a sense of purpose to an impoverished and aggrieved people.

Much has been written about the extent and purpose of German infiltration in Spain both before and during the Civil War,[51] but what is important here is not only the extent to which Britain was able to maintain her supplies of iron ore and pyrites, but also the degree to which the question of Spanish ores was at all a factor in the formulation of British Government attitudes. In relation to the question of minerals two separate problems emerged. First, there was the comparatively unimportant but nuisance value of the repeated claims from certain mining companies for compensation or protection. But, second, underlying these routine considerations was a developing awareness that British policy could open the way to German exploitation of Franco's position, thereby gaining control of minerals, 'presumably', as Lord Cranborne minuted, 'for the manufacture of munitions which may well be intended ultimately for use against us'.[52]

Pyrites

First let us consider the importance of pyrites. The term 'pyrites' is, in fact, a generic one used in commerce.[53] The ore is prized above all for its very high sulphur content, since the by-product, sulphuric acid, is regarded as the most important single ingredient in the chemical industry, and is used in the manufacture not only of iron, steel and munitions but also of petroleum and fertilisers, etc. Average world production of pyrites between 1934 and 1938 was nearly 10 million tons, of which the mines of southern Spain produced roughly 20 per cent rising to 25 per cent in the immediate pre-Civil War years. Of Spain's total production of 2,500,000 tons, Britain imported 205,264 long tons in 1935, or approximately 65 per

Table 9 Imports of pyrites into the United Kingdom, 1935–9 (in long tons) [* 55]

Country	1935	1936	1937	1938	1939
Cyprus	12,000	18,000	28,138	29,344	34,596
Other British countries	–	–	–	1	1,464
Total British	12,000	18,959	28,138	29,345	36,060
Norway	65,377	58,171	50,764	33,238	56,601
Portugal	21,347	36,082	11,744	8,273	18,094
Spain	205,264	197,883	290,418	325,324	236,314
Other countries	4,831	–	21,119	5,178	5,327
Total foreign	296,819	292,135	374,045	372,013	352,396
Total	308,819	311,085	402,183	401,358	388,456

cent of her total pyrites imports.[54] For Germany the position was slightly different in that her percentage import at 55 per cent was lower than the British, although her actual imports at roughly 562,000 metric tons were far higher. Both countries therefore relied heavily on Spanish pyrites, but whereas for Britain alternative sources would have been an inconvenient but possible substitute, for Germany with her monetary and exchange problems Spanish

Table 10 Pyrites imports from Spain by principal importing countries and Italy, 1934–6 (in metric tons) * [56]

Country	1934	1935	1936	1937
Germany	**49,343	562,584	464,232	835,708
Netherlands	**674,852	136,712	192,202	209,320
USA	376,678	422,000	337,000	not available
France	263,179	292,436	326,946	96,785
Belgium	214,602	not shewn	135,843	142,546
Italy	15,844	17,482	nil	22,591

* One long ton equals 0.984 metric tons.
** Shipments to Holland were re-exported to Germany.

pyrites were essential, providing the source for 80 per cent of her production of sulphuric acid.[57]

The two major mining companies of southern Spain, the Rio Tinto Company and Tharsis Sulphur and Copper Company, were both British. In August 1936 came announcement from Burgos of Restrictions to be placed on mining companies in the Huelva district. On 26 August, the rebels had captured the Rio Tinto mines and claimed to hold the coast between Gibraltar and Portugal, including the port of Huelva from where the ores were shipped.[58] Requisition orders for ore followed on the 27th and 28th, signed by General Cabanellas (head of the temporary administration at Burgos set up by the rebel faction on 24 July). On 29 August it was announced that all copper and copper precipitate in the mines was to be requisitioned by the military.[59]

The full import of these measures was brought home to Rio Tinto with the receipt of 'authoritative information' that the German Government had held a meeting on 10 September 'with the object of organising direct barter of compensation trade between Germany and the territory occupied by insurgent Spain'. Rio Tinto was in any case normally a supplier of pyrites to Germany, but it was feared that these measures were not merely for the duration of the war, but might become a permanent arrangement. The decrees were, however, qualified by the announcement that although there would be requisitions of all minerals and the products of mines according to the needs of the insurgent troops, the rights of mining companies would be safeguarded and strict settlement made at average market prices for products seized.[60]

From this point on, Sir Auckland Geddes, Chairman of Rio Tinto, acting often as spokesman for all the companies of Huelva, made it his mission to involve the British Government in a stand against Nationalist intervention. His belligerent attitude was actually antipathetic to the non-interventionary stance of the Cabinet and he later went so far as to persuade Eden of the necessity of a military response, perhaps half-wishful that this would spark off a far greater conflagration. Yet the first complaints of the Huelva companies, placed before the Board of Trade by a deputation of representatives led by Capt. Charles of Rio Tinto, had been swept aside. Geddes himself seems rarely to have been taken wholly seriously by the Foreign Office at this time, for he had too often made too much fuss at too little provocation. Even before the Civil War, the Foreign Office noted that complaints from that quarter were 'not always justified and in some cases deliberately exaggerated', and that Rio Tinto was reasonably well treated despite their complaints of Spanish Government discrimination against them.[61]

Nevertheless, after initial scepticism, the detailed memorandum stressing the importance of pyrites, prepared by the mining companies and presented by the deputation, had some impact, and an interdepartmental meeting was arranged for 4 September. The situation raised legal and political as well as economic questions. However, with the grip of war tightening on Spain, the Legal Department was forced to admit that although in theory requisitions were without validity, they were in practice a question of *force majeure*.

There were two major problems involved. First, the very large British consortium ICI drew its entire supply of pyrites for the manufacture of sulphuric acid from Spain. Ores from other possible sources would require the adaptation of British furnaces. The second aspect of the situation was the financial burden imposed on companies faced with paying twice for cargoes of ores, since the rebels demanded payment in foreign currency before the ships were cleared from port.

Nothing concrete ensued from this meeting and, as so often happened, the matter was allowed to drift. At this stage it was not thought worthy of discussion at Cabinet level, despite evidence of considerable German interest in Spanish pyrites. Already, a cargo from the SS *Girenti* had been requisitioned and diverted to Hamburg. It was known that the German Government was very apprehensive regarding the provisioning of chemical works, such as those of the *Duisburger Kuferhütte* and *I. G. Farben Industrie*, the largest consumers of Spanish pyrites, who took approximately 500,000 tons out of the annual total of 625,000 tons from Spain. France, too, was believed to have less than three months supply, and Rio Tinto feared more requisitions would follow.[62]

Possibly the knowledge that other European countries were equally affected by the inevitable disruptions to exports allayed British Government fears in this matter, for not until the beginning of the new year was any real concern as to the extent of German ambition in Spain expressed. Only then was it noted:

It is a fairly safe assumption that one of the reasons for the help given by the German Government to General Franco is the intention to extend Germany's economic interest in Spain. I wonder if we should now begin to consider how far, in the event of his maintaining or improving his position, the carrying out of this interest is likely to conflict with similar British interests.

However, doubts were expressed by H. M. G. Jebb[63] as to whether there was much that could be done to prevent Germany enlarging her economic interests in Spain, although he recommended departmental discussion of the problem. His view, supported by others, was that if Britain tried to prevent German expansion in Spain she would merely alienate Franco and force him to associate himself more closely with Germany. The time for Britain to assert herself, he suggested, would be when – and if – Franco won.

Meanwhile German negotiations with the insurgent authorities proceeded apace, largely through the agency of two organisations, the *Compañía Hispano-Marroquí de Transportes*, more commonly known as HISMA, and the *Rohstoffe-und-Waren Einkaufsgellschaft*, or ROWAK. The first of these, HISMA, had been constituted on 31

July 1936 in continuation of a private partnership already in existence and registered in Tetuán. Its sister organization, ROWAK, handled the German end of transactions, while the whole German project of systematic infiltration and exploitation of Spanish mines was known as the 'Montana' project.[64]

Despite the somewhat complacent attitude at the Foreign Office, the Board of Trade hoped to take a more positive stand. Nothing could be done about transactions already completed, but the Board was determined to pre-empt excessive demands from Germany by taking up large contracts for pyrites. This decision was reached after study of the extent to which Germany was dependent on Spanish pyrites. It was estimated by the Department of Overseas Trade that in 1935 Germany had produced $1\frac{1}{2}$ million tons of sulphuric acid of which 80 per cent was produced from pyrites. Yet only one-eighth of this could be met from German sources and imports of the ore in 1935 had totalled nearly 1 million tons, derived as follows:

Spain	562,584
Norway	268,589
Cyprus	106,259
Italy	65,954
Greece	12,360
Sweden	1,875

Already figures for German requisitions of pyrites in December 1936 were given as

Rio Tinto	51,000 tons
Tharsis	32,000
Pyrites de Huelva	20,000
Total	103,000

compared with a monthly average in 1935 of 47,000 tons. Moreover, Rio Tinto had received demands for a further 90,000 tons, whilst the other two companies were required to provide 40,000 tons each. This would bring Rio Tinto's contribution to 190,000 tons of pyrites (plus 500 tons of copper) in little over three months. The price had been fixed at between 14s. and 16s. per ton according to quality, compared with the purchase of pyrites by I. G.

Farben Industrie from Rio Tinto at 17s. Payment was to be made in pesetas at 42 pesetas to the £1.[65]

The Board of Trade proposed a contract with Rio Tinto to purchase 20,000 tons of pyrites per month for an initial period of six months. The cost of this enterprise would be borne by the War Office – an arrangement not much appreciated in that quarter. It was, interestingly, believed that the Germans would raise no objections if they knew that it was a British contract, a conjecture apparently based on information of recent German manœuvrings designed to cut off the French from the pyrites so essential to their rearmament programme.[66] In January 1937, the French, too, had concluded successful negotiations with Franco for pyrites. Yet a month later all export of pyrites to France was banned by the insurgent government.[67] The prohibition served to underline the force of the Foreign Office contention that to attempt directly to prevent further economic expansion by Germany would achieve only the opposite effect. As it was, the Board of Trade was prepared to sanction negotiations between Rio Tinto and German interests provided the projected contract for 20 million tons of pyrites was kept up. Of the stocks which would be thus accumulated, Rio Tinto agreed to store between 80,000 tons on sites adjacent to their copper smelter at Port Talbot.[68]

Even this arrangement did not satisfy Geddes. Writing to Vansittart on 24 February 1937, he claimed that the quantity was insufficient, and advised the accumulation of no less than 250 million tons – an amount he believed well within the company's capacity to supply. He recalled the emergency stocks which Rio Tinto had accumulated during the Great War, and warned how aerial and submarine activity would effectively stop imports from other countries. For good measure, he also pleaded the case of the unemployed of Port Talbot where refining had ceased from 15 October 1936; and the financial strain put on the company, forced to accept payment in pesetas at 42 pesetas to the £1 and to accumulate worthless currency. Geddes argued that if the British Government were to take diplomatic action, they should be prepared to back this, if necessary by force. 'I personally believe', he wrote, 'that to see the matter through will involve at least the exhibition, possibly the use, of naval power'.[69]

His belligerent plea met with a degree of sympathy from the Foreign Secretary, who from the end of 1936 had begun to recognise the danger for democracy in the Spanish conflict. He therefore included Geddes's memorandum in a Cabinet paper on 'The Position of the British Mining Companies in Spain'.

Increasingly anxious to make a stand against the dictators, Eden argued that German requisitions were equally relevant to the northern mines, which seemed likely in the future to receive similar treatment. Legally, Britain was entitled to claim compensation under the 1922 Treaty for requisitions made. Furthermore, it had been hoped that the commercial arrangement of 4 December 1936 would bring about a more accommodating attitude on the part of the Burgos authorities. This had not proved the case, and although a British representative was shortly to enter discussions at Burgos, the Foreign Secretary doubted if the negotiations would be successful. Retaliatory trade measures would be impossible, since the insurgent government was in a position to do far more harm to Britain than vice versa, and Eden, therefore, was in favour of Geddes's proposal for strong measures. He now proposed that since Britain was in a position to use her warships to intercept any ship which left Huelva carrying ore to Germany and Italy, this should be made plain to Franco from the start, even though exhaustive diplomatic methods should be carried through before resorting to direct action.[70]

Eden's memorandum had been precipitate, and his proposal brought forth an immediate, hostile and successful rebuttal from the First Lord of the Admiralty. The effectiveness of the Foreign Secretary's proposals, he countered, would depend entirely on the nationality of the ships concerned. For although British and insurgent ships might be controlled in peacetime, ships of other nationalities could not. It would be contrary to international law, and could well be regarded as a *casus belli*, in which case, Hoare warned, the League might hold Britain as the aggressor.[71]

Later, Hoare cited this incident as an example of the 'irresponsibility of the FO', complaining that even the legal advisers had not been consulted – nor, of course, had the Admiralty. Of Eden's proposal he wrote triumphantly, 'My memo killed it'.[72] The difference between the two men was essentially political and serves to illustrate a further step forward in the polarisation of opinion within the Cabinet as to the way in which the increasing aggression of the dictators was to be met. Hoare's assessment of the probable attitude of the League was no more than plausible, and came ill from the co-author of the Hoare-Laval pact. In retrospect the likelihood of provoking war at that stage seems remote, but in the light of available knowledge it was not then an unreasonable fear.

More relevant to Cabinet support of Hoare would seem to have been, once again, the general expectation of imminent Nationalist victory – although in the event these hopes were dashed.[73]

Yet the divergence between the two men was also highly personal. Shortly after this episode the First Lord wrote to Chamberlain advising him to make his new government 'as unlike the old as you can'. And, he continued:

> Do not let anything irrevocable or badly compromising happen in foreign politics until you are in control. I say this because I am convinced that the Foreign Office is so much biassed against Germany (and Italy and Japan) that unconsciously and almost continuously they are making impossible any European reconciliation.[74]

The duel between Admiralty and Foreign Office had been carried one stage further and would soon be continued over the question of the blockade of Bilbao, the Spanish Civil War thus providing not only a battleground for the opposing ideologies of Europe, but also for the internecine antagonisms of His Majesty's Government.

Eden had chosen to advance his case on the rather uncertain basis of economic necessity and had been defeated by the priority of international considerations, foremost of which was the wish to stand well with the victor in Spain, although the Cabinet agreed to make strong representations to Franco. Within a fortnight Hoare's stance was vindicated in as much as economic pressures had eased. The Foreign Secretary was obliged to report to the Cabinet that the negotiations under way at Burgos were going well. Moreover, this news was shortly followed by the promise that the United Kingdom would receive all the minerals she required provided pyrites were not sold to France.[75]

There is no doubt, however, that while Britain managed to maintain, even to increase substantially, her imports of pyrites from Spain (see Table 9, p. 82), the mining companies themselves suffered financial loss as a result of hostilities in Spain. Yet even before the Civil War, Geddes had been unhappy about the position of Rio Tinto in Spain and the 'disproportionate loss of pyrites business' there, which he attributed among other causes to the development of new mines in other countries and to preference for non-arsenical pyrites.[76] One year later the situation was so bad that Rio Tinto was only able to keep its head above water thanks to development in Northern Rhodesia.[77] As financial pressure increased so did Geddes's expectation of attention from the Foreign Office and Board of Trade, his petitions becoming ever more unrealistic. In November 1938 he tried to persuade Lord Halifax that the Spanish conflict had its origin in communist and fascist rivalry over Spain's raw materials. The only solution to this situation would be found, he submitted, in a cessation of hostilities. This might be brought about, he suggested, by payment of a 'subsidy' to Franco of £1 million in return for which Franco would engineer the restoration of the monarchy, the sum being paid through Rio Tinto.[78]

Preposterous as the scheme was it received due attention, and indeed may even have had some attractions to the Foreign Office, although it is doubtful if these would have been the same as those which commended the scheme to Geddes. Moreover, as venality does not at this stage appear to have been among Franco's shortcomings, the scheme was absurdly ill-conceived. Pointing out that Britain had had no difficulty in obtaining supplies of pyrites, and that the War Office had managed to accumulate a reserve of 125,000 tons in the latter part of 1937 and early part of 1938, with a further 50,000 tons promised, the Board of Trade presented a memorandum entirely refuting Geddes's pessimistic view. Even if Spanish supplies were cut off it was pointed out that increased amounts would be obtainable from Cyprus, although these, it was admitted, would not suit all types of furnaces. Moreover, as a last resort pyrites could be imported from the USA. As to the increased amounts exported to Germany, these had been obtained largely at the expense of France for whom all Spanish pyrites exports were refused. Lord Halifax's reply to Sir Auckland was tactful but firm: 'It would not appear that the actual position is at present so gloomy as was painted at the time when the material for your memo was being collected'.[79]

The Board of Trade and the Foreign Office had dutifully considered each claim or petition from Rio Tinto, but although the problem of pyrites was given due weight there is no evidence that it was ever a factor of prime importance in the formulation of government policy. It is, however, a measure of Sir Auckland Geddes' flair for publicity that the fortunes of Rio Tinto were followed so avidly in press, Parliament, and thus, later, by historians. With no such colourful figurehead to publicise their plight, the difficulties of the iron-ore mines of the north of Spain and

Morocco have remained relatively obscure, but it was here, if at all, after March 1937 that the concern of the British Government focused with regard to Spanish minerals.

Spanish Iron Ore and Mercury

Whereas pyrites, although an essential ingredient in the production of armaments, may also be used in a wide variety of other manufactures, the vast amounts of iron ore which Germany began to import from Spain were blatantly, and menacingly, used, in large part, to feed Germany's growing rearmament programme. Indeed, it was estimated that some 50 per cent of all steel production in Germany was 'earmarked for army purposes'.[80] But potentially as alarming from the British point of view was the growing German exploitation of the Riff iron mines of North Africa. Foremost of these was the *Compañía Española de Minas del Rio*, whose output of ore was increasing spectacularly, having risen, as Major Morton of Industrial Intelligence noted early in October 1936, from 485,409 tons in 1933 to 692,011 in 1934. The German presence in North Africa posed a serious strategic problem since the Riff mines not only faced Gibraltar, which was now brought within range of German guns, but also threatened French North Africa. This was a point on which the French were especially sensitive, having half their army stationed on the other side of the Mediterranean. Prompted by rumour of the possible concession of Spanish Morocco to Germany as a *quid pro quo* for aid, a report was compiled by Morton setting out the economic attraction of that area to Germany.

Morton's report revealed that by January 1937 – when the iron-ore mines of northern Spain were still in government territory – Spanish Morocco had become Germany's chief source of iron ore. In January 1936 Germany had imported 150,000 tons of iron ore. In the same month one year later she imported 206,000 tons, but of this 180,000 tons were taken from Spanish Morocco. There was good reason to believe that Germany would seek to increase her imports further from this source. Other sources were becoming closed to her, partly as a result of Germany's inability to offer an acceptable exchange, but equally as a result of pre-emptive purchases by other nations, for example, British purchases in Sweden. It was not yet known whether the British contract had affected German imports, but Germany was believed to be very short of ore, having probably less than four weeks supply.[81] Hitherto Spain had been a comparatively minor source of ore for Germany, but since 1934 imports from there had increased, and there was every reason to believe that they would now be stepped up significantly, although Germany could never meet all her requirements from that source. British imports, too, were increasing, and Britain was ostensibly more dependent than Germany on Spanish ore (see Table 11 below).

Table 11 Principal countries importing iron ore from Spain
(in European metric tons)

Country	1933	1934	1935	1936 (Jan. – April)
Belgium	22,981	25,191	31,266	23,068
Germany	70,868	61,968	227,796	59,593
France	118,893	72,712	33,198	24,653
United Kingdom	876,454	1,235,407	1,084,856	427,412
Holland	22,981	25,191	31,266	23,068
Total	1,411,156	1,778,451	1,893,370	775,235

Spain had so far been quite able to meet increasing demand, her total production rising from 1,786,811 (long) tons in 1933 to 2,591,570 tons in 1935.[82] There was as yet no evidence that increased German demand was in any way curtailing British imports of iron ore, and indeed the chief iron-producing mines lay well behind Republican lines.

Yet for the first time the Cabinet did display some interest, chiefly because certain aspects of the problem were relevant both to Britain's strategic position in the Mediterranean and to the race to rearm. The degree of German organisation already achieved, and the clear expectation of further gains were certainly alarming. It was known, for example, that arrangements had been made for the Bicker Company, agents of the *Vereinigten Stahlwerke*, to carry out distribution of ores in Germany; that the metallurgical industrial working day would be raised in March 1937 from 8 to 10 hours a day; and also that all stocks of iron ore in northern Spain, as and when taken by Franco, were to be requisitioned and shipped to Germany.[83] But it was the strategic implications of German infiltration into Morocco which drew the attention of the Cabinet. It was suggested in the Cabinet on 27 January 1937 that if the Republic won the Spanish Government might not wish to retain the

North African colony, which had been a continuous drain on the finances of previous Spanish Governments. Interestingly, the implication that France might then extend her influence in that sphere was unpalatable to the Foreign Office. But nor did Britain want to see any other great power established in Spanish Morocco.[84]

The Chiefs of Staff were therefore asked to examine the question in detail. Their view merely endorsed Eden's view that the African coast opposite Gibraltar should never come under the control of any other major power, for it would be possible to establish batteries there for the bombardment of Gibraltar. Equally, the possession of naval bases in the area would constitute a threat to shipping. Strategically, the best situation would, the Chiefs of Staff believed, be for Britain herself to control Spanish Morocco, although experience had shown that Morocco was a source of endless friction. The Chiefs of Staff were reluctant to compare the disadvantages of French, German or Italian control, regarding them alike, in the long run, as a threat to British interests.[85]

What is revealing here is the apparent consensus of opinion between Cabinet, Foreign Office and the armed forces that France was still at least as firmly cast into her ancient and traditional rôle of Britain's enemy, as was Germany. Indeed, rather more so, since Germany was already ensconced in Spanish Morocco and appears to have been regarded, at least temporarily, as the lesser evil. This was an important factor (although rarely so openly expressed) in the formulation of more general policy towards Spain.

As to the economic importance of Spanish iron ore, although some anxiety was expressed on this score in mid-March[86] and it remained a cause for concern throughout the summer of 1937, Spain was already a less important source of iron ore to Britain by 1936 – although in that year British total imports of iron ore actually increased (see Table 11).

At roughly the same time as the memorandum of mid-March noted that 'There is no doubt that the principal gainer [of iron ore] was Germany and the principal sufferer, the United Kingdom', General Franco, troubled by the extent of German infiltration, sent assurances to Britain through A. J. Pack that instructions had been sent to Tetuán to ensure full compliance with the existing contracts for exports of iron ore to the United Kingdom. This was to be done, Pack was told, in order to retain 'old customers' and not to be dependent on a temporary demand from 'certain quarters

Table 12 *Relative decline of Spain as a source of iron ore for Britain*[87]

	Imports from Spain	Total imports	Imports Spain (%)
	(in '000,000 tons)		
1935			
United Kingdom	1.38	4.54	30
Germany	1.32	14.06	9
France	0.11	0.43	25
Holland	0.13	0.42	30
1936 (first 11 months)			
United Kingdom	1.14	5.53	18
Germany	1.03	17.11	6
France	0.11	0.29	37
Holland	0.15	0.44	34

which might fall away once the war was over'.[88] Fears that Britain might lose out to Germany to the detriment of her rearmament programme were therefore allayed; the Board of Trade noted, however, that although no action was called for in the immediate future, it might be necessary to act later if Franco were to capture the mines of Bilbao or Almeria.[89]

No doubt Franco's assurances of safeguarding British iron-ore supplies had been made partly with a view to obtaining in return the promise of some further degree of recognition from the British Government. In this he was disappointed,[90] and a period of tension ensued, exacerbated by the humiliation of Guadalajara and the confounding of hopes of an early Nationalist victory. This, combined with the problem of exporting ore from an embattled and blockaded area meant that many difficulties were experienced by shippers and mine-owners alike. Here, too, the largest mining company of the area, the Orconera Iron Ore Company, was British, with capital of £2 million and exporting mainly to British steel manufacturers. The four next most important mines were the:

Sociedad Franco-Belga de Somorrostro, Paris. A French company exporting both to continental and British steel manufacturers.
Parocha Mine. Joint Spanish and British ownership.
Sociedad de Triano. Spanish owned, but exporting principally to the United Kingdom.
Sociedad de Dicido (sic). Spanish owned.

Of lesser importance in terms of British imports, were three more British companies:

Aquifa Mines Company of Granada.
Baird's Mining Company.
European Iron Ore (merchants with purely financial interest).[91]

By midsummer Franco's forces had advanced considerably. Bilbao fell on 19 June 1937, and once more the Nationalists seemed anxious to nurture their tenuous relations with Britain. After a meeting with the Duke of Alba on 28 June, in which the Nationalist representative confirmed that Britain would be able to have without difficulty as much iron ore as was wanted from the Bilbao area, Lord Cranborne was able to report a decided thaw in relations with Nationalist Spain.[92] Yet there is no doubt that at the time these words seemed to have little resemblance to the reality of the situation in the north where shippers, mine-owners and merchants alike experienced continued obstacles under the new administration of the *Comisión de Rugulación Económica de Vizcaya y Santander* which controlled imports and exports. The British commercial representative in the area, T. W. Pears, was informed that while British contracts had not been cancelled they had been 'shelved for the time being in view of the special circumstances resulting from war'.

By July 1937 it was almost impossible to obtain shipping permits, and those which were granted were heavily penalised. Shippers were obliged to credit to the Nationalist Government through a London bank the full value in sterling of the cargo, and in return were reimbursed in pesetas at 42.50 pesetas to the £1. It was indicated that sterling was required to liquidate large coal purchases from Britain, both then and in the future – a fairly persuasive argument at the Board of Trade. Pears reported that it was generally believed that the Germans, on discovering the heavy nature of contracts for Bilbao ore held by Britain, and in view of the low production of the mines, had brought pressure to bear on Franco to cancel or suspend contracts temporarily. Although Franco had resisted as long as it seemed likely that belligerent rights might be granted, he was no longer prepared to co-operate.[93]

Doubtless recognition would have been a great convenience for both Britain and Franco, and in August it was again considered by the Foreign Office, partly in relation to economic problems, although more as a release from the deadlock in which the NIC had by then found itself over the questions of recognition of belligerency and withdrawal of volunteers. Once again, however, unilateral rapprochement was abandoned on the grounds that the fall of Santander to the Nationalists had made any move towards further recognition of Franco too controversial to be promoted at that time, and that, as Eden noted in a draft of the statement delivered to the meeting of ministers at the beginning of September, 'political considerations must for the time being override the practical ones mentioned in my earlier memorandum.'[94] By the time the appointment of a British Agent to Spain was officially announced in November 1937, Britain's economic relations with Nationalist Spain had probably eased as much as was compatible with war conditions. This did not, however, deter the Government from presenting economic arguments in favour of an appointment which was widely regarded with deep suspicion. For, as Lord Cranborne had suggested, the appointment 'could easily be defended in the House of Commons on the score of British interests'.[95]

The capture of Gijón at the end of October placed yet another large group of mines in Nationalist hands and production was immediately stepped up yet again. Output soared, despite the

Table 13 Increase in Basque iron-ore output and exports[97]

	Workers	Output (tons)	Exports (tons)	Home consumption (tons)
1937				
July	1,000	20,000	–	10,000
August	1,500	40,000	45,000	20,000
September	2,100	50,000	100,000	25,000
October	3,000	90,000	120,000	35,000
November	3,500	120,000	105,000	40,000
December	4,000	140,000	120,000	50,000
Total		460,000	490,000	180,000
1938				
January	4,300	145,000		
February	4,500	147,000		
March	4,700	160,000		
April	5,000	162,000		
Total		614,000		

evacuation of half the Basque miners, but only at the cost of great
hardship to the many prisoners-of-war used in the mines as slave
labour.[96] The target set for 1938 was 1½ million tons, and it was soon
evident that this would easily be reached and even exceeded. Not
only would Germany's requirements be fulfilled, but Britain too
would see her contracts met. Indeed with the removal at the end of
July 1937 of the ban on ore exports, little more was heard of the
problem of iron ore, first deliveries arriving at Cardiff on 28 August.
By mid-1938 it was equally clear that Franco was treating his
German allies with extreme caution and that most of the recent
mining concessions taken up by Germans were of relatively little
long-term value. All mining rights acquired after 18 July 1936 were
nullified on 9 October 1937, and foreign ownership was later limited
to 40 per cent.[98] One more area of difficulty remained, however,
and this was at Almadén, where the mines which supplied some 80
per cent of the world's, and 99 per cent of Spain's mercury were
situated. For the greater part of the war the mines lay just inside
Republican territory and inevitably hostilities interrupted the flow
of exports to the outside world. Yet this does not seem to have
aroused concern in Britain, at least until mid-1938. By the end of
October that year Britain had managed to obtain only 7 per cent of
her total imports from sources other than Spain. What little had
been brought from Spain had been transported mainly in British
vessels. As the Nationalist blockade tightened around the southern
and eastern ports of Spain the question arose as to whether steps
should be taken to protect the mercury transport ships. It was
believed, however, that any such measures would 'be unlikely to
make the Burgos authorities disposed to grant permission for the
export [of mercury] to the United Kingdom even of such quantities
as are reaching us at present, in the event of their troops capturing

Table 14 Imports of mercury into Britain, 1935–September 1938

Year	Quantity ('000 lbs)	Value (£'000)
1935	1,419	209
1936	1,404	222
1937	2,599	419
January–September		
1937	2,363	382
1938	2,236	327

Almadén.[99] This strategy of restraint evidently paid off to the satisfaction of the Government, for on 2 May 1939 in answer to a question in the House, Mr Oliver Stanley of the Board of Trade said that no indication had been given that industry in Britain was unable to obtain adequate supplies of mercury.[100]

Clearly the British Government, prompted by the Board of Trade, followed the vicissitudes of Anglo-Spanish trade and British investments in Spain with much concern. But at no point can it be demonstrated that economic factors were the sole inspiration for specific policy decisions on Spain, except insofar as these were an extension of the generally anti-communist attitudes which had first inspired the policy of non-intervention, a policy maintained in the first instance for strategic reasons and later for the rather broader purposes of 'appeasement'. For the British Government the major query regarding this policy was whether or not to recognise Franco's administration, and on several occasions economic factors were advanced as grounds for doing so. But these grounds were never sufficient in themselves to bring about recognition, nor were they even potent enough to persuade the British Government to give Franco the one concession he desired above all other: the recognition of belligerent status.

However, it is true that despite the leadership of a man who had made considerable personal financial sacrifice for his country,[101] the left remained convinced that pressure from financial interests was influential in the formation of British Government attitudes towards the Spanish conflict, and certainly Government connection with Anglo-Spanish trade or investment was much in evidence.[102] Both Rio Tinto and its subsidiary, European Pyrites Corporation (jointly owned with *Metallgesellschaft A.G.*), had contacts with the House of Commons through their respective directors, Capt. A. H. Ramsay (Conservative MP for Peebles) and Col. the Hon. Henry Guest (Conservative MP for Drake) who was also a director of the Orconera Iron Company – both rabidly pro-Nazi. The latter company was partly controlled by Consett Spanish Ore Company which, again, had powerful political connections through the Hon. W. L. Runcman, son of Lord Runciman, President of the Board of Trade (7 June 1935 – 28 May 1937); and by marriage through the Rt. Hon. Capt. Euan Wallace (Conservative MP for Hornsey), occasional Chairman of the Non-Intervention Committee[103] and Parliamentary Private Secretary at the Overseas Trade Department where he acted as spokesman for the Department on the occasion of the suspension of the clearing agreement with Spain.[104] Wallace was described by the Soviet Ambassador as wanting 'to stress in every possible way that his sympathies were entirely on the side of Italy and Germany'.[105]

Neville Chamberlain himself had once been a director of Birmingham Small Arms, and of Elliot's Metal Company (a subsidiary of the prime sulphur consumer, ICI),[106] and this connection, though severed, suggests at least a degree of sympathy towards the problems of the firms concerned. Baldwin's own fortune was based on iron and steel firms amalgamated by his father.[107] Both Capt. Ramsay and Col. Guest spoke frequently in the House on Spanish affairs,[108] and Chamberlain was evidently very much in agreement with members of his coterie such as David Margesson, Conservative Chief Whip ('A victory for the Rebels in Spain and a successful meeting of the Locarno Powers would be splendid . . .'), on whose advice Euan Wallace was promoted to Parliamentary Private Secretary at the Board of Trade on 28 May 1937.[109]

Against this, however, must be balanced not only the influence of the French branch of the Rothschild family, major shareholders in Rio Tinto[110] and patently anti-Nazi, but also a growing body of professional opinion, such as that voiced by *The Economist* which consistently argued the demerits of a Franco victory in which Germany and Italy would play a major part:

> The last of the Spanish rebellion will not be heard with the fall of Madrid and when it is heard, it will prove highly unpalatable, we fear, to the British and French Governments.

As to the belief that the German yoke would easily be sloughed off, and that, as Eden predicted, Spain would not allow foreign domination, *The Economist* warned, 'This may well be so, but it is not the long view that guides the Fascist powers.'[111]

Moreover, increasingly prevalent as the war moved into its second year was the realisation among merchants that a better deal would be obtained from the Republican Government, which went as far as possible in the circumstances to accommodate British traders and investors. Nor was this true only of those engaged in shipping and rail (although these were outstanding cases),[112] or of those investors, such as the holders of Madlon bonds, fortunate enough to receive reimbursement.[113] The *Financial Times* welcomed the news that the Spanish Government had made arrangements for the payment of a second instalment of the post-clearing credits acknowledging that this was not only 'commendable' but a 'considerable sacrifice in the existing situation', especially since the payments were for debts accumulated in Nationalist as well as in Republican territory. It was noted that the insurgents, on the other hand, showed

> no signs of wanting to pay. They pay cash for current deliveries but nothing on debts. Foreign creditors stand a better chance of payment from Government Spain in the case of Government victory than from Franco in the case of a Nationalist victory.[114]

In effect, the natural instincts of the market place were reasserting themselves, and it was found to be no less congenial to trade with Republican Spain than with, say, communist Russia.

Thus, economically, as regards both a short and long term view, opinion began to tilt in favour of a Republican victory. Had economic reason alone prevailed in 1938, the last and the grimmest six months of the war might have taken on a very different aspect. As it was, it was considered far too late politically to change course in post-Munich Anglo-Spanish relations. Franco's blockade of Barcelona would be allowed to hold out against British merchantmen and the Republican Government starved to its defeat.

4 Naval Attitudes to the Spanish Civil War

If, as is suggested here, there was less interest and a higher degree of ambivalence in British Government attitudes to economic aspects of the Spanish Civil War than was once thought, this is not true of Britain's naval policy. For it is now clear that the response of the British Government to naval problems contributed positively to Franco's ultimate victory. In an area of policy where confusion and *ad hoc* decisions tended to mask the full vehemence of much ministerial hostility towards the Spanish Republic, naval policy was exceptional in its blatancy. This was largely because, unlike the Foreign Office where some genuine disagreement on the Spanish question existed, and the pro-Republican position of Anthony Eden after December 1936 muted official advice on other aspects of Spanish policy, the Admiralty under Sir Samuel Hoare was consistently and emphatically anti-Republican.

Despite Britain's adoption in August 1936 of a policy of non-intervention aimed at isolating and containing the Spanish imbroglio, ships of the Royal Navy were engaged throughout the Spanish Civil War in intensive operations of evacuation and patrol off the coast of Spain. From mid-1937 these activities were mostly of an international nature, either under the terms of the non-intervention scheme or the terms of the Nyon Agreement. This did not, as had been hoped, deflect criticism of British Government policy towards Spain, which came under vigorous attack for its unwillingness to ensure that the Royal Navy carried out its traditional role as protector of Britain's merchant fleet, an unwillingness believed to reflect pro-Nationalist bias. Yet during this period the British Admiralty itself was fighting, not only for swifter and broader rearmament, but also for a greater degree of independence in ordering naval affairs in peacetime, and this accounts, in part, for the admiralty response to the Spanish Civil War.

Until Baldwin's retirement in May 1937, the senior civil and military posts at the Admiralty were filled by men of forceful opinions and personality. Sir Samuel Hoare had regained a position in the Cabinet as First Lord of the Admiralty only six months after his resignation in December 1935 following criticism of the Hoare-Laval negotiations. In Cabinet discussions he was invariably forthright in support of Franco, favouring recognition of the Nationalists and reconciliation with Italy. His service counterpart at the Admiralty, the First Sea Lord and Chief of Naval Staff, Admiral Sir A. Ernle Chatfield, was also currently Chairman of the Chiefs of Staff Committee. If Chatfield inclined 'more to the "White" than the "Red" in Spain',[1] his overriding aim was that the Royal Navy, then sorely depleted in both men and ships, should be rebuilt. To this end the Spanish Civil War became for Chatfield, as the Abyssinian war had also been, a stick with which to beat the Government. To add Spain to Britain's potential enemies would, he believed, be ' . . . the last straw on the military burden, imposed by an unbalanced and unrealistic outlook'.[2]

Each of these men found in the other's views support for his own policies. Thus Hoare warned that the Navy would not be able to cope in the face of the Nationalist blockade of Bilbao, while Chatfield maintaied that if Britain interfered with a beleaguered port, that action would be interpreted as taking sides and might provoke Germany and Italy.[3] This close alliance stood in direct opposition to Eden as regards the war in Spain, and because naval support was so important to every aspect of British foreign policy, it could not but have exceptional influence. It is significant that, in the spring of 1937, Eden had the utmost difficulty in prevailing against the Admiralty, and succeeded only in forcing minimal protection for British vessels, whereas in the autumn with the more malleable Duff Cooper at the Admiralty, the Foreign Secretary was able to fulfil his long-felt wish to 'show a tooth in the Mediterranean' by bringing off the Nyon Agreement on the control of submarine activity in the Mediterranean.[4]

There was, however, much justification for the position adopted by the First Sea Lord. The British navy had been severely reduced after the Great War, and until the mid-thirties there remained two major obstacles to any naval expansion. The first of these had been the Ten Year Rule, abandoned only in 1932, by which the Government maintained that war was not contemplated for at least ten years, and large-scale rearmament was therefore unnecessary. The second was the series of conferences resulting in treaties setting stringent limits to naval expansion. By the Washington Treaty of 1922 and the London Treaty of 1931 (both due to expire on 31 December 1936), all signatories agreed to limit their ships in number and tonnage and to adopt a one-power standard, that is, that each navy would be equal to that of only one other great power.[5] The size of the Royal Navy was thus tied, until December 1936, to that of the USA, although there was no comparison, at that time, between the American naval responsibility and the worldwide commitments of Britain.

Yet even when these limitations were eased at the London Naval Conference of 1935, there was considerable opposition to the degree of expenditure which would have been required to rebuild a fleet in which one battleship alone might cost as much as £10 million. Thus it was, as Chatfield pointed out, that when war broke out in 1939, Britain possessed no capital ships newer than the *Nelson* and the *Rodney* whose keels had been laid in 1923. Moreover, although the 1936 White Paper indicated that cruiser strength should be increased to seventy ships, so many vessels had to be scrapped that little headway was made, as Table 16 shows. At the same time, by

Table 15 Proposed strengthening of the Royal Navy[6]

	1936	1937
Capital ships	15	15
Aircraft carriers	5	5
Cruisers	52	53
Destroyers	175	164
Submarines	57	52
Minesweepers	68	70
Flotilla leaders	18	

The Navy was strengthened in that many old vessels, e.g. thirty destroyers, had been scrapped. But overall numbers were down.

the Anglo-German Naval Agreement of June 1935 Germany was allowed to increase her naval strength to 35 per cent of the British strength; 60 per cent of British submarine strength; or, in certain circumstances, 100 per cent of British Empire submarine strength.[8] Worse, that spring the Japanese withdrawal from the London Naval Conference indicated a fresh threat to British security in the Far East, and one which severely restricted the scope of naval activity elsewhere, and especially in the Mediterranean. 'We are in no position', Vansittart wrote in August that year, 'to take a strong line in the Mediterranean – anyhow not for some time'.[9] In exasperation, Chatfield warned that

> however willing the Navy is to do all that is required of it and more, we cannot make bricks without straw and nine months on a war footing, without mobilisation, is more than even the most willing administration can cope with without help.[10]

Following the withdrawal of sanctions against Italy in June 1936, the Admiralty had successfully requested the release of thirty ships from duty off Alexandria. It was as these ships were making their way back through the Mediterranean for leave and refitting that the Spanish Civil War broke out and they were diverted to Spain. Once

Table 16 *Comparison of Italian and French naval forces in 1936*[7]

	Italian naval forces	French naval forces
Battleships	6	7 (and 1 obsolete vessel)
Aircraft carriers	–	1
Cruisers	29	16
Flotilla leaders and Destroyers	64	30
Torpedo boats	61	17
Motor torpedo boats	65	–
Submarines	83	76
Minelayers	15	2
Minesweepers	38	4

again the British navy was fully extended. Now, however, in addition to its numerical weakness, the Navy had been severely humiliated at Alexandria and was anxious thereafter to avoid any similar situation. As Cadogan later remarked of the British naval position in general, 'No good blustering unless we are sure we can carry out our threats.'[11]

The report of the Chiefs of Staff on 'The situation in the Western Mediterranean arising from the Spanish Civil War', called for by Cadogan in August, further demonstrated the degree of frustration felt in naval circles at the Government's dilatory attitude to rearmament, but also new respect for Italian ruthlessness. Both these factors were to play an essential part in the formulation of

Cabinet attitudes to events in Spain during the coming year. Given Spain's geographic position, flexibility of policy was very dependent on willing support of the Admiralty. As Eden later pointed out, 'The First Lord's technical objections impressed my colleagues, most of whom had no experience with which to counter them.'[12] Faced with their own culpability in having failed to secure a naval force sufficient to Britain's requirements, Cabinet members were doubly sensitive to Admiralty arguments and loath to risk another public débâcle such as had followed the Abyssinian crisis.

EVACUATION

The first British naval involvement came within twenty-four hours of reports of the rebellion, when the Senior Officer, Gibraltar, signalled the Commander-in-Chief of the Mediterranean Fleet, Admiral Sir William Fisher, 'In view of strained relations suggest fast warship be sent urgently, view to protection of British lives and property.'[13] The Fleet, already homeward bound from Alexandria, made swiftly towards Spain and the Balearics. By 24 July thirteen ships were distributed around the Spanish coast.

The most immediate, and indeed continuing, task was the evacuation of the British who wished to leave, and it was later agreed between the British, French, Italian and German representatives at a conference aboard HMS *London* on 28 July to evacuate nationals of each other's countries.[14] By July 1937 the British had evacuated a total of 27,700 refugees.[15] 'This', recalled Chatfield, 'was the Navy's chief and happiest work.'[16] Others found the work less congenial.[17] Nevertheless this great humanitarian work continued intermittently throughout the war, culminating in the evacuation of the Republican Government. It was work of political value too, in that it underlined the neutrality of Britain's position, particularly in the early phases when rebel as well as republican refugees were aided.

By 4 August, Britain had twenty-eight men-of-war in Spanish waters, and the main evacuation of Barcelona had been completed, only three hundred British subjects remaining voluntarily. Taking advantage of the temporary lull if the situation, Admiral James requested permission to release some of his ships. The Foreign Office agreed, but asked for sufficient ships to lie ready at consular ports.[18] The lull was shortlived. Before the end of the month the Chiefs of

Staff report had spelled out Britain's interest in the Spanish situation. Furthermore, the Spanish Government had issued warning of intention to blockade rebel ports. All ships, whatever their nationality, would be attacked if suspected of arms smuggling, and port and neighbouring districts would be in danger of aerial bombardment. By the end of August there were again twenty-four British naval vessels keeping, as Chatfield put it, 'watch and ward on the Spanish coast, from the Bay of Biscay to Marseilles'.[19] From now on there would be no respite for the Royal Navy.

THE REPUBLICAN BLOCKADE

If from the outset political and strategic factors predisposed Admiralty attitudes in support of non-intervention, these were more than confirmed by the actions in support of the Republican Government of counter-revolutionary crews of the Spanish navy. Refusing to obey the orders of the Spanish Minister of Marine, José Giral, many commanding officers incited their crews to support the military rebellion. As soon as this was known they were dismissed by official order, and control of the ships was given to loyal junior officers and crews. Clearly such a major reversal was not to be accomplished without resistance, and many higher-ranking officers were killed or imprisoned.[20]

For the Admiralty, the mutiny at Invergordon in 1931 was of sufficiently recent memory for this episode to be especially shocking, and although the Republican Government had acted in accordance with 'procedural etiquette',[21] the event was undoubtedly prejudicial to good relations with the Republic. Naval reports from Spain referred unabashedly to the 'Reds' and the 'Whites', and certainly first impressions did nothing to convince British naval officers on the spot that the counter-revolution was not part of a communist plot.[22]

As the significance of naval operations to the outcome of the war became clearer, British policy grew more distinctly pro-Nationalist. This was demonstrated in the difference between the response to Republican blockade warnings of July and early August 1936 and the later warnings issued by the Nationalists. On 24 July the *Gaceta de Madrid* published a decree declaring that the Spanish Protectorate of Morocco and its territorial waters were zones of war. On 10 August blockade warnings were extended to the Canary Islands, Lugo, Corunna and Ponte Verde, and one week later to Almeria and Alicante.[23] Accordingly, two days later the German ship *Kamerun* was held forcibly by the Spanish Government on suspicion of arms smuggling. Germany naturally contested the right of the Republicans to take such a step.[24]

One solution open to governments wishing to adopt a neutral position towards foreign conflicts is to formally recognise the belligerency of rival forces and to concede to them belligerent rights. This allows those parties in the course of blockade to stop and examine ships suspected of carrying arms to their opponents. The right to take such action is, however, accompanied by the responsibility for any loss caused by delay or damage. Without the award of such rights any irregular activities by either party may legitimately be regarded as acts of piracy. The British Admiralty, which did not relish the prospect of British ships submitting to the blockading activities of the 'communistic' Republican navy, and did not believe that fleet capable of enforcing a blockade, refused in August to countenance the recognition of belligerency.[25] Consequently, partly in response to Admiralty reluctance to submit to a Republican blockade and partly because they were anxious that no hitch should delay progress towards an agreement on non-intervention, the British Government followed Germany's firm lead.[26] The Foreign Secretary warned the Spanish Ambassador that if a Spanish warship had stopped the *Kamerun* on the high seas, His Majesty's Government viewed the action as incorrect and British ships would be protected from any such interference.[27] In fact, the warning was almost certainly superfluous at that stage since there was little danger that British ships would be in any danger from deliberate attack whilst the Republican Government so earnestly sought to enlist Britain's support for her cause.

Yet already on 16 August precise instructions had been issued to Royal Navy ships regarding the Republican blockade. First, Britain did not recognise Spain's claims that her territorial waters extended six miles from her coasts. Outside the three-mile limit a Spanish man-of-war might ask where ships were bound but was not entitled to search. British ships were to signal 'stop interfering' if there was any attempt to hinder. If a Spanish ship were to fire she was to be engaged 'until she ceased to do so'.[28] These instructions represented the predictable response of a great power to the presumptuous aggressions of a lesser. Initially, of course, the British Government had nothing to fear from the Republican navy, and the Nationalist navy was virtually non-existent. However, with the advent of considerable support from Italy and Germany to the Nationalists, the naval situation changed, and so did Britain's attitude to Spanish blockades. Over the next months the concise instructions issued to British ships in August were to be amended and altered so often that they became almost meaningless, placing an intolerable burden on junior commanding officers and resulting in the inaction which was to provoke an outcry in press and Parliament.

The fact was that the British Government had to balance two wholly incompatible policies. On the one hand it was essential, as the Chiefs of Staff's report made clear, to remain on, at worst, strictly neutral terms with whichever party emerged victorious in Spain. On the other hand, the report also stressed the need for giving no offence to Italy. As 1936 drew to a close it became increasingly obvious that these requirements were irreconcilable. Having taken a firm line with the Republican Government over their declaration of blockade, the British Government could scarcely abandon that position without offending the Republican Government, and this was doubly evident when, contrary to expectation, Madrid did not fall to the rebels that year. At the same time the Spanish Nationalist navy was increasingly in a better position to carry out its threats and was receiving practical aid from Italy.[29]

Neither of the Spanish navies would in the normal way have presented any challenge to the Royal Navy. However, in early November it was learned that Mussolini had openly declared his intention of waging 'an ideological war against bolshevism in Spain', and that solid backing for the Nationalist cause had been sent in the form of two Italian submarines which were making for the eastern Mediterranean with orders to be ready for immediate action. In the western Mediterranean, too, activities of Italian warships indicated that they were probably preparing to intercept Russian ships bound for Spain.[30] If the rapprochement with Italy which the British Government sought were to be achieved – and negotiations were soon under way for an Anglo-Italian agreement – it would have to be accompanied from now on with as much accommodation of the Spanish Nationalist cause as was compatible with the maintenance of sufficient semblance of neutrality to avoid alienating the Spanish Republican Government.

Meanwhile *bona fide* British shipowners, confident of British naval protection, continued to ply to and from Spain, and were joined by many others anxious to take advantage of the British flag. For the

Table 17[31] *Disposition of Spanish naval forces as assessed by the Admiralty*
on 28 August 1936

Vessel	Government	Rebel	Uncertain
Battleships	*Jaime Primero*	*Espana*	
	(both due for modernisation)		
Cruisers	4	3	1
Flotilla leaders	9	–	1
Destroyers	1	1	–
Submarines	12	–*	–
Torpedo boats	3	1	–
Gunboats	1	2	2

* Jane's also gives the rebel navy as having no submarines. They had in fact two, although both very old, according to Admiral Sir Peter Gretton (Reading University Seminar, 1972).

British Government the position was further complicated by the consideration that recognition of belligerency which the Admiralty, having performed a complete *volte face*, now strongly advocated, would, in terms of international law, have implied that Britain placed both sides on the same footing, and this they were not yet prepared to do openly.[32] While the Cabinet debated this delicate question, the Nationalist blockade was intensified. Temporary orders were therefore issued to British naval ships off Spain to help them in what had become a most arduous task of protection. The provisional orders stipulated that until the Cabinet had reached a decision on belligerent rights

> in order to avoid incidents, instructions should be provisionally modified to the extent that it is no longer necessary for you to protect ships flying the British flag from visit and search or (if they are carrying war material destined for Spain) capture by Spanish warships . . . The main objectives are on the one hand to avoid any incidents between His Majesty's ships and the Spanish warships, and on the other to avoid giving the impression that HMG are not prepared to afford full support to unobjectionable activities of British ships.[33]

In order to meet the latter requirement British shipowners were not informed of the new orders, and for two days British merchant ships continued to sail, unaware that they no longer enjoyed naval protection.[34]

So provocative a position was clearly untenable, and a meeting of ministers was hastily convened on Sunday 22 November at the instigation of the Foreign Secretary, who was opposed to the flabbiness of the new orders.[35] As a result of this meeting the temporary orders were rescinded, but a bill, which became law on 4 December 1936, was swiftly introduced to prohibit

> the discharge in, or trans-shipment for, Spanish territory of weapons and munitions of war and other articles from certain ships, to prohibit the carriage in such ships consigned to, or destined for Spanish territory, and for the purposes connected therewith.[36]

For the future the Royal Navy would defend, if at all, only those ships which carried cargoes inoffensive to either side in Spain, and thus Franco's right to blockade, although not formally recognised, was tacitly admitted.

By late November, Eden had become convinced by War Office reports that Italian intervention in Spain was a positive danger to the democratic powers. During the closing weeks of 1936 he watched the growing influence of Italy on the rebels' struggle in Spain, and particularly in Majorca, and noted with frustration the fruitless efforts of the NIC to make any practical progress on the agreed principal of naval control. Meanwhile, negotiations went forward with Italy for the 'Gentleman's Agreement' which was finally signed on 2 January 1937, and which pledged the preservation of the *status quo* in the Mediterranean. On returning to the Foreign Office after the Christmas break, Eden learned of fresh consignments of Italian troops disembarked in Spain.[37] Sickened by Mussolini's perfidy, he produced a compelling memorandum expressing his fear that

> the extent and character of the intervention now practised by Germany and Italy have made it clear to the world that the object of these powers is to secure General Franco's victory whether or not it represents the will of the Spanish people.

He went on to warn his colleagues:

> . . . in the language of the Nazi Party any adventure is a minor adventure. They spoke thus of the Rhineland last year, they are

speaking thus of Spain today, they will speak thus of Memel, Danzig or Czechoslovakia tomorrow.

Wanting to take positive action, he suggested that it might be possible to hasten agreement on naval control if the British Government offered the services of their own fleet for the purposes of preventing either volunteers or war material reaching Spain. The operation could be conducted with the co-operation of the French in the closing of the Franco-Spanish border, and, Eden hoped, of the Portuguese who would be urged to do likewise.[38] Having found, as he believed, provisional support for his scheme from both Baldwin and Halifax,[39] Eden presented and defended his proposal at a meeting on 8 January of the principal ministers involved. But although his paper made sound sense politically and strategically and had the approval of the Prime Minister, Eden suffered a major personal defeat at the hands of Sir Samuel Hoare. The First Lord, who resented the lack of consultation between the Foreign Office and the Admiralty on an issue so directly concerning the latter, advanced detailed geographic and technical objections to Eden's proposal which so convinced his colleagues that, as Hoare later noted, 'the whole Cabinet turned Eden down'.[40] The Foreign Secretary's scheme was rejected in favour of Hoare's proposal of an international scheme under the auspices of the NIC.

Although he agreed to work out a scheme on these lines with the Admiralty, Eden was clearly disappointed. He was not, he admitted, much interested in the naval aspect *per se*, but in the wider power struggle being fought out in Spain. The danger did not arise from what happened at sea, but if Germany and Italy were not checked in their Spanish ambitions then, he believed, Britain would find a situation in which those two countries would in effect conquer Spain. For both men the political issues were paramount, but the controversy was also tinged with strong mutual antipathy. The occasion was a victory for Hoare, who warned his colleagues that the Cabinet

appeared to be getting near a situation where as a nation we were trying to stop General Franco from winning. That was the desire of the Left, but there were others, including perhaps some members of the Cabinet who were very anxious that the Soviet Union should not win in Spain.[41]

Of Eden's proposal the First Lord recorded triumphantly, 'I destroyed it'.[42]

THE INSURGENT BLOCKADE IN THE NORTH

The new merchant shipping act had been passed with the intention of shoring up cracks in the Non-Intervention Agreement which gave rise to the danger of incidents at sea, and was to be a stop-gap measure until such time as the Non-Intervention Committee came up with a workable and acceptable sea control scheme, or until a suitable opportunity for an award of belligerent rights occurred. Yet despite the new legislation ships remained vulnerable to attack, and indeed the danger was increased. In the early months of the war there had been relatively little hazard of aerial bombardment. This was partly for reasons of political tact on the side of the combatants, but probably as much because, in order to conserve the few aircraft available to either side, pilots flew too high for accurate aim on targets to be taken.[43] But from the autumn on this was no longer so, and the build-up of both aerial and sea blockade with Italian help[44] was testified to by the torpedoing of the Republican submarine C3 off Malaga in December, and by the sinking of the Russian supply ship *Komsomol* in the same month.

Both episodes were severe blows to the Republican Government, which was quite unequipped to deal with the emergency. Nor could the Russians easily defend their own merchant ships in the Mediterranean. Maisky, the Soviet Ambassador in London, was therefore instructed to sound out British views on international action to deal with attacks on shipping. The request met with some sympathy at the Foreign Office, although no practical comfort could be given.

> This is a nasty looking business. . . . it cannot be disputed that the Soviet Government are in the right and the sinking of the *Komsomol* was completely unjustified and might be regarded as an act of pure piracy, minuted Sir William Malkin.

Meeting no active opposition, the Nationalists renewed blockade warnings and intensified minelaying activities. On 20 December Franco warned that the main northern ports of Bilbao, Santander and Gijon were to be closed (although actual closure would be postponed until a proposed exchange of prisoners had taken place.[45] Further, unofficial notice of minelaying operations off Cape Creus and Cape Negri came from Admiral Francisco Moreno at Palma on 22 February. The admiral revealed 'in confidence' that he did not propose to mine the entrance to the harbours of Valencia and Barcelona because he would not then be able to enter them himself.[46] Dramatic confirmation of this warning came when the British liner *Llandovery Castle* hit a mine 1½ miles off Cape Creus on 25 February. Following this incident, however, the Government was assiduous in issuing warnings, no matter how unofficial or, indeed, unconfirmed.[47]

Yet since the naval initiative had passed almost entirely to Franco's forces, British Government warnings now inevitably appeared to support the Nationalist movement, and certainly the Admiralty played a dominant rôle in the formulation of the Government's political attitudes at this point, being (as was later admitted) excessively scrupulous in their acceptance of insurgent mine and blockade warnings, despite reassurances from the Basque Government that the ports of northern Spain were clear. 'To give them credit,' admitted one naval report, 'I feel that they probably are clear, but Ferrol contains several minelayers ready for service.' In fact, there was good reason to believe that the northern harbours themselves generally had not been mined, for as Admiral Moreno had pointed out to his British officers, mines would hinder the rebels' own access to ports in the event of victory. Moreover, the Basques had succeeded in postponing for some time the threatened closure of ports by extending negotiations on the exchange of prisoners with the Nationalists.[48]

Nevertheless there remained a degree of uncertainty, and evidence suggested that if the ports themselves were not mined, large stretches in the approaches were.[49]

In addition to the problem of minefields, there was growing opposition from the Admiralty to their task of protecting vessels which, although legally within the Board of Trade's definition of 'British', belonged often to foreign speculators, and were frequently of sub-standard, unseaworthy condition. 'I sympathise with the Admirals', wrote Lord Runciman, President of the Board of Trade, 'and well understand that they do not want more *soi-disant* British ships to look after.'[50]

THE BILBAO CRISIS, APRIL 1937

At sea, British naval officers continued on amiable, if unofficial terms with the insurgent naval authorities, their sympathies, according to Chatfield, 'lying in the main with the Rebels', victims of a 'most savage mutiny'.[51] However, at the beginning of April, an incident occurred which was impossible to overlook. Early on 6 April the Nationalist ship *Almirante Cervera* stopped and detained the British SS *Thorpehall* until action by HMS *Blanche* forced the withdrawal of the Spanish warship. Nevertheless the captain of the *Blanche*, Cdr Caslon, warned his superiors that in his opinion the blockade was effective and that either reinforcements should be sent or British ships stop trading to Bilbao.[52] In the event the latter proposal was adopted despite the assurances of the British Consul at Bilbao, Mr R. C. Stevenson, which supported earlier evidence of Capt. McGrigor of HMS *Campbell* that the Bilbao approaches were swept clear of mines and the harbour defences in good order. More influential were the opinions of Admiral Blake, Commander of the Home Fleet, who feared further minelaying might take place,[53] and of the British Ambassador, Sir Henry Chilton, although the latter could in fact do no more than pass on from his temporary embassy at Hendaye[54] the dubious warnings relayed to him by the insurgents. As a result of this advice British ships were advised that they should not proceed to Spanish Government ports on the north coast and that if they did, they would receive no protection within territorial waters.[55]

The new instructions were clearly contrary to the explicit statement of policy given to the House of Commons on 11 March 1937 to the effect that British merchant shipping was entitled to naval protection against any illegal interference by either party in Spain, and the Government prepared to meet considerable opposition from the House of Commons when the new orders became known. Once more Hoare and Eden met in combat. The First Lord stressed the grave risks and dangerous consequences which might arise from the protection of British vessels in Spanish territorial waters and maintained, moreover, that such protection would amount to intervention by Britain on behalf of the Spanish Government.[56] Yet Admiralty Intelligence was well aware that illicit arms traffic concentrated not only at Santander, but also at Nationalist Pasajes.[57] To refuse to escort food ships into Bilbao therefore constituted a far greater intervention than the continued performance of the Royal Navy's traditional task of protection could ever be, since it would serve actively to starve the local Basque population while arms continued to pass freely into Nationalist ports.

Encouraged by the evident pusillanimity of the British Admiralty, the Military Governor of Irun, Colonel Troncoso, warned that any attempt by merchant ships waiting at St. Jean-de-Luz to proceed to Bilbao would be resisted by force.[58] When informed of this threat by Chilton, Cdr Caslon immediately ordered all ships to remain at St. Jean-de-Luz. Such was the gravity of the situation that an emergency session of the Cabinet was called on Sunday 11 April, when it was decided that a compromise statement should be issued informing Franco that while Britain did not recognise belligerent rights in this affair and could not tolerate interference with her ships, in view of the prevailing conditions ships would be advised not to go to Bilbao for the present.[59] A Foreign Office official summed up the humiliating position thus:

> General Franco has got us all on the run over this. Owing to his threats and big talk about mines and what his warships will do, he can now sit back and watch us complete the starvation of Bilbao . . . By their instructions to HM ships the Admiralty are getting behind the Government's decision to keep the high seas open to British ships and are, in fact, trying to prevent them from getting into these ports.[60]

As expected, the Opposition demanded a parliamentary debate, which took place on 14 April. Called in to brief the Government for the debate, the Admiralty advised that, although it would be possible to protect shipping if the proper forces were available, the undertaking would be 'definitely a full-dress operation of war'.[61] Speaking for the Government in the debate on the 14th, Sir John Simon repeated Hoare's argument that to break the blockade would amount to intervention on the side of the Spanish Government.[62] While thus so firmly set on a policy of withdrawing naval protection for shipping bound for Bilbao it was something of a shock for the British Government when the same day a signal was received from the navy off the Basque coast: 'It is not considered that insurgent blockade can be effective. Only one warship seen at a time.' Indeed, the blockade was now believed to be effective 'only

by threat'.[63] Dumbfounded, the Admiralty demanded an explanation from the navy off Spain, pointing out that 'the whole policy
of His Majesty's Government as expounded at length in the House
of Commons has been dependent on this'.[64] Yet their Lordships at
the Admiralty had been dupes only of their own and of certain of
their naval officers' prejudices, choosing to ignore the advice of the
Foreign Office representative and of one of their own senior officers
on the spot.

Four of the ships detained at St. Jean-de-Luz now decided to test
the situation for themselves, and on 19 April sailed without harm for
Bilbao, which they reached the following day. Two days later there
followed an attempt by two Nationalist ships to stop three more
British ships, but HMS *Hood* and HMS *Firedrake* which were in the
vicinity proved to be quite adequate protection. It was now
admitted by the Royal Navy that 'the term "effective blockade"
was a misnomer and should never have been used'.[65]

Following this incident it was learned from General Franco that
he too wished to avoid incidents at sea and was anxious to find a
modus vivendi with the Royal Navy. In order to achieve this, new
orders were formulated by the Admiralty which were, as Lord
Runciman, the President of the Board of Trade, protested, a
considerable departure from previous policy 'in that unqualified
protection was no longer to be given to British vessels on the high
seas'.[66]

There can be little doubt that conciliation of Franco was the first
objective of the Government during this crisis, and Cabinet
ministers went far further in defending their policy before
Parliament than even Admiralty advice gave them grounds to do.
The Home Secretary, for example, suggested during the debate in
the Commons on the 14th, that there would be grave danger from
mines, although the Admiralty had clearly said this was not so. At
the same time the Admiralty had accepted unquestioningly the
assessment of a junior officer as to the effectiveness of the blockade
itself, and the Cabinet had eagerly followed Sir Henry Chilton's
interpretation of events even though St. Jean-de-Luz was 'acknowledged to be full of Franco's agents'[67] and his sources of information
might therefore have been recognised as dubious.

The naval situation at Bilbao had arisen directly as a result of the
British Government's acceptance of Foreign Office advice that an
award of belligerent rights would be 'politically impossible'[68] and
that to grant such rights would be a complete reversal of previously

announced policy. In the event, the tortuous policy the Government was forced to adopt in order to continue the policy previously formulated towards the Republican blockade witout offending Franco brought great disrepute upon the policy of non-intervention which was proffered by the Government to the Commons as a universal scapegoat. As to naval attitudes, their Lordships were concerned during this crisis not only to demonstrate the overall inadequacy of their forces, which was real enough, but also to push for a far greater degree of autonomy in decisions affecting the distribution of the Fleet. Recent experience in the Abyssinian crisis had convinced Admiral James that

> though the Foreign Office must have the last word when international relations are strained, the Admiralty should be free to dispose the Fleet as they think fit when the tension becomes acute.[69]

In this respect the Spanish Civil War was to offer still more opportunity for demonstrating both the inadequacy of the Fleet and the Admiralty's determination to have a greater say in the distribution of its ships, for naval problems were far from over.

THE NYON AGREEMENT[70]

Public attention which had been much aroused by incidents such as the *Thorpehall* affair was shortly distracted by the coronation of George VI on 12 May. 'Foreign affairs and the state of our defences', Churchill commented, 'lost all claim upon the public mood'.[71] The British Government, however, was not so easily quit of the problems of its shipping around the coasts of Spain, although by the constant efforts of both British and Nationalist navies it was possible for a while to avoid a direct confrontation such as had occurred in April. As the situation around Bilbao intensified, shipping for the Republic was diverted to Gijon or Santander, where delays in turn-round were sometimes up to three weeks and had it not been for the co-operation between the two navies the crush of vessels would have been exceedingly vulnerable to attack.[72]

Since the British Government had announced its firm intention to protect all British merchant vessels, ships of many origins had flocked to take advantage of the shelter afforded by the British flag, although as was pointed out, often the only truly British part of the ships was the Red Ensign. An investigation in July 1937 into complaints of this nature revealed that at least twenty-five such ships had transferred to the British registry in recent months. Typical of the shipowners complained of was J. A. Billmeir, who controlled the Stanhope Steamship Company. In 1935 he had owned two ships; by 1937 he owned twelve, all trading to Spain, and several of which had previously been of foreign registration. A similar case was that of a Greek shipowner named Kokotos, holder of 999 out of 1000 £1 shares in a company owning two ships, neither of which was of British origin and which held only provisional British certificates.[73]

In August, British naval restraint was pushed to breaking point as the increasing number of ships requiring protection coincided with the stepping-up of the Nationalist sea campaign in an effort to stop fresh consignments of oil and arms known to be on their way from Russia. Franco approached the Italian Government for aid. Although Count Ciano, the Foreign Minister, refused to sell outright, he agreed to send four 'legionary' submarines complete with crews to be placed directly under Nationalist command.[74] By the second half of August the vessels were fully operational, and the work of these in conjunction with intensified air operations pushed the number of incidents involving shipping beyond the level at which connivance or restraint were possible responses for the British Government. The Royal Navy had itself suffered more damage to its own ships than might normally have been considered acceptable in peacetime.[75] Private owners would not be so easily silenced.

A survey of the last three weeks of August 1937 revealed that altogether there had been attacks on twenty-six ships. Seven of the eight British ships listed had been sunk after 23 August, and of these five had been sunk by 'unknown submarine' or rather, as the Admiralty knew, by submarines of the Italian Navy.[76] These statistics followed hard upon the news of Mussolini's self-congratulatory telegram to Franco on the fall of Santander on 23 August. The conjunction of the increased attacks on shipping, the inflammatory telegram, and the fall of the last Republican bastion on the north coast of Spain finally shook the British Government from its summer torpor. In France, too, Mussolini's boastful advertisement of Italian involvement in Santander campaign had placed the Chautemps Government in a very difficult position, making their further co-operation in the regeneration of the Non-Intervention Pact extremely doubtful.

Eden had until then been in a particularly difficult position, since he was well aware of Chamberlain's determination to patch over past differences with Italy and by establishing friendly relations with Mussolini to detach him from Hitler's sphere of influence. Despite this, several warnings had been given to Italy during the course of August, though without avail. Following an air attack on the tanker *British Corporal* on 10 August, Sir Robert Vansittart had spoken to the Italian Chargé d'Affaires, Sig. Crolla, and advised him that the Foreign Office was well aware that air attacks emanated from Palma where the Italians had an air base. The interview had no satisfactory outcome, however, as the now familiar response putting blame on the 'Reds' was given.

Feeling ran high at the Admiralty against the burden imposed upon the Royal Navy, and there was no desire to retaliate in the face of increased attacks but rather to opt out completely by awarding belligerent rights to both sides. Nor had Chamberlain's appointment of Duff Cooper as First Lord in any way altered Admiralty opinion as to the merits of either side in the Civil War. Indeed, the First Lord's remark that ' . . . so long as I am in control of the Admiralty, I am determined that not another British sailor shall fall in a cause not worth fighting for'[77] had caused jubilation on the Nationalist side and a considerable lessening of tension in Anglo-Nationalist relations.[78] It was something of a triumph for the Foreign Secretary, therefore, that a meeting of ministers summoned by him on 17 August to discuss both the attacks and the Admiralty views on how to meet the new situation resulted in a firm and public warning. Not only would His Majesty's ships continue to protect British shipping, but if any British merchant ship were attacked by a submarine without warning, the Royal Navy was authorised to counter-attack the submarine. When this too failed to effect a decrease in the number of attacks on shipping, a more direct warning was given in Rome by the British Chargé d'Affaires, Maurice Ingram.[79]

A series of discussions then took place between Eden and representatives from both Foreign Office and Admiralty. It is clear that the Foreign Secretary very much wanted to make a stand, but his suggestions were met with scepticism verging on ridicule by the Admiralty. He had, Admiral A. B. Cunningham, Acting-Chief of Naval Staff, noted, proposed having 'a few aircraft flying about from an aircraft carrier'. The Admiralty view was still that belligerent rights awarded to both sides would be the simplest solution. Furthermore, with the situation in the Far East rapidly deteriorating, it was now argued that if, as seemed likely, Britain should wish to make such an award to the belligerents in the Far East, then recognition of belligerency should go first to the Spanish combatants, for the latter war had been in progress for over twelve months.[80]

It is doubtful if Eden would have been able to prevail against the Admiralty and win his colleagues to his point of view had it not been for the extravagance of Italian policy in the last week of August. As a result, the French Chargé told Eden that the French were determined that some public condemnation of Italian intervention should be made, either at a meeting of the Non-Intervention Committee or before the League of Nations. In a formal note delivered by Cambon it was suggested that in the latter case the Mediterranean powers, Great Britain, France, Yugoslavia, Greece, Turkey and Egypt should be summoned. The inclusion of the Black Sea powers would be a matter for discussion. This, as Eden says, was the genesis of the Nyon Conference.[81]

Yet the Foreign Secretary did not, find either of the proposals entirely satisfactory. Any attempt to haul Italy before the Non-Intervention Committee could only hasten the demise of that body, and this Eden was not yet prepared for. On the other hand, to summon a conference of powers which excluded Italy but possibly would include Russia – or even, as the French later wanted, the Spanish Republican Government – would be equally divisive, driving the powers even more clearly into two camps. He still preferred, therefore, to explore the possibility of delivering a short, sharp shock to Mussolini, and during the last two days of August continued his discussions with the Admiralty as to how this might best be done. One suggestion, that the Nationalist cruiser *Canarias* should be sunk in retaliation for any further attacks on ships, plainly horrified the Admiralty, who feared that if the venture miscarried Britain would suffer tremendous 'loss of prestige and become a laughing stock'. The ships required to carry out the operation would necessitate alteration to the cruise programme of the Mediterranean Fleet, and possibly the Home Fleet. Moreover, Franco was in a position to retaliate himself by bombarding the dockyard and harbour of Gibraltar and there was no defence against this, short of landing an army in Spain. Finally, it was argued that since both Italy and Germany had shown their intention of seeing Franco win in Spain, any drastic action taken such as sinking the *Canarias*

would be regarded as distinct aid to the Government forces, i.e.
may involve us in conflict with these Powers . . . Japan would
profit by our entanglement and adopt a high-handed attitude in
the East knowing us hopeless to protest effectively.

Other possible actions more seriously considered were:

1. a blockade of the Nationalist coast;
2. raids of insurgent seaports – rejected as 'rather hunnish';
3. seizure of Majorca;
4. intensive operations with a view to sinking offending vessels.[82]

Of these, the first two would not have hit directly at Italy, and only
the very last would have done so legitimately since Majorca
remained nominally Spanish territory despite virtual military
takeover by Italy.[83] As to whether or not it was desirable to take
retaliatory action directly against Italy, the Foreign Secretary and
the Admiralty were at odds, the latter believing that 'in view of
Italian involvement, the Foreign Secretary's policy runs directly
counter to the Chiefs' of Staff recent recommendation to improve
Anglo-Italian relations'.[84]

Meanwhile practical steps had been taken to avert the necessity
for any such direct action. Franco was warned that unless
immediate and effective action was taken to prevent any further
incidents on the high seas, retaliatory action would be taken.
However, this was followed by a flurry of further attacks in the last
days of August. On 30 August the SS *Carpio* was attacked off
Valencia by an 'unknown' submarine. On the following day the
Soviet SS *Timiriasev* was attacked, as was the SS *British Dominion*.
The fate of the British ship was uncertain, but the captain of the
Soviet ship did not hesitate to state that the attack on his ship was
the work of an Italian submarine. Most decisive of all from Eden's
point of view was an attack on HMS *Havock* on 31 August, again by
an 'unknown' submarine.[85]

It was therefore in an atmosphere of public outrage that Eden
attended a meeting of ministers on 2 September, called to discuss the
grave situations in both the Far East and in the Mediterranean.[86] In
the absence of Chamberlain the meeting was presided over by the
Chancellor, Sir John Simon. Ministers heard how attacks in the
Mediterranean were now widespread, occurring not just off the
south-eastern coast of Spain but off the African coast, in the central

Mediterranean, and as far east as the Dardanelles. Even the combined numbers of submarines belonging to Republican and Nationalist forces could not have covered so wide an area in so short a space of time.

Added to the determination of the French to see the Italians publicly denounced for their intervention was the Spanish Government's declared intention of bringing the whole Spanish question before the League. The Spanish Ambassador warned Lord Cranborne, Parliamentary Under-Secretary at the Foreign Office, that this would involve not only the question of attacks on Spanish shipping but also the very delicate question of Spanish re-election to the League Council. Clearly some step had to be taken to satisfy both these countries, but warnings to the Italian Government had failed, and neither of the French proposals was satisfactory, the one because it aimed to exclude Italy and the other because it would finally kill non-intervention, which had, declared Eden, 'by no means proved completely ineffective'.[87] The Foreign Secretary's position was further strengthened by the news received immediately before the meeting of the sinking of the SS *Woodford* with loss of one life and injury to six of her crew members.[88] It was finally agreed, therefore, that the French should be discouraged from bringing the question of Mussolini's telegram to Franco before the Non-Intervention Committee. Although the French proposals were unsatisfactory as they stood, discussions among the powers would be acceptable to the Cabinet if Italy were also invited. As an immediate measure four destroyers were sent to strengthen the Mediterranean Fleet.[89]

Behind the scenes the Admiralty had now to convince their staff that a multinational solution to the situation would be workable. Strong opposition came from the Commander-in-Chief Mediterranean, who urged that a convoy system should be used instead. He suggested that the convoys, if adopted, need not be too liberal 'in view of the dubious character of the ships, and the highly remunerative nature of their business'. That the mass arrival of ships in government ports might provoke insurgent air raids, he regarded as a legitimate hazard, suggesting that this would offset the indirect assistance afforded the Spanish Government by the convoy system.[90] However, neither the French nor the British naval staff was prepared to approve the idea of a convoy system, and the principle of patrols of hunting destroyers was adopted instead.[91]

Preparations for the forthcoming conference had begun immediately after the meeting of ministers on 2 September. The following day Eden was visited by both the French and German Chargés d'Affaires, who in turn discussed the list of powers to be invited.[92] After what Eden later referred to as 'somewhat acrimonious controversy' with the French, the 'Valencia' Government was omitted from the list but Russia was included.[93] Finally, invitations were sent jointly from France and Great Britain to the following countries: Germany, Italy, the Soviet Union, Albania, Yugoslavia, Greece, Turkey, Egypt, Bulgaria and Romania. All were invited to send representatives to the conference to be held at the small town of Nyon on Lake Geneva on 10 September.

Faced with the prospect of a conference at which she would have only the ambiguous support of the French,[94] and incensed by two recent attacks on her merchant ships, the Soviet Union delivered a sharply worded note demanding compensation for the attacks and punishment of the guilty. This was the first open and formal accusation against Italy for her part in the recent submarine activity in the Mediterranean. It was clear, therefore, that if Italy appeared at the Nyon conference further recriminations would occur. Italy therefore declined to attend and Germany followed her example.[95]

Anticipating just such a contingency, Eden had told his colleagues at the Cabinet meeting of 8 September of his intention to keep Italy informed of all the conference's conclusions. Chamberlain, anxious above all to avoid any division of the powers into blocs, went further, and asked that Italy should be informed in advance of the various proposals to be discussed.[96] Despite this setback the conference convened, and in a remarkably short time agreement was reached, although considerable work on the details of the patrol system which had been adopted remained to be done. Discussions on this continued in Paris between the British and French naval staffs whom the smaller powers had agreed should undertake the organisation, and indeed the chief weight of the work. This came about largely because the smaller powers had little to offer in the way of practical assistance, but were strongly against any arrangement which would give Russia legitimate rights of patrol in the Mediterranean. For her part, Russia accepted the majority wish of the convention and agreed to waive her claim to participate in the patrols. Predictably, the British Admiralty was most emphatic that it would be impossible to carry out the Nyon patrols as well as those of the Non-Intervention Scheme, and the latter therefore ceased.[97]

The final agreement allowed for the Mediterranean to be divided up into six zones, each covering the major shipping routes, to be patrolled by units of the British or French navies.[98] In deference to Chamberlain's wish to accomodate the Italians, the Tyrhennian Sea zone was reserved for the Italians should they later want to join the scheme. Despite Ciano's cynical boast that by this gesture the Italians had passed from ' . . . suspected pirates to policemen of the Mediterranean – and the Russians, whose ships we were sinking, excluded!',[99] the arrangement limited the Italians to patrolling only their western offshore waters. Any suspicious activity east of a line between Sicily and Corsica would, in theory, be quickly detected.

The basic settlement had been achieved with remarkable rapidity. Eden wrote in triumph to Chamberlain on 14 September, the day on which the Nyon Agreement was signed. He was careful to point out to the Prime Minister that despite her refusal to attend, ' . . . the Italian Government has been kept in touch and has been treated with more courtesy than any other Power which refused to attend a Conference in similar circumstances', adding that he felt the Italians appreciated this.[100]

Yet as with the Non-Intervention Agreement and Scheme, reality differed somewhat from the intention of the original agreement. It was known in London even before the conference began that the Italians had been sufficiently impressed by the threat of international action for Ciano to order the suspension of operations against Republican-bound shipping from 4 September[101]. However, Ciano, probably realising that the conference was simply another version of the NIC, had recovered himself sufficiently by 15 September to have agreed to supply Franco immediately with two submarines, with the promise of two more to follow.[102] The difference this time was that these vessels would be under Nationalist control. Appearances were, of course, everything, and behind the scenes at a conference which took place on HMS *Barham* at Bizerta on 30 October, the British, French and Italian navies came to a mutual understanding concerning their several activities.

The main point at issue was the clause from the Nyon Agreement reading:

The other participating Governments possessing a sea border on the Mediterranean undertake within the limit of their resources to furnish these fleets (i.e. the British and French) any assistance that may be asked for, in particular that they will permit them to take action in their territorial waters and to use such of their ports as they shall indicate.

During the talks which succeeded the signing of the agreement at Nyon the Italian Government had consented to join Britain and France by taking up her option of the Tyrrhenian sea patrol zone, but France and the Balkan states were adamant that this option should not be extended to the privileges outlined in the clause above, as they did not wish to allow Italy access to their ports. The compromise solution reached on board the *Barham* demonstrates yet again the accommodation afforded to Italy and the degree to which the Admiralty was permitted to arrange matters itself. In essence, the agreement now reached was that since the Italians were denied access to foreign territorial waters, both the French and the British would waive their rights to access also.[103] The atmosphere in which the settlement was reached was described as extremely cordial, and is best summed up by an Italian naval officer who remarked that 'agreement was always easy where naval authorities were concerned, but that *sono i diplomatici che sono terribili*'.[104] The new arrangement was, of course, a substantial deviation from the original agreement, yet it was agreed in the Foreign Office that there would be no 'necessity for the Nyon Powers to have this matter brought to their notice at all'.[105]

The swift conclusion of the agreement in September had forestalled an attempt by Chamberlain to halt arrangements for Nyon and to follow up instead an Italian proposal that the question of piratical attacks be referred to the Non-Intervention Committee.[106] Probably only Chamberlain believed there to have been any worthwhile purpose in such a meaningless gesture. Despite Eden's triumph at Nyon he was greeted less than enthusiastically, therefore, by the Prime Minister, who was perhaps aware of the encouragement his Foreign Secretary had received from Churchill and Lloyd George.[107] In fact, in many ways Nyon was not the success that is sometimes claimed. Not only did the final arrangements not go as far as the agreement of 14 September allowed, but the Foreign Office belief that the Nyon Conference had made it 'quite safe for Russian, Spanish, Greek and other ships to bring supplies of arms and foodstuffs to Valencia'[108] was not sustained, as Table 18, submitted in 1938, shows.

The preliminary agreement signed on 14 September had been amended on 29th to bring in the Italians, and the signatures to the

Table 18 Ships calling at Spanish ports, October 1937[109]

Nationalists	Government	Nationalist
German	–	70
British	53	35
Danish	–	25
Dutch	1	10
Norwegian	–	5
Italian	–	14
Finnish	–	2
Belgian	–	1
Greek	–	4
French	11	1
Latvian	–	1
Portuguese	–	5
Irish Free State	3	–
Swedish	–	1
Total	68	174

final details were not given until 30 October. In his initial moment of triumph Eden had laughingly assured reporters that if there was another attack he would 'eat his hat',[110] and for three months his optimism was unchallenged. Then on 31 January 1938 the SS *Endymion* was sunk, and this attack was followed by the sinking of the SS *Alcira* on 4 February and attacks on other ships.[111] The new outbreak of piracy cut across an understanding between the Nationalist and British navies that Admiral Bastarreche, and later his successor Admiral Moreno, would inform the British where their submarines were operating, and they would not be hunted 'so long as they behaved themselves'. There was no question but that the *Alcira* had been sunk by German planes manned by German pilots, and although Admiral Moreno at first admitted responsibility for the *Endymion*, blame for this was later placed on a floating mine. The Admiral did, however, admit responsibility for the SS *Conclara*, and the SS *Lake Geneva*, attacked on 19 and 22 January, offerring full compensation and punishment of the offenders.

So well had their navies' mutual understanding worked that the First Lord told the Foreign Affairs Committee, which discussed the question, that he was loath to take action against the Nationalists. The Nyon patrol had been eased in January as a result of a period of comparative safety for shipping. The new activity was Franco's reaction to the increase in traffic to Barcelona of ships, many of which carried vital coal supplies. He defended the Royal Navy's sympathy for Franco on the grounds that 'one of the first actions taken by his opponents in the war had been to murder all the Spanish naval officers they could lay their hands on'. Having argued his department's case, however, Duff Cooper was fairly receptive to Eden's far-sighted exposition of the situation.

The Foreign Secretary believed that if some action were not taken against the Nationalists, blame for the attacks would tend to be laid at the door of Italy, since it was known that they emanated from Majorca which was popularly (and with justification) believed to be under Italian sway. This, Eden argued, would be disastrous when, at last, Italy seemed disposed to move cautiously towards the British camp. He believed that Italy viewed the recent changes in the German Government (giving Hitler supreme command of the armed forces)[112] with apprehension, fearing that these would affect Italo-Austrian relations. Count Grandi had actually expressed support for British action in the Mediterranean, when he had spoken to the Secretary of State the previous evening, and promised that he would adopt similar measures. It would mean, Eden told his colleagues, that Italy would be depriving Franco of the use of his submarines used in the blockade of south-eastern Spain. On this he placed the most optimistic interpretation, and despite considerable opposition from his colleagues was able to persuade them that the Nyon patrols should be intensified.[113]

Both Eden and Chamberlain were agreed on the need to separate Italy from Germany, but where the former was prepared to stalk his prey cautiously, the latter knew no such subtlety, as the events of the succeeding days were to show.[114] The Nyon Agreement had been a consistent development of Eden's policy towards the dictators over the previous nine months, but, despite its faults, it was also the summit of that policy: the first, and last, real attempt to take swift and aggressive action against illegal and bullying tactics of either Italy or Germany until World War II.

THE BLOCKADE OF BARCELONA

After Eden's resignation in February 1938[115] the focus of attention shifted from Spain to Czechoslovakia, although the problems of the former could not entirely be sloughed off. Throughout the year the

Republic hung on with sufficient determination and just enough success to make the outcome still open to question. In a final effort to starve the Republic into surrender, the Nationalist blockade was again stepped up in the summer. Throughout the autumn British ships came increasingly under attack to an extent which seemed to threaten the spirit of co-operation even between the British and Nationalist navies. Naturally, throughout September the Cabinet had no time to think of Spain, as the situation in central Europe dominated all else. When, however, ships of the Nationalist navy pursued and sank Spanish ships in the North Sea off Norfolk, the question of shipping was once more dramatically raised.

On 9 November Lord Halifax, Eden's successor as Foreign Secretary, told his Cabinet colleagues that

> provided the sinking was carried out by *bona fide* ships of war, that the normal rules in regard to preliminary warning and so forth were observed, and that no action was taken within territorial waters, the Foreign Office were disposed to regard the proceedings as irregular (inasmuch as we had not agreed to give belligerent rights to Nationalist Spain) but not amounting to acts of piracy.[116]

Further acts of piracy, or 'irregularity' took place, notably the detention at Palma of Greek ships chartered in the United Kingdom and bringing wheat into Britain. When asked to consider what action should be taken to secure the release of the ships if Franco did not respond to a formal request to free them, the first Lord replied that any action 'might involve us in awkward complication'. It was therefore decided to avoid similar difficulties in the future by informing the Nationalist authorities of the positions not only of all British ships, but also of all foreign ships under charter to Britain.[117]

Certainly, as Chatfield himself openly admitted, political prejudice at the Admiralty favoured the Nationalist cause. However, beyond this the central principle on which Admiralty policy was based was the need to avoid direct action for which the Royal Navy was below strength, and which might easily lead to embroilment with the major powers and further humiliation of both Great Britain and her navy. To political prejudice and inadequate force was added, in the autumn of 1938, the recognition that in time of war Britain, too, might be obliged, as in the Great War, to resort to blockade tactics similar to those of General Franco. If Chatfield over-emphasised the weakness of the Navy with regard to the Spanish situation, he did so only in order to impress upon the Cabinet the need for swifter rearmament. It was the clear duty of the Admiralty to put these facts before the Government.

Yet finally it was the Cabinet which took the major policy decisions, and it would be misleading to suggest that the Admiralty alone was responsible for the British Government's reluctance to take firm action against increased bombing and other acts of piracy by Nationalist forces towards ships believed to be carrying food supplies to beleaguered Barcelona. In the autumn of 1938 that port and the surrounding countryside were crowded with refugees from those parts of Spain recently taken by the Nationalists.[118] Malnutrition was almost universal by November, and starvation commonplace. On the 14th of that month the Spanish Ambassador, Pablo Azcárate, approached the Foreign Office and requested that the British Government should use its good offices to assist the import of food for the refugees.[119]

Chamberlain, however, was most anxious to reach an early settlement of the outstanding issues between Britain and Italy and regarded the Spanish issue as the major obstacle to his achievement of this. The more speedily the Spanish war could be concluded the sooner understanding with Italy might be reached. Moreover, victory for Franco would settle once for all the prickly question of belligerent rights.[120] There could in this analysis be no question of taking firm action against Franco's blockade in order to force ships through to Barcelona. The issues involved in this decision were never more clearly nor more harrowingly set out than in the following report from the British Chargé in Barcelona, Ralph Skrine Stevenson.[121] Explaining that only those of the rich who had previously suffered from internal complaints deriving from their former life-style were benefiting from an enforced diet, and had taken on a new lease of life, he continued:

> But the children suffer. Government hopes are pinned on humanitarian help from abroad. The more food that is imported for children and non-combatants, the more food there will be for the army. As long as the latter can be reasonably fed, and as long as the sufferings of the civilian population are not great enough to react on the morale of the men at the front, the situation can probably be held.

Humanitarian work in such circumstances comes perilously

near intervention. It means, in fact, taking from Franco's hands the very weapon which we used against Germany with such grim effect twenty years ago. But it is a weapon of which the use is very painful to watch at close quarters . . . A military decision is unlikely unless the food situation which is bad, and is rapidly deteriorating, causes a break up here.[122]

During November some dozen British ships were bombed in Republican harbours. Since these were largely aerial attacks there was little that the British navy could have done in those particular cases, although Franco's boldness was the result of long-standing tolerance on the part of the British Admiralty and Government. Food had never been defined as contraband cargo by the NIC, although at the time of the bilbao blockade Hoare had suggested it should be so.[123] Yet despite eloquent appeals from respected figures such Gerald Brenan,[124] and pressure from such groups as the Spanish Emergency Committee, the blockade of Barcelona was allowed to stand and failure to obtain food supplies marked the beginning of the end for the Republic. Government policy towards the blockade had been formulated in July. It had been suggested then by the Foreign Office that

> any British action such as reprisals for the bombing of British ships would help keep open the Spanish Government lines of communication by sea and its effect would be to prolong the war. The longer the war lasts the greater the risk of Germany obtaining a strong position in Spain, particularly if prolongation is attributed to British intervention.[125]

On 5 July Chamberlain told his Cabinet that he did not propose to repeat an earlier warning to Franco. According to the Cabinet Conclusion:

> What he had in mind was a verbal communication intimating to General Franco that if he must bomb the Spanish Government ports he must use discretion and that otherwise he might arouse a feeling in this country which would force the Government to take action. Such a situation was by no means beyond the bounds of possibility if the sinkings were to reach, say, one ship a day.[126]

It is difficult, therefore, in the light of this and subsequent inactivity on the part of the British Government to escape the sombre conclusion that in the stressful circumstances of late 1938, the Cabinet declined to take steps to protect their merchant shipping and connived at the starvation of Barcelona in the hope of hastening the end of the war.

Chatfield had claimed that the Navy's happiest task was the evacuation of refugees,[127] and this continued throughout the war with the grave exception of the days immediately following the bombing of Guernica, when the Foreign Office actually discouraged evacuation.[128] From the diplomatic point of view, the most encouraging aspect of the Navy's work was undoubtedly the renewed co-operation and goodwill between the French and British navies as a result of the Nyon Agreement. For the future, however, the greatest gain probably lay in the experience gained in the field of naval Intelligence, which led to the expansion of the Operational Intelligence Centre established in 1936.[129] There were then some positive gains for the Navy from the years spent patrolling the seas around the Iberian Peninsula. However, when the Spanish Civil war had first begun, the Anglo-German Agreement was just one year old, and Germany could not yet be regarded as a first-class naval power. Even one year later, Eden still believed it possible to challenge Italian ambitions with the combined navies of Britain and France, but he achieved the Nyon Agreement only after considerable opposition from the Admiralty. Although the Foreign Secretary insisted again in February 1938 that the Admiralty should face the recrudescence of submarine attacks firmly, it was clear that after his resignation, Admiralty reluctance to deploy naval forces in what was regarded by them as a lost cause would go unchallenged. When the Spanish Civil War ended in April 1939, Germany had had four years in which to bring her navy up to scratch, and Admiralty fears were nearer reality.

5 Intervention – the Problem of Volunteers

ARMS AND MEN

The breakdown of non-intervention in the summer of 1937 focused British Government attention on the long-standing problem of foreign troops fighting in Spain – 'volunteers', as without distinction regarding side they were called.[1] For in providing that the volunteers should be withdrawn as a *quid pro quo* for the granting of belligerent rights to both sides, these two essentially unrelated aims became inextricably although illogically linked in the British Plan of July 1937. Thus, although for Spaniards foreign aid in the form of tanks, planes and arms was generally – and certainly ultimately – the most decisive form of foreign intervention, in terms of international relations it was the question of volunteers which most exercised the British Government and which contributed to the resignation of Anthony Eden in February 1938.

At first, despite protests from Italy, the volunteers had been considered as irrelevant to the wider question of arms traffic, and were not included under any prohibition of the NIA. Not until the end of 1936 did numbers reach such proportions as to warrant special consideration as a form of direct intervention. By then, what had begun as a comparatively small number of aviators of Italian, German, French and British aircraft, together with enthusiastic but orderless supporters of the Republican cause, had reached considerable numbers on both sides, with the undeniable professionalism of the insurgents' foreign forces pitched against the slowly but increasingly better organised International Brigades of the Republicans.[2] Yet no formal measures to stem the flow of volunteers to both sides were taken until February 1937, by which time the problem had grown from the comparatively manageable proportions of foreign participants of the early autumn of 1936 to the armies of foreign troops who fought at Guadalajara in March the following year.[3] However, before examining that aspect of non-intervention in more detail it is necessary to consider the general escalation of intervention in Spain and the extent of British Government information on this aspect of the war.

Throughout the first autumn of the war the build-up of foreign aid and troops to both sides was widely publicised, and it was with interest and considerable scepticism on the Opposition benches that the House of Commons on 19 November heard the Foreign Secretary declare:

> So far as breaches [of the NIA] are concerned I wish to state quite categorically that I think there are other Governments more to blame than those of Germany and Italy.[4]

It was true, of course, that Russian commitment to the Republic was considerable, and was known in the Foreign Office to be so from information garnered from Royal Navy ships off Spain. After the acrimonious meeting of the NIC on 9 October during which the Soviet representative had threatened to withdraw from the agreement if violation of the NIA were not immediately halted, Eden had surveyed all the information on Soviet intervention with the intention of bringing it before the Committee, if necessary, to counter Soviet allegations.

Quite apart from the monetary contributions, made up from subscriptions drawn from Soviet workers' salaries, food supplies had been sent to Spain in the Russian ships *Kuban* and *Neva*. The Foreign Office had also received information, later confirmed, regarding the landing of 50 tanks with crews at Cartagena, and 1,500 regular Russian troops at Alicante. Other military aid reported to have arrived by 16 October included Whippet-type tanks and 20–25 large cases of the sort used to crate aircraft.[5] The War Office calculated that the first major consignments of aircraft and tanks had arrived in Spain in time to be in action by 20 October. 'I fear there is little doubt', minuted Roberts on one report of 150 large Russian aeroplanes landed at Cartagena, 'that the inequality of the Government forces is being rapidly redressed'.[6]

Certainly by mid-October Eden believed that Soviet supplies to the Republic outweighed aid given by Italy and Germany to the rebels. At his first meeting with the new Spanish Ambassador, Pablo Azcárate, on 15 October, Eden asked if the Ambassador was 'really certain that the operation of the agreement acted against them'. He was doubtful that it did, and the French, too, he said, were far from convinced. The Ambassador replied that Spain's crying need was for arms and aeroplanes and they could get neither. However, his next words could have served only to confirm the British Government's adherence to non-intervention:

> He said [minuted Eden] that he appreciated that it was difficult for me and many others in this country to understand how it came about that he, a man of liberal opinions, should be now representing the Madrid Government in London. He did not contest my statement that neither the Government of Barcelona, nor the present Government of Madrid could be described as liberal. On the other hand, his Excellency himself strongly maintained that it was only through a victory of the Left elements that democracy in Spain could be saved and any liberal element come back into the Government.[7]

By 26 October the Foreign Office had firm evidence of ten instances of Soviet infractions of the agreement,[8] and evidence that the Mexican Legation in Paris was prominent in the organisation of arms traffic to Spain from, for example, Lithuania.[9] By the same date only three instances of Italian contraventions had been confirmed. Based on this information Eden's accusation against the Soviet Union in the House of Commons on 19 November was undoubtedly made in good faith, but unfortunately his earlier briefing was already very outdated. A War Office report of 6 November had noted the 'continued flow of aircraft and tanks to the insurgents from Italy and Germany'[10] and at the time of his speech the situation regarding foreign intervention was known by the War Office to have changed radically.

On hearing the Secretary of State's allegation that there were other governments more to blame than Italy and Germany, Maj. C. S. Napier of the War Office, whose task it was to collate information of intervention, expressed his surprise to Roberts that Eden should speak thus. The Foreign Secretary's statement was not, he said, borne out by the evidence available, and he feared that the words would be seized upon by Germany and Italy to justify to their own nationals their policy in Spain. As a result of this conversation he was asked to draw up a detailed report in conjunction with the Air Ministry of all known breaches of non-intervention.[11] The report, dated 23 November 1936, which Napier was able to produce very quickly since most of the information in it had been available for some time, concluded pointedly: 'The War Office has no evidence to show that there are other governments more to blame than those of Germany or Italy'.[12]

Indeed, in summary, the indications of the extent of Italian intervention were extremely alarming, although, as the report made clear, the evidence, although from 'unimpeachable' sources, was not such as could be put before the NIC with any hope of conviction, and neither would Britain be prepared to reveal her sources of information. Before signing the Agreement on 28 August, Italy had sent between 50 and 60 aircraft with bombs, pilots and mechanics to Spain. On 1 September Franco had asked for armaments for the cruiser *Canarias* and two days later had requested a further 24 aircraft. These had been promised. Since 28 August he had received at least 75 aircraft and a suitable amount of bombs. Not only had the *Canarias* been supplied with guns and machine-guns, but other ships had been armed at Spezia. He had probably received about 100 tanks.

German intervention was believed to have been less than the Italian, but the evidence was admitted to be incomplete. Before signing the agreement on 24 August, Germany had supplied 26 aircraft to Franco, with bombs and mechanics, and cargoes of material had followed. During September and October at least 35 aircraft and 4,000 incendiary bombs had been sent, with at least 500,000 rounds of aircraft machine-gun ammunition. On 1 November two German ships had been reported at Hamburg loading tanks and munitions. Copper was being shipped to Germany in large quantities, partly, it was thought, in payment for arms.[13]

With easier access than Germany, but with far less to offer, Portugal did her best for the rebels, although Salazar, who despised Hitler, was not anxious for the insurgents to forge closer ties with either Germany or Italy.[14] Portuguese recognition of the insurgents on 23 October was probably a pragmatic move as much as a political one, since by then all the territory along the Portuguese border was under the control of the Nationalist General Yagüe. Portugal was at this time, however, hoping to negotiate with Britain for arms and training facilities for her own outmoded army. Any equipment supplied would have to be used strictly for Portuguese defences and would be supplied to her as a long-standing British ally. After learning of the activities of the German ship *Kamerun* which was reported to have landed arms at Lisbon in August,

Britain received assurances from Portugal that she herself was in no position to aid the insurgents.[15] However, negotiations between Portugal and Britain for military aid were protracted throughout the first half of the war in Spain, partly because Britain herself had difficulty in meeting Portuguese requirements, but also because the British Government had reservations about arms sales to the Iberian Peninsula.[16] Furthermore, once Franco had secured the ports of Cadiz in the south and Ferrol and Vigo in the north there was little point in taking the longer voyage to Lisbon to discharge cargo, except in the interests of secrecy. But this, too, was of dubious value in view of British naval facilities in that port. On the other hand, it was later shown that there was, despite all obstacles, a constant trickle of arms across the border,[17] and there is no doubt that the insurgents were helped considerably in the first months by the unofficial embassy set up in a hotel in Lisbon and administered by Nicolas Franco, General Franco's brother.[18] More important to a movement with cash problems was the much-reduced rate of exchange offered by the Salazar Government to the insurgents.[19] As to volunteers Sir Richard Hodgson, Britain's representative in Nationalist Spain from November 1937 to March 1939, later claimed that altogether there were as many as 20,000 Portuguese troops fighting in Spain at one time or another,[20] although these figures are challenged by a more recent account which places the number as low as 3,000.[21] However, for Franco the greatest advantage was undoubtedly that, unlike the Pyrenees, the Portuguese border provided a secure backstop for his movement.

As regards Russia, on the other hand, although a substantial volume of goods was known to have been sent, little was known of the details of the cargoes. According to War Office reports, war material was believed to have reached Spain about 1 October, and to have been in service by 20 October. Seventy-five aircraft, probably a hundred tanks and several thousand tons of ammunition and small arms were believed to have been sent. Napier's report stressed, however, that arms obtained from illicit sources could not be brought under control, but that although the bulk went to the Spanish Government, these were mainly small arms and were relatively insignificant as regards the progress of the war. Much more important were the modern weapons such as aircraft, anti-aircraft guns, tanks, etc. which the rebels had received, for it was with these that the war would be won.[22]

The report was circulated in the Foreign Office and provoked a degree of controversy strangely at odds with the bland sentiments of neutrality previously expressed on Spain. In particular it occasioned a sharp exchange between Laurence Collier, Head of the Northern Department, and Owen St. Clair O'Malley of the Southern Department. Apologising for interfering in the affairs of another department, Collier seized the opportunity to lambast those of his colleagues who as 'Conservatives first and Englishmen after' were prepared to tolerate the spread of facism as an 'antidote to communism'. He expressed concern at

approaches being made to Signor Mussolini for a Mediterranean Agreement without any stipulation (so far as I am aware) that the first condition for such an agreement must be the cessation of his activities in Spain and the abandonment of the doctrine that he is entitled to intervene wherever he fears that a 'Marxist' government may be established in another country.

Collier was careful to point out that by 'Marxist' Mussolini meant any government of the left, and he reminded his colleagues that the government against which Franco had revolted was not a communist government. His chief fear was that, as had happened over Abyssinia, the public might feel they were being kept in the dark over the intervention of the powers, and that this could result in the loss to the British Government of 'the united front of public opinion which might in a crisis be vital to her'.

O'Malley, stung by the reference to Conservatives, refused to wear that 'party-coloured cap', but nevertheless expressed the view that the Soviet Government had been 'asking for trouble' in a great many countries for years, and had 'initiated a special movement in Spain at least as early as the beginning of 1936.' (Evidence of Comintern intervention was confirmed by C. J. Norton, private secretary to Sir Robert Vansittart.) O'Malley mocked Collier for taking the NIC 'more seriously than I supposed anyone did. I had thought it was generally admitted to be largely a piece of humbug. Where humbug is the alternative to war it is impossible to place too high a value upon it.' He believed that the best policy was to protect specific British interests, but for the rest, taking rather an Olympian point of view of foreign squabbles. Both he and Mounsey felt that in view of Soviet activities, the Foreign Secretary's statement in the House had done no more than redress the balance – an opinion with which Vansittart wholly concurred.[23]

MAJORCA

Already large numbers of Italian troops had disembarked in peninsular Spain, and shipments of these were stepped up after Italian recognition of the insurgents on 18 November. Italian military resources were now stretched to their limits by the launching of the Spanish venture, whilst at the same time holding down the new conquest of Abyssinia. On 24 November, therefore, all leave from Italian ships and bases was halted.[24] Some 10,000 Blackshirts, reported to have been recruited in Rome, were dispatched to Seville, and a further 15,000 were said to have landed at Algeciras. Indeed, Mussolini's methods of recruitment illustrate well enough his desperate requirement for fresh supplies of men. Volunteers from Catania and Messina were offered pay at the rate of 50 lire per day for soldiers and 150 lire for lieutenants. It was reported that of 5,000 men who left Florence many were convicts while others were unemployed men threatened with loss of unemployment benefits if they did not 'volunteer'. For those who did join up there was mention of a 1,000-lire bonus in addition to pay.[25]

Much more serious, as Eden realised, was the build-up of Italian forces on the island of Majorca. The first confirmation of this trend came towards the end of October in a naval cypher noting the persistent infiltration of Italians, an increasing proportion of whom were officers. At the same time the leader of the Italian contingent, Arconovaldo Bonaccorsi, better known as Count Rossi, began a series of inflammatory propaganda speeches which convinced Vice-Consul Hillgarth[26] of the possibility of an Italian *coup* in the island. On 17 October, for example, Rossi had announced that now the Italians were in Majorca, they would never be ejected. Hillgarth suggested secret service agents should be sent to the island, and in view of the very detailed accounts of Italian activity in Majorca which shortly followed, it seems likely that this request was acceded to. The Foreign Office also advised that British warships off Barcelona should display themselves at Palma.[27]

Following Collier's memorandum, Eden reviewed the situation in Majorca, and was concerned that the intervention of the Soviet Government might afford Italy an excuse for disregarding her previous assurances to Britain concerning the *status quo* in the Mediterranean.[28] Moreover, great publicity was now being given to all Italian troop movements. In the House of Lords on 26 November Lord Cecil asked that the texts of all Italian assurances to Britain should be given. This the Government was not prepared to, and indeed could not do, since all assurances had been verbal.[29] As important, no doubt, was the consideration that French opinion of all political shades was most sensitive to the threat posed by the Italian presence in Majorca.[30] The French feared that an Italy allied to Germany would have in Majorca not only the essential link in an aerial chain from the Canaries, through Majorca, Sardinia and northern Italy, to Germany but also, a stronghold athwart French communications with North Africa where half the French army was stationed. Indeed, so concerned was Rear-Admiral Godefroy of the French Naval Staff with whom the British Naval attaché was detailed to discuss the problem, that the Admiral suggested the possibility of taking a leaf from Italy's book by occupying Minorca.[31]

Already Mussolini's threats were becoming more explicit, and he warned that 'if a Soviet State independent of the rest of Spain were set up in Catalonia, this would be regarded by Italy as a disturbance of the *status quo* in the western Mediterranean.' It was now clear that Mussolini was also dictating his conditions for a Mediterranean settlement, and refusing to include France in the proposed exchange of notes. Eden was strongly advised by his department to accept these dictates. The Head of the Western Department reminded him of the advice of the Chiefs of Staff in their report on the Abyssinian war, that 'it would be unwise to allow public opinion here or in France to assume that if France were to put Italy in the dock over this question and invoke the Covenant, we should take action by force to restrain her.' Instead, Sir George Mounsey suggested that extra naval vigilance should be exercised and pressure put on the French to make their own representations in Rome.

In a minute which expressed the dilemma the British Government faced, Vansittart pointed out that although it would be possible to ask formally for the removal of Count Rossi he did not advocate such a step unless the Government was prepared 'to see the thing right through', adding that Britain might win just as much respect by 'finesse'. He complained that the Chiefs of Staff were 'very tepid' and strongly advised Eden to do no more 'unless we are really prepared to show our teeth'.[32] He continued in familiar vein:

I do not agree with them once more. If we allow Italy to take over

Majorca, we are sunk in the Mediterranean. Yugoslavia will no longer stand out against Italy, and the map of Europe will alter disastrously for us in the long run. But if we are going to threaten Italy with war about the Balearic Islands . . . we have got to rearm much quicker than we are doing now.

Piling contradiction on contradiction, he concluded that although he agreed with the Chiefs of Staff that the Government should take no action they were not prepared to back by force, keeping the Italians out of the Balearics was 'essential on grounds of highest politics'.[33]

Despite this confusing advice Eden firmly agreed with Vansittart's final recommendation, and drafted a paper on the extent of Italian infiltration in Majorca for the benefit of his Cabinet colleagues. By mid-November, he noted, there were 17 new Italian aeroplanes on the island, with probably a further 40 or 50 assembled. With these there were 50 Italian aircrew, of whom 27 were pilots and the rest engineers. All were in Spanish Foreign Legion dress.[34] Moreover, Italian works in Majorca would provide lucrative employment for the local workforce for many years to come, and the local people were beginning to take a pride in their knowledge of the Italian language which was now being taught in schools.[35]

Above all, the speeches of the Italian Count Rossi, chief of the 20,000 strong Majorcan *Falange*,[36] were quite intolerable, for he was also head of public security with 200 Italian experts under him employed in espionage and administration, both civil and military. He was known to have been sent to Majorca with 'a direct personal mission' from Mussolini to organise the Fascist party. Despite representations to the Italian Government concerning his removal, it was now believed that he was to become the first Italian Military Governor of the island. Already his title following a visit to Rome on 11 November was *Generalissimo di Majorca*.

Although the Chiefs of Staff had argued that Italian occupation of the Balearics would not vitally affect British interests, they had agreed that the menace to the Straits and to Gibraltar would be increased. That conclusion had been based, Eden contended, on the premise, no longer valid, that there were no military air bases on the islands. Britain's position in the Mediterranean was maintained, he argued, by that 'imponderable element called prestige', and this had suffered badly at the time of the Abyssinian crisis. Any further move by Italy in the Mediterranean would create a grave risk to Britain's position:

> Nothing that we could say in explanation or justification of passivity or of merely ineffectual remonstrance would be credited. I doubt whether we could convince ourselves, I am certain we could not convince others, that we had not from anxiety or timidity, or from a sense of our own weakness, been obliged to acquiesce in an Italian move which was, if not in immediate, at any rate in definite ulterior conflict with a vital British interest.

He admitted the possibility that in the event of a war in which England and France were engaged against Italy, Germany might either join with Italy or continue to build up her own strength. But this he believed was balanced

> by the probability that the relations with Germany could, for the future, be conducted with very much greater advantage to ourselves if we demonstrated beyond all possibility of doubt that in the Mediterranean there is a point beyond which the United Kingdom cannot be driven by sapping and mining or by blusters and threats, and that where a vital interest is threatened, the English will be found, for all we speak so often and so smoothly of compromise and conciliation, not to be at heart a meek nor in action a timid people at all.

Eden saw the main hope for joint action with the French in the recent strong representations made by the French Chargé in Rome against Italian intervention in the Balearics.[37] At the same time he recognised the folly of contemplating war with Italy without taking into account the possibility of Germany assisting her.[38] As usual little in the way of firm resolution emerged from the Cabinet meeting two days later when the Foreign Secretary's memorandum was discussed, although the Chiefs of Staff were asked once again to review the situation.[39] Eden's memorandum had, once again, defined the dilemma, but had offered no clear or immediate solution. He had made it clear that he had no wish to impede the progress of the arrangements for the exchange of assurances on the *status quo* in the Mediterranean, but nevertheless the British Ambassador, Sir Eric Drummond was instructed once more to speak to Ciano on the matter of the continuing propaganda of

Count Rossi. Furthermore, Eden proposed that the declaration to be made by the two countries should make clear their intention to 'disclaim any desire to modify, or, so far as they are concerned, to see modified, the national status of the territories in the Mediterranean area, particularly the territories of Spain'.[40] In fact, the decision to recall Rossi had already been taken, and he left Majorca on 23 December. Far from being a triumph for British diplomacy, his removal made way for a formal Italian Military Mission.[41]

The formal exchange of notes, or the 'Gentleman's Agreement', as it was called, took place on 2 January 1937, and included in slightly modified form Eden's clause on the maintenance of the *status quo* in the Mediterranean.[42] No sooner was this done than news of Mussolini's latest dispatch of 4,000 troops to Spain was reported. Eden, whose attitude to the Spanish conflict had changed considerably since his speech in the House on 19 November, now came out firmly in favour of either a Republican victory or a compromise settlement, and was definitely against a victory for the insurgent forces, at any rate whilst they were under the influence of Italy and Germany. As he himself recorded, 'From the early months of 1937, if I had had to choose, I would have preferred a Government victory.'[43]

The Foreign Secretary immediately set to work to persuade his colleagues of the seriousness of the situation in Spain for Britain, and especially in regard to Anglo-German policy. For he believed that if interference were not checked in Spain it would not be checked elsewhere: 'It follows that to be firm in Spain is to gain time, and to gain time is what we want. We cannot in this instance gain time by marking it.' In his view it was now imperative to stop intervention in Spain, both in war materials and in volunteers.[44] Never again would he be persuaded of Italy's good faith unless firm evidence were provided.

VOLUNTEERS

From early November the NIC had considered methods by which the carriage of arms to Spain might be prevented, and although progress was slow, the basis of a scheme had been worked out. In contrast, the question of volunteers had so far been dealt with mainly by diplomatic negotiation, but no progress had yet been made. As a result of Italian intervention, it was this aspect which now attracted attention. At the beginning of December the matter had been raised in the NIC by the Soviet Union, which was by then much the keenest nation to secure a total ban, since the Republic had scored a temporary success in repulsing the Nationalists at Madrid, but this could all to easily be reversed by further dispatches of troops from Italy.

Both Germany and Italy, as was to be expected, objected to the Russian call for a ban on volunteers, pointing out that they themselves had asked for such a measure much earlier.[45] Yet with the signing of the Anglo-Italian Agreement so imminent it was clear that some move towards a ban was necessary and Eden therefore negotiated behind the scenes with representatives. In an endeavour to allay British apprehension as to Russian objectives in Spain, Maisky assured Eden that it was not part of the Russian plan to set up a communist régime in Spain, but merely to see a set-back for the aggressors.[46] In retrospect this seems to have been a realistic interpretation, for initially Stalin hoped that by displaying an attitude of 'non-intervention' similar to that of Britain, that country would look more favourably on Russian moves towards rapprochement and take a stronger line with Germany and Italy. Maisky believed that in view of the division of opinion in Germany, in which the Reichswehr were opposed to the greater intervention which Hitler and the Nazi Party favoured, it was the right psychological moment to impose a ban. Certainly, evidence suggests that Hitler, having provided transport aeroplanes to ferry Franco's Army of Africa across the Straits to mainland Spain in the first crucial weeks of the war, was now content to leave major intervention to Italy.[47]

Finally, on 22 December, the NIC agreed to set up a further sub-committee to report on methods of controlling the entry of volunteers to Spain.[48] Meanwhile Lord Plymouth called on all governments to take interim measures to stop foreign nationals from leaving or passing through their countries. The problem of volunteers was now, he declared, 'by far the most important arising out of the war in Spain'.[49] Little came of this *démarche*, however, the USSR, Italy and Germany being equally obstructive. Indeed, it provoked hostility in Germany where it was regarded as yet another attempt to 'perpetuate the vicious system of Anglo-French tutelage over Germany and other countries'.[50]

Yet both France and Britain were anxious to impose control on volunteers almost as much with a view to solving the problem from a domestic angle as from the international one. Indeed, in view of mounting criticism at home, the French Government had already taken unilateral action, instructing local prefects to eradicate local recruiting offices. This was to prove particularly difficult on the Riviera where even the local *mairies* were reported to have their walls 'plastered with posters' exhorting men to enlist for Spain.[51] Nor was Britain guiltless in the matter of volunteers, although in comparison with other nations far fewer Britons were yet involved. Nevertheless, in her position as host country to the Non-Intervention Committee these few were an increasing embarrassment. It was not, of course, an actual contravention of the Non-Intervention Agreement to enlist in the International Brigades, nor, for that matter, for Germany or Italy to send whole armies to Spain if they so wished. But it was clearly against the spirit of the Agreement, and if, in order to save the Non-Intervention Committee, Britain wished to encourage others to join in a general ban on volunteers, it was evident that she should quickly take steps to control recruitment in England.

Equally embarrassing were the numbers of questions now being asked in Parliament as to why the Government had so far taken no steps to restrict recruitment, especially in view of the fact that Britain was already possessed of the legislation necessary to do this under the Foreign Enlistment Act of 1870.[52] Potentially dangerous, too, was the situation which might arise if the 2,000 Irishmen now fighting for the insurgent forces should ever line up against British volunteers.[53] Indeed, the Irish Premier, De Valera, made it plain that he was anxious to adopt any measures the British Government might take to prevent volunteers from going to Spain.[54]

However, it was by no means certain that the provisions of the Foreign Enlistment Act were relevant to the Civil War in Spain, and at the beginning of December it had been pointed out by Shuckburgh that since no warning had been issued to the public and no prosecutions made under the act so far, the act was to all effect a dead letter. The only practical measure taken had been for the Passport Office to refuse visas for Spain except for those on *bona fide* missions. Visas were also refused for other European countries if it was suspected that there was any intention to continue to Spain.[55] Yet it was still comparatively easy to reach Spain, travelling quite legally to France on a forty-eight hour 'weekend ticket'. Many volunteers went from there with papers provided by communist agencies in Paris, or travelled with no papers at all, making their way via Marseilles to Barcelona and Alicante or over the Pyrenees into Catalonia.[56]

Although no direct action had yet been taken, recruiting agencies were closely watched by MI5 on account of their communist basis.[57] New schemes were devised, such as stamping passports 'not valid for Spain', or making the issue of passports conditional upon a deposit of £10 in the belief that the unemployed, thought to number prominently among the volunteers, would not be able to afford such a sum.[58] In the event, neither scheme had been adopted, and by January the situation seemed to threaten the future of Britain's non-intervention policy. British ratings were known to be serving in Spanish warships at Cartegena, and British volunteers had been arriving in batches of eighty to ninety, at the port of Dunkirk alone, every ten days throughout December.[59] Britain could scarcely adopt a high moral tone with the other major powers while she herself was guilty.

As to foreigners in Barcelona, now numbered at 20,000, all were believed to have been recruited in France and nearly 50 per cent were French nationals.[60] There had been much propaganda concerning the number of Russians in Spain, notably from the Nationalist 'radio' general, Quiepo de Llano, in Seville, who put the number of Russians at the absurdly high figure of 35,000. The more scrupulous reports of Ogilvie Forbes suggested that there were no more than 2,000 Russians in the capital itself, although there were a number of Russians in civilian dress in the Ministry of War, the Census, and other departments of state. Forbes had been denied access to the 'International Column' at Albacete, but had been told that the Russians manned the tank corps and to some extent the artillery, while others were in depots at Guadalajara and Alcalá. In the Republican navy a similar infiltration had been observed, with one or more Russian officers serving in each of the three cruisers and three flotilla leaders.[61]

On available figures, then, the USSR appeared to be one of the chief offenders after Italy and France. Indeed, Sir Orme Sargent believed that Britain had been 'duped' by the Soviet Union in the matter of volunteers, and that the Soviet Union hoped Britain would place Germany and Italy in the dock while Russia posed as a 'good European'. The only difference between the three, he contended, was that Russia had been successful in reversing the situation in Spain. 'If we are fated to quarrel with Germany', he went on, 'everyone will be agreed that it should be a quarrel of our own choosing and not one prepared for us by M. Litvinoff.' But that there could be no solution to this problem without close French co-operation was abundantly clear.

Table 19 *Information on volunteers available to the Foreign Office on 8 January 1937*[62]

Nationality	Location	Numbers	
French	Barcelona	c.12,000	at the beginning of December 1936.
		c.10,000	various nationals collected in France.
	Madrid	c.10,000	but a total of at least 20,000 foreigners, mostly recruited in France.
Germans	Seville	c.6,000	
		c.3,500	known to have left Munich.
Italians	Cadiz	14,000	
		4,000	known to have left Italy.
Russians		15,000	admitted by Soviet Union one month before.
		2,000	in Madrid itself according to Ogilvie Forbes.
British	Madrid	350-400	known to the Communist Party. Several hundred more believed in Barcelona.

Furthermore, Britain was reluctant to take unilateral action in the matter of volunteers. First, it was believed that individual action would lessen the chance of securing an international agreement on the control of volunteers. Second, the Foreign Enlistment Act was believed then – and indeed more recently in the case of the Angolan civil war – to be of unsound application to that particular case,[63] i.e. in case of civil war. Open recruitment in Scotland and England had so far not been stopped for fear that the Labour Party would complain that such action was to the detriment of the Spanish Government. The ambivalence of British Government attitudes threatened to be exposed by the return to England of volunteers. Those returning on leave could expect a hero's reception from supporters of the Republican cause; those who had sought and been given grants from public funds to enable their repatriation were likely to rouse the ire of Franco's supporters in Britain. Neither would bring credit on the British Government. Perhaps the final spur to action was the headline in the *Daily Mail* on 7 January 1937, which read 'How Reds Lured My Son to Spain'.[64] Eden, who had previously been reluctant to raise the matter with the Cabinet 'not on account of criticism at home, but because it will in fact weight the scales against the Government in Spain',[65] now raised it at consecutive meetings of the Cabinet on 8 and 9 January 1937. On the Saturday morning, 9th, agreement was reached not only on the outline of the new Non-Intervention Scheme for the prevention of the carriage of war material to Spain, but also on the necessity of invoking the Foreign Enlistment Act. The French Government, it was learned, were to introduce similar legislation on the following Thursday.[66]

As an exercise in pure diplomacy the move had some effect, for the powers, guided by the appointed sub-committee, acquiesced in the notion of control of volunteers for sufficiently long for full agreement to be reached, and as from midnight on 20 February 1937 the Non-Intervention Committee's prohibition on recruitment of volunteers became effective.[67] Neither provision, as had been foreseen by the more cynical, had the slightest effect. At no time during the Spanish Civil War were there any prosecutions under the Foreign Enlistment Act,[68] and far from restricting recruitment the extension of the Non-Intervention Agreement to cover volunteers seemed almost an irresistible challenge. Certainly, War Office reports for the next few months indicated that although no large consignments of troops were sent, small batches continued to be dispatched, presumably to maintain numbers as they were depleted by casualties or leave,[68a] and, although in a speech on 3 July 1937 Eden claimed that 'not a single volunteer has left this country since the ban was imposed', volunteers continued to pass in and out of Britain without hindrance.[69]

THE BRITISH PLAN FOR THE WITHDRAWAL OF VOLUNTEERS

Forewarned with the knowledge that definite action would be taken by the Non-Intervention Committee, Italy began to build up her forces in Spain, intense movements of Blackshirts to Spain continuing up until 14 February. At that point, what was now recognised in the Foreign Office as a full expeditionary force in Spain, was regarded by Mussolini as complete, and the embarkation commissions at Naples and Spezia were ordered to be dissolved. The total number of Blackshirts believed to have arrived in Spain since 22 December was now put at 70,000.[70]

Open participation of these troops in the Guadalajara campaign which began on 8 March brought wide publicity to Italian intervention, and hoping to take advantage of this, the Spanish Ambassador called on Eden on 12 March with the request that the matter be brought before the Non-Intervention Committee. If that body could not cope Spain would raise the matter at the League of Nations.[71] In a formal note the Spanish Government had set forth the extent of Italian intervention. To counter this move the Italian and German Governments referred to the matter of Spanish gold on which they had been calling for action since the New Year. Caught in this cross-fire the Foreign Office was reluctant to have the subject raised at the NIC.

Since the French Government, now in an almost permanent state of crisis, would not act without Britain, the Spanish Government turned once more to Russia. At the plenary session of the NIC on 24 March, Maisky, to Plymouth's discomfiture no doubt, announced his government's desire to deliver an urgent message – later deposited with the Committee as an official note. First Maisky asked the Committee to investigate the validity of charges against Italy brought by the Spanish Government. Next he called for two special commissions to be sent to Spain to investigate the landing on Spanish territory on 20 February of Italian volunteers, and to investigate allegations of Italian army intervention. Nationalist supporters on the Committee immediately protested.[72]

The Soviet note, once again, opened endless vistas of accusation and counter-accusation. Indeed, Ribbentrop warned Eden on 9 April that he himself could speak for five hours on the subject of violation of the Agreement. The following day Grandi told Eden that the main objection to the withdrawal of volunteers was now the Soviet note. He naturally denied Soviet allegations and warned Eden that he too had information of French and Russian infringements of the Agreement. He also denied that Italians fighting in Italy were other than true volunteers, reminding the Foreign Secretary that since there were at that time in Italy some 300,000 men demobilised from the Abyssinian war it was relatively easy to collect volunteers. Furthermore, as every able-bodied man, including himself, belonged to local militia units, it was easy, but not strictly true, to accuse the men of having a military background. Grandi admitted that he had been tempted to agree with the idea of an impartial commission to go to both sides, but was unable to do so as the idea had been presented in the first instance by the Soviet delegate. He therefore suggested that if Eden would arrange for Lord Plymouth to ask Italy if she were ready to discuss volunteers, Italy would now consent, on condition that Russia agreed to withdraw the offending note.[73]

Besides this diplomatic manœuvre Grandi complained to Eden of the way in which supposedly confidential material had leaked from the meetings of the Chairman's Sub-committee, and openly accused the Soviet representative, Maisky, of acting 'in truth, as little else than the correspondent of the *Daily Herald*, the *News Chronicle*, and the *Manchester Guardian*'.[74]

The Chairman's Sub-Committee now recognised the impossibility of achieving total confidentiality for their meetings, and it was agreed that full stenographic records, which had ceased after the fifth meeting, should be resumed.[75] A second irritant, the question of Spanish gold, was also tackled. The Chairman's Sub-Committee had agreed on 16 March that a Committee of Jurists should be appointed to

> examine the use outside Spain of Spanish capital assets, including the use outside Spain since the outbreak of the present conflict in that country, of gold, which prior to the outbreak formed part of the reserve of the Bank of Spain; to report whether any, and if so what, legal problems are raised by such use; to report on the bearing, if any, of these problems on the question of non-intervention in the Spanish conflict up till now.[76]

This committee now convened, although the project was abandoned by tacit agreement after only five meetings.[77]

More important for the future of the NIC than either press leaks or Spanish gold was the resumption of serious consideration of the practical and political aspects of a scheme for the withdrawal of volunteers.

By the end of May almost complete agreement had been reached on the question of volunteers, with the exception of the problem of 'definition'.[78] Nationalist supporters were anxious that every foreigner who had fought in Spain since 18 July 1936 should be categorised as a volunteer, but many who had fought on the Republican side had since acquired Spanish passports and could not be deported. On the other hand, those who sympathised with the

Republican Government were determined that Moors fighting for Franco should also be included in the numbers of volunteers. Whether these objections might have been overcome will not be known, though it may be doubted, for there followed the Republican attacks on both Italian and German ships at Majorca which killed six Italians and twenty-two Germans. On 31 May Grandi announced Italy's withdrawal from the naval supervision scheme and from further NIC meetings until guarantees against any such recurrence were given. Germany and Portugal followed suit. Not until 21 June, when the three countries consented to rejoin, were discussions of withdrawal resumed.

It was clear, however, that many hurdles remained before the scheme for withdrawal could be accepted. It was now the Russian representative who seemed determined that no agreement should be reached. However, the points he raised were by no means unreasonable, and were, after all, for the protection of the legitimate government of Spain. He asked that:

1. there should be no withdrawal without consent of both parties;
2. Moroccan troops should be included in the term 'non-Spanish nationals';
3. allocation of expenses should be on a *pro rata* basis;
4. simultaneous withdrawal should be of proportionate numbers of volunteers, not of equal numbers.

The latter point Maisky amplified by explaining that General Franco had roughly 100,000 volunteers, the Spanish Government only 15,000–18,000. Therefore, if, for example, 5,000 were taken from each side, Franco would lose only 5 per cent while the Republic would lose 33 per cent. He agreed, however, to accept the scheme which the Technical Sub-Committee had now devised, as a basis for discussion.[79]

However, the Russians were not alone in disliking the plan for withdrawal, which was almost universally unpopular. It was proposed that the committee should send two commissions, one to each side, to count the numbers of volunteers, and to arrange the evacuation of those who chose to comply and the deportation of, or concentration camps for, those who refused to do so. The Poles presented a particularly difficult case, since at least 3,000 were believed to have lost their nationality and would be refused repatriation. Expenditure involved in transporting men to the coast would be borne equally by the five principal powers.

Meanwhile, the crisis created by the withdrawal of the dictators from the Non-Intervention Scheme was watched anxiously by other powers. Despite the attack on the *Deutschland* off Ibiza, arrangements had gone ahead between London and Berlin for an official visit to London by Baron von Neurath, the German Foreign Minister, albeit in face of considerable opposition from the German Ambassador in London, von Ribbentrop, who did not believe Germany should resume her seat on the NIC.[80] The mysterious torpedoing of the German warship *Leipzig* on 15 and 18 June[81] ruined the efforts of Eden and Neurath to bring about an Anglo-German rapprochement. In the aftermath of the incident, the veracity of which, incidentally, was doubted by the British Admiralty, the visit of the German Foreign Secretary was cancelled. Instead, a meeting was hastily convened between representatives of the four major powers on 19 June, at which Ribbentrop demanded that the powers should take the strongest possible action against the Spanish Republic.

Like the British, the French Admiralty doubted the truth of the German story of the attempted torpedoing of the *Leipzig*, and despite the difficulties created by the fall of the Blum Government[82] the French Ambassador received firm instructions to reject the German demands and to demand a full inquiry into the episode. On 21 June the Germans and Italians pressed for an early decision, and on that day, therefore, the Foreign Policy Committee met to consider how the crisis should be met.

Clearly Germany would not agree to submit to the inquiry called for by France, but equally the German demands were, Halifax suggested, quite unacceptable. On the whole, however, Chamberlain and the committee felt that the French proposal was right and should be followed. Britain would also consult with the other naval powers as to what measures, if any, could be taken for the further protection of vessels engaged in control duties.[83]

Later that week the French Ambassador approached Eden with a proposal that Britain and France should jointly undertake to fill the gap in the naval patrol scheme left by the withdrawal of Italy and Germany. (It should be noted that the Sea Observation Scheme, which relied on mixed nationalities for its observation officers, was affected by the withdrawal of the dictator states from naval patrol but did not cease to operate.)[84] At the Foreign Policy Committee meeting on 28 June the Committee endorsed the French proposal, with the reluctant support of the First Lord. Inevitably, the Anglo-French proposals were unacceptable to Germany and Italy, and at the Chairman's Sub-Committee meeting on 2 July Ribbentrop countered with alternative proposals. Two days earlier the German Ambassador had suggested that although the naval patrol could not be agreed upon, it might be possible to continue non-intervention and combine it with a grant of belligerent rights to both parties. Eden had replied that the world would not be convinced of the efficacy of a non-intervention scheme that was not supervised, but that it might be possible to combine a non-intervention scheme with a grant of belligerent rights if all foreigners could be withdrawn from Spain. Here then was the fatal conjunction of two essentially disparate conditions for international agreement on Spain.

At the Foreign Policy Committee meeting on 1 July, members were informed that French public and parliamentary opinion was hardening over Spain, and a less effective policy of non-intervention would not be tolerated. On the other hand the French were against using belligerent rights as a bargaining counter. It was (wrongly) believed that[85] in Germany extremists such as Dr Goebbels and General Goering had gained the upper hand, and had persuaded Hitler to adopt a forward policy in Spain, one which would enhance his prestige if France and Britain gave way before him.[86] Other countries watched anxiously also, as Britain faced a critical choice. The Portuguese Government had sought assurances from Franco that his policy would remain 'within the orbit' of British policy and these had been given. The Nationalist leader had given assurances, moreover, that his indebtedness to Italy and Germany would be paid only in the commercial sphere, and that no territorial concession was contemplated or would be granted. The General had also asserted that he would be willing to agree to a withdrawal of volunteers and that, while there was some resentment against Britain, it was nothing like that against France.[87] In obtaining these assurances from Franco, Salazar had hoped to smooth over differences between the British Government and the Nationalists, for the victory of the latter was regarded as 'a matter of life and death' to the Portuguese. Meanwhile, believing that the 'equilibrium of non-intervention had been broken', the Portuguese suspended the facilities which had been granted to British observers on the Portuguese border.[88]

In response to the Portuguese *démarche* the French Foreign

Minister informed the British Ambassador that the French Government would not on any account allow control to continue over the Spanish frontier, unless strict control were resumed over the Portuguese frontier. He added that strict naval control and a serious beginning to the withdrawal of volunteers was essential before there could be any talk of granting belligerent rights to Franco. Delbos was supported by both the Turkish and Yugoslavian representatives who ominously made the point that if Britain and France showed themselves strong, Turkey and Yugoslavia would stand by them to the end. If not, both states would find it difficult to 'resist the attraction of strength elsewhere'.[89]

No words could have more clearly illustrated the alternatives which faced the British Government, but Chamberlain was already committed to a policy of rapprochement with Italy, hoping to separate that country from German influence. It has been suggested that 'every decisive principle of British policy in relation to that [Spanish Civil] war was laid down before Chamberlain became Prime Minister with unanimity in Cabinet and Party'.[90] While this is essentially true, it should be recalled that Baldwin was not much interested in foreign affairs, and formative decisions on Spain were taken when he was most occupied with the Abdication crisis. Formulation of foreign policy had fallen frequently on the strong triumvirate of Chamberlain, Hoare and Simon. Eden's attitudes, however, now deviated significantly from his rather acquiescent views of the previous autumn. In a speech on 3 July, he said that although Britain had remained disinterested, 'this must not be taken to mean disinterestedness where British interests are concerned on the land or sea frontiers of Spain, or the trade routes that pass her by'.[91] Lacking confidence now in his Foreign Secretary's ability to smooth the path to Italian friendship, Chamberlain began from this point to bypass Eden and the Foreign Office, preferring to deal directly with Mussolini. Thus, at this most sensitive point in European relations, the Prime Minister twice saw Grandi and without Eden's knowledge gave the Ambassador private letters couched 'in friendly terms' for Mussolini.[92]

At the Foreign Policy Committee meeting on 1 July Lord Plymouth had been instructed to repeat the British Government's offer to continue joint naval patrol with France, and to ask if Italy and Germany would consider placing neutral observers in their ships. The general aim, it was suggested, was 'to gain time'. Thus, while it was not expected that belligerent rights would be granted in return for the strengthening of the control scheme, Plymouth was instructed to state, if asked, that he was willing to consult his government.[93] A long plenary session on 9 July brought interminable set-piece speeches from the major representatives during which Maisky drew the Committee's attention to what he described as 'nothing but a thinly veiled Italo-German war' in Spain. In Italy, *Il Popolo d'Italia* published casualty lists of those killed in Spain, and General Franco's praise of those Italians who had fought in the assault on Bilbao had been widely publicised. Turning to Germany, he reminded his colleagues that on 27 June Hitler had made a speech in which he declared: 'Germany needs to import iron ore. That is why we want a Nationalist Government in Spain, so that we may be able to buy Spanish ore.' No solution having been reached that morning, the plenary session of the NIC reconvened the same afternoon and in order to break the stalemate the Netherlands representative suggested that the British Government should draw the two positions together. Since most parties had agreed that non-intervention should continue at all cost, Britain accepted this responsibility.

One week later Lord Plymouth outlined to the Committee the proposals which became known as 'the British Plan'. Essentially this fell into two parts. First, a system of supervision similar to that in operation before the Italo-German withdrawal would be rein-stated. It would, however, be reinforced by the placing of observation officers in Spanish ports. Supervision, in addition to various reinforcements, would be further strengthened by a grant of belligerent rights, subject to certain definite conditions, when the arrangements for the withdrawal of foreign nationals were working satisfactorily and when substantial progress in withdrawal had been made. All members announced their governments' preparedness to accept the plan as a basis for discussion.[94] The second section of the plan was, of course, all-important. It not only provided the Chairman's Sub-Committee with ample scope for the further creation of what Maisky called 'diplomatic spaghetti',[95] but exacerbated the rift which was already forming between Chamber-lain and Eden. For the Foreign Secretary became increasingly determined that 'substantial progress' in the withdrawal of volun-teers from Spain was an essential gesture of good faith on the part of Mussolini, without which a grant of belligerent rights should not be made.

Although behind the scenes the Chairman's Sub-committee

continued to meet, no further plenary sessions were called until 4 November. The situation now was that France had withdrawn facilities for observation of the Franco-Spanish border as from 15 July. Portuguese facilities were withdrawn until such time as non-intervention should be completely re-established. Britain and France alone continued the naval patrol of the sea approaches to Spain. Italy and Germany stood firm on their insistence on a grant of belligerent rights. Britain remained pledged to the withdrawal of volunteers.

DIVERGENT ATTITUDES OF CHAMBERLAIN AND EDEN

That the linking of the question of volunteers with that of granting belligerent rights would cause endless delays and would effectively postpone any positive action by the NIC was perfectly well appreciated by the Foreign Office, and especially by Eden. Indeed, the prevarication that would result was a positive aim of the Foreign Secretary's policy at this juncture, and followed closely the line suggested to him by his personal private secretary, Oliver Harvey. In a letter to Eden at the end of July, Harvey advised Eden that Britain's chief interests now lay in prolonging the war, which the longer it lasted 'the more expensive, unpopular and damaging it must be for the dictator countries'. Arguing that Soviet aid at least counterbalanced, if it did not exceed, that of Italy and Germany, and therefore a long war, if not a stalemate, seemed likely, and Britain's own genuinely neutral attitude would be all the more appreciated, he went on:

> If, therefore, our object should be, as I think it should, to prevent either side from winning a quick victory with foreign aid and to neutralising if we cannot eliminate the foreign aid on either side, then we should endeavour to hold the present situation as long as we can. We should insist on linking the grant of belligerent rights with the withdrawal of volunteers . . .[96]

Thus while Eden had previously believed that time for rearmament could not be bought by 'standing still', he now believed it could be gained by a prolongation of the war, although in the long run he did not desire a Franco victory.

Throughout the summer feeling in France ran very high against

Italian intervention in Spain, and was only mildly assuaged by the Nyon Agreement in September. In response to rumours that Italy was contemplating sending in still more troops, Chautemps retaliated with a threat to open the French border on a formal basis, which would have meant, in effect, a declaration of withdrawal from the Non-Intervention Agreement. Eden, who clearly shared Oliver Harvey's views as well as France's fears, told the Cabinet on 29 September that in his opinion no victory on either side could be purely Spanish, and that if Franco won he would not be able to control the situation without Italian assistance. He shared the French belief that the Italians sought submarine bases in Spain, either for bargaining purposes or to put pressure on other nations in case of war. British interests would best be served, therefore, by a stalemate leading to a compromise solution. It was against Britain's best interests that Franco should win in Spain so long as he was dependent on foreign aid, and above all that he should win during that year. Like many of his colleagues, Eden was also convinced that while non-intervention did no more than allow Franco to survive, its abandonment would mean even greater aid for the Nationalists.[97]

If non-intervention were to be upheld, positive steps now needed to be taken by the British Government. Eden agreed, therefore, to make a joint *démarche* with the French to the Italians, inviting them to the talks then in session in Paris, following Nyon, offering as bait the hope of opening Anglo-Italian conversations in the near future. It would be stressed that the British Government shared French anxieties and endorsed the French threat to open the frontier if further dispatches of troops were made to Spain. In the event, however, a much milder note than Eden had intended was drafted under the guidance of Chamberlain and contained no reference to the French threat. The Prime Minister also deleted from Eden's original draft all reminders of previous Italian assurances that Italy would keep no troops in Spain or the Balearics once hostilities ceased.[98] There followed a humiliating rebuff. The following day Ingram was told by Ciano that Italy would not be ready to enter into conversations without consulting Germany.[99] The French responded to the rejection with near panic, and Delbos told Eden that 'the one thing Britain and France could not do was to take an Italian refusal to discuss volunteers lying down'. Again, it was suggested that *prises de gages* should be taken. This time it was suggested that since Spanish Morocco had originally been ceded to the Spanish Government, who were no longer in possession of it, it should be reclaimed.[100]

Alarmed at the threatening tone of the French, and fearing a rapid escalation of the situation, Charles Howard Smith, Assistant Under-Secretary, circulated a memorandum in which he suggested that the Spanish issue was not one in which Britain could afford to become involved. Referring to the theme of Eden's recent plea for a protraction of the war, he wrote:

> It is understood to be the policy of this country that General Franco should not win in Spain, or if this is impossible to prevent, the longer his victory is postponed the better, because in the interval we shall be getting stronger . . . This is a realistic and cold-blooded policy because it seems that we care nothing for the sufferings of the wretched Spanish people through another winter or longer of war.

The Under-Secretary did not believe that a totalitarian régime of the right would ultimately be established in Spain, but that if one were it would not necessarily be more menacing to Britain than, for example, that of Portugal with whom Britain enjoyed good relations. Moreover, he questioned whether Britain was in fact prepared to accuse Italy of breaking her word, and to turn her out.

> In a word, will this country fight for anything except the Colonies and the Channel ports? Personally I do not think they will. Totalitarianism has come to Europe. We may not like it but we have to live with it in two forms, Fascism and Bolshevism . . . Surely it all boils down to this, that it does not matter two straws what occurs in Spain unless the Chiefs of Staff say that the presence of the Italians, who will (following the projected conversations) have promised to clear out, is of real strategic danger.[101]

Although the views expressed by Howard Smith were broadly shared by the Cabinet, almost every paragraph of his paper received the most scathing attentions of Sir Robert Vansittart. In particular he contended that what was strategically dangerous to France must be strategically dangerous to Britain. Nor would his Foreign Secretary accept Howard Smith's assertion that if a war broke out over Spain Britain would be fighting with a 'distracted and bankrupt ally'. France, he said, was not as near bankruptcy as Italy, and had at least as good a navy. Indeed, it was as much on the question of the Anglo-French relationship as on Spain and Italy that discord between Eden and members of the Foreign Office and Cabinet can be discerned. The aim of Howard Smith's memorandum was to persuade the Cabinet that a strict warning should be given to the French that 'if they open their frontier, and if the dangers which we foresee flowing therefrom come to pass, we will have no part or lot with them and they must face the consequences alone.' Vansittart believed this was going too far, even though he admitted that the opening of the border would only serve to help Franco.[102] The influence of the Permanent Under-Secretary was, however, swiftly waning, and after his appointment to the sinecure of Chief Diplomatic Adviser, a post where he saw few papers and had virtually no influence, British interference in the internal affairs of France increased.

Chamberlain, however, now held no doubts as to the correct policy to be pursued. He regarded his private correspondence with Mussolini as an unqualified diplomatic success, one which had 'created a very deep impression of rejoicing and relief throughout Italy'.[103] Yet there was little reason for such optimism. The War Office report for September indicated an increase in armaments for Spain from Italy including Fiat fighters, destroyers, and two or three more submarines (two others had been withdrawn). In the same period the Nationalist blockade was estimated to have reduced Soviet aid to negligible proportions.[104]

The formal reply to the Anglo-French note was given by Italy on 8 October, having first been scrutinised in Berlin. Although Ciano had intimated that German approval would be necessary, he now claimed that the delay in replying was caused by the speech given by Alvarez del Vayo at Geneva. In a speech later acknowledged to have been a tactical error, the Spanish Foreign Minister was interpreted as saying that the International Brigades had been incorporated into the Spanish Army and could not, therefore, be included in any scheme for the withdrawal of volunteers. Members of the International Brigades held Spanish nationality and would replace the *Tercios*, or Foreign Legionaries, as units in the Spanish army.[105] The speech aroused so much opposition that the Spanish Government amended the Foreign Minister's statement on 10 October, pointing out that precisely because the volunteers were now under the full authority of the Government they could be withdrawn at any moment. Azcárate was authorised to tell the Foreign Office that an objective criterion such as that of mother tongue would be acceptable to his government in arranging withdrawal.[106]

The Italian reply intimated that there could be no question of talks without Germany, and furthermore that to attempt to deal with the Spanish question outside the NIC would add to misunderstandings. Italy therefore advocated a return to that body for discussion. But there could be no question of including Germany in the talks since both France, Russia and Poland were opposed to the idea. That project was therefore abandoned.[107] Instead, the French proposed that one more meeting of the NIC should be called at which a modified version of the British Plan should be studied. If the Anglo-French proposals contained in the plan were not accepted, then the NIA should be suspended and the French frontier opened.

At the Cabinet meeting on 13 October it was learned that the French had since slightly modified their demands and would not necessarily regard the failure of talks as terminating the work of the Committee. The chief outstanding question, Eden told his colleagues, was that of the proportional withdrawal of volunteers favoured by the Republican Government. He assured the Cabinet that he had been careful not to commit Britain in any way to the French proposal that if the talks failed the French frontier then could be formally opened. Clearly the Cabinet as a whole was most disturbed by the recent manifestations of French independence. Inskip, the Minister for Co-ordination of Defence, complained with some accuracy that the 'whole of the French policy was different from ours'; whilst Malcolm Macdonald (Dominions) voiced a fear common to all parties in reminding his colleagues that Blum had declared his object was to get Great Britain and Russia together. He did not, however, think that British public opinion was at all anxious for that. As so often happened, no formal conclusion was reached, and the Foreign Secretary was left to approach the ambassadors of the powers concerned on the lines of the Cabinet discussion.[107a] This allowed Eden a degree of latitude, which he now took.

The following day the Foreign Secretary saw Maisky and warned him that Britain's next appeal to the NIC for withdrawal of volunteers would be her last effort to seek a peaceful solution through that body. In turn Maisky cautioned Eden that a return to the NIC and support for the Anglo-French proposals could only be agreed if no further substantial concession was asked in the future. Despite this exchange the Chairman's Sub-committee met on 16–19 and 20 October without any concession being made on the part of the Russian representative, who insisted that nothing significant had happened since July to change matters.[107b] Nevertheless, the withdrawal, as peaceably as possible, of the Italian troops became daily more necessary as a crisis in France developed once more. For as Sir Eric Phipps, the British Ambassador in France, warned, the fall of the Chautemps Government would not necessarily herald the return of a government willing to follow a less independent line, but would probably result in the return of the Blum Government. The former Premier E. P. Flandin had warned Chautemps and Delbos that if the French Government decided to open the frontier he would demand the immediate summoning of the Assembly, but, once again, Delbos had proved to be the only member of the Government willing to listen, and was counting on the restraining influence of Great Britain. Other members of the Government were boasting that they could put pressure on Britain to follow a more forward policy by means of a press campaign in papers such as the *Daily Herald*, but Flandin assured the Ambassador that in case of real trouble the French peasants 'would not march'.[107c]

So critical was the position that Eden himself presided on 26 October at two further meetings of the Chairman's Sub-Committee at which it was proposed that the British Plan of 14 July should be accepted as a whole, subject to such modifications as seemed necessary. Plymouth asked that both parties in Spain should be approached for their concurrence on six specific points covering their co-operation in withdrawal, their reception and co-operation with the two commissions, an award of belligerent rights, etc. Still Maisky would not make any concession on the point of a grant of belligerent rights,[108] despite considerable diplomatic activity by both Britain and France in Moscow.

At the beginning of October Lord Chilston British Ambassador in Moscow, then in London, had discussed the position of the NIC with Laurence Collier, and had been warned that action might soon be necessary. Chilston assured Collier that

Litvinov at least realises we have never acted in bad faith and could be relied upon to keep any assurance given. What he and Stalin complain of is that we have been weak with Hitler, Mussolini and the Japs, and let them do what they like in

Manchuria, Abyssinia, Spain and China, and in the case of Spain have tried to dissuade the French from taking up a stronger attitude. The greatest bugbear is the Four-Power Pact. A statement that we will never make such a pact might have a decisive effect on their attitude.

In view of the deadlock in the committee Eden cabled Chilston in Moscow on 27 October:

> Position in the NIC is so critical and the possible consequences of the Soviet attitude so serious that I must now take steps foreshadowed in Mr Collier's conversation with you on 6 October and ask you to apply for a special personal interview with M. Stalin. If this is absolutely refused you should in the last resort accept an interview with M. Litvinov.

Stalin was to be made to appreciate that the position Russia had adopted was one which could only further isolate her, while uniting the other four major powers. The consequences, said Eden, far transcended the Spanish issue. If asked about a Four-Power Pact, Chilston was not to give a definite guarantee but was to point out that the British and French Governments had hitherto refused to consider any general agreement which would ignore the interests of the Soviet Government in Eastern Europe, and had done their utmost to make possible Soviet collaboration on the NIC and in the international sphere generally. If asked whether, if the Soviet Union met Britain's wishes, they could be sure no further concessions would be asked, Chilston again was to give no guarantee but should make clear:

> from statements made when the Anglo-French plan was presented and from subsequent acceptance of all its principles by Italy and Germany, that there is no likelihood of any concession which will prevent it attaining its main objects: an impartial estimate of the number of volunteers to be accepted by all parties, and their speedy removal thereafter, without grant of belligerent rights until it has made substantial progress.[109]

In the event, Chilston was unable to see Stalin, who always refused to see all foreign representatives other than foreign ministers. He was, however, able to see Litvinov, who as predicted was afraid that further concessions would be asked. He did not believe that the Italians would accept the estimates of numbers given by the commissions, or that they would withdraw their troops in substantial numbers. Furthermore, there was no guarantee that they would not send more troops. In fact, Russia believed that more were being sent at that moment.[110] However, in order to break the deadlock, Litvinov offered a considerable concession: Maisky would abstain on the clause covering belligerent rights.[111]

This was at first misunderstood, but was clarified by Maisky at the next meeting, when he cited League's rules as a precedent for an abstention not precluding a technically unanimous decision. By this piece of wizardry the British Plan was saved. However, the Russian representative informed the Committee that since his government regarded control as useless it was not prepared to continue to contribute to its funds in the present form. Since many other governments had withdrawn from the existing control scheme this was not regarded as an insuperable obstacle, and arrangements went ahead, at last, for a plenary session of the NIC on 4 November.[112] At the twenty-eighth meeting of the NIC on 4 November it was resolved to adopt, as recommended by the Chairman's Sub-Committee, all nine points of the British Plan of July 1937, and to approach both parties in Spain for their approval of the scheme for withdrawal of the volunteers. Thus by Eden's skilful negotiations with Moscow the French did not formally open their border and the NIC was saved.

During that month Eden was able to discuss the scheme with Litvinov who, like Eden, was in Brussels for the Nine-Power Conference. The Russian Foreign Minister suggested that on the question of withdrawal Britain, Russia and France should start negotiations with a figure of 80 per cent, fall back to 70 per cent and stand firm on 65 per cent. This having been informally agreed, Litvinov said Russian reservations on the scheme would be withdrawn, and the difficulties presented by the term 'substantial withdrawal' would not be mentioned until raised in the Committee. The reason for Russia's new enthusiasm for the scheme is not difficult to find. The USSR was now very occupied with events in the Far East. The peak eagerness of foreign volunteers for the Republican cause was over, although small numbers of recruits would continue. Italy, on the other hand, seemed to have endless supplies of cannon fodder she was willing to expend in Spain and, though very few in number, the technical skill of the German

Condor Legion contributed a ruthlessly efficient force it was hard to match. Moreover, with the fall of Gijon on 21 October, 130,000 Nationalist troops were released for duty elsewhere.[113]

Table 20 *Russian shipments of arms to Spain during the summer of 1937 according to British Intelligence*[114]

	(tons)	
May	13,000	
June	10,000	
July	3,750	
August	2,000	(of which only 750 believed to have arrived in Spain)
September	0	
October	0	(2 shipments were reported but neither reached Spain)

The Spanish Government reply to the new proposals was received on 30 November, and although certain reservations were appended, Azcárate assured Cranborne that these were no more than a request for information on certain difficult points.[115] The Foreign Office, however, was as unenthusiastic for this scheme as it had been the previous autumn when discussing the first NIC scheme. Britain's estimated share of the cost of withdrawal, £40,000, was unquestionably out of all proportion to her liability, and would, it was thought, be difficult to explain to Parliament. There was a strong tendency, therefore, to 'go slow' on the scheme. This was made easier by the Nationalist reply to the NIC proposals, for it suggested that belligerent rights should be awarded in return for a token withdrawal of 3,000 Italians. While advisers in the Foreign Office were not against this and suggested the Republic should do likewise, Eden, who had been appalled by the latest figures of Italian intervention, remained adamant, and minuted firmly: 'Equality is not equivalent'.[116]

THE RESIGNATION OF THE BRITISH FOREIGN SECRETARY

While the NIC mulled over organisational problems, information of a more serious nature engaged the Foreign Office. This was contained in a report drawn up from very secret information supplied by the Joint Intelligence Committee.[117] The report listed five concessions which Italy had demanded and was believed to expect to receive shortly from Franco:

1. Her special interests were to be recognised in the Balearics, and on the Spanish Mediterranean seaboard;
2. Italian interests under the guise of a Spanish *coup* would be entrusted with the constitution of naval and air bases in her areas;
3. Italy would contribute a naval and air mission to Spain;
4. She would supply the nucleus of a new Spanish fleet;
5. It was suggested she might fortify Columbretes and form a seaplane base there.

In effect, while not altering the territorial *status quo* of Spain, Italy would receive extensive naval and air facilities, and it was believed she intended to develop a network of commercial airlines over the western Mediterranean. This was particularly alarming, and Vansittart, regarding the report as 'well within the bounds of possibility', asked the Chiefs of Staff to review the situation. The Chiefs of Staff, however, took a different view. They considered the report to deal in 'hypothetical contingencies . . . so numerous and nebulous that no good purpose would be served by attempting a detailed forecast either of what might happen, or of how British interests might be affected'.[118] However, the Joint Planning Committee which examined the report further did not report to the Chiefs of Staff until 19 January 1938. By that time Vansittart had been promoted out of harm's way and Eden's own position was extremely shaky.

The report had highlighted once again the fundamental divergence of opinion in Foreign Office and Cabinet on how Mussolini might best be prised from Hitler: by firmness or by acquiescence. By and large, Chamberlian had supported his Foreign Secretary in Cabinet during the crisis of the autumn, but over the succeeding months all common ground was whittled away, not least as a result of vicious attacks on the Foreign Secretary in the Italian press, often accompanied by warm praise of the Prime Minister himself: '. . . we only wish that other British politicians, and not only on the Opposition side, knew how to follow his example.'[119] Constant references were made to the 'two voices from London'. Following his success at Nyon, Eden, against Chamberlain's wishes, made a speech at Llandudno on 15 October in which he said that if the situation in Spain did not improve he would not be disposed to criticise any nation which felt obliged to resume its liberty of action. The speech received praise in France, although it was criticised in certain sections of the press for not going far enough.[120]

Eden's immense popularity both at home and in France was attractive to king-makers such as Oliver Harvey. 'The Cabinet cannot use A.E.'s popularity, and sabotage his foreign policy,' he wrote, adding, 'The majority of the Cabinet are against A.E., and the Cabinet are far too right, both of the House of Commons and of the country.'[121] At the beginning of November a group of influential Foreign Office members met at Eden's house to discuss their position. Of these Leeper, Cadogan, Sargent and Strang favoured Chamberlain's policy of rapprochement with Italy, while Cranborne, Eden and Harvey opposed any further move towards Italy 'until the Spanish question is cleared up'. Harvey's voice was perhaps especially persuasive in urging Eden to take a firmer line with Chamberlain: 'If you left the Cabinet the Government would fall . . . You should speak to the Prime Minister with some "appalling frankness".' When Eden did this on the following day, however, he received a firm rebuff, although Chamberlain did agree to call a Foreign Policy Committee meeting the following week to hear his complaints.[122]

Further support for Eden's attitude towards Italian intervention in Spain came at the end of November during the visit of the French ministers. The French Foreign Minister expressed the view that although France would prefer a Republican victory, French interests would not necessarily be threatened by a Nationalist victory. The only danger lay in the continued presence of Italy and Germany.[123] This was a position with which Eden, and others of many shades of political opinion, could find little fault.

Chamberlain was now anxious to conduct conversations with Italy. The chief obstacle to Anglo-Italian accord remained the withholding from Italy of formal recognition of her conquest of Abyssinia, but although Eden was not in principle against recognition he believed that some gesture of good faith was essential from Italy. Moreover, although no formal promises had been given to the USSR for her accommodating attitudes at the NIC in the autumn, Lord Chilston had given certain assurances and the Russian delegates had been quite adamant that there should be no further concessions to Italy until 'a substantial number' of foreign volunteers were withdrawn from Spain. Thus although, strictly speaking, recognition of Abyssinia was outside NIC affairs, it was likely to be taken as a direct affront by Russia.

In the summer of 1937, mild interest displayed by the USA in the European crisis occasioned by the Civil War had led to tentative suggestions in the Foreign Office that the USA should be approached with a view to filling the gap left by the withdrawal from the naval scheme of Italy and Germany. At that time, given her isolationist position, it had been decided not to risk the rebuff which would almost certainly result.[124] However, with the outbreak of war in the Far East and attacks on shipping in which the USS *Panay* was sunk, the question of possible co-operation with the USA was raised once again. Sir Ronald Lindsay, the British Ambassador in Washington, was authorised to tell the Secretary of State, Mr Cordell Hull, that Britain would send eight or more capital ships to the scene if the USA would do the same. Roosevelt, who was eager for staff conversations to take place, responded in the new year by sending a naval officer, Capt. Ingersoll to London for discussions with Eden.[125]

However, while Eden was building bridges with the USA, Chamberlain was no less diligently nurturing his friendship with Italy. For far from trusting his Foreign Office, Chamberlain was convinced that only by bypassing his appointed advisers and acting on his own initiative could peace be preserved. He was supported in this by many in his Cabinet, but drew for inspiration to an inordinate extent upon the extraordinary correspondence between himself and Lady Ivy Chamberlain, widow of Sir Austen Chamberlain, Neville Chamberlain's stepbrother. Mussolini, who had been a great admirer of Austen Chamberlain, encouraged Lady Chamberlain to act as an unofficial go-between, passing messages from him to Chamberlain and even, in one instance, dictating the contents of Lady Chamberlain's letter to the Prime Minister.[126] Most faithfully did Lady Chamberlain report the strong feeling against Eden which was undoubtedly rife in the capital. 'Nothing will covince them', she wrote, 'that it is not he [Eden] who is preventing the conversations from starting. They believe you are friendly, but that the Foreign Office is working against you.' More dangerously still, she reported that the US Ambassador, William Phillips, 'begged me to tell you to start conversations at any cost', because he believed this might have prevented Italy leaving the League.[127] That such a statement did not appear incompatible with Roosevelt's latest moves, or that if it did, Chamberlain was unperturbed, is perhaps an indication of his naïvety in foreign affairs.

Eden, much encouraged by Roosevelt's emissary, cancelled his Madeira holiday, travelling instead to the south of France to be more readily available. Before leaving he asked the Foreign Office to draw up a list of *desiderata* to be asked in return for recognition of the Abyssinian conquest. Of the two possible courses presented he gave his support (with the approval of Cadogan, Orme Sargent and Harvey) to recognition given 'as a gesture to which would be coupled an Anglo-French declaration of collaboration in the Mediterranean, and an invitation to Italy to negotiate outstanding questions'. He then departed for France, leaving the Foreign Office in the charge of Chamberlain.

Ten days later the Foreign Office learned of Roosevelt's hope for world discussion. The President intended to launch his plan within the week, but first sought approval of the British Government. With only four days in which to draft the reply, Cadogan, who did not share the Foreign Secretary's enthusiasm for rapproachement with the USA,[128] approached Chamberlain. He proposed replying that, as discussions with the French on *de jure* recognition of Italy's Abyssinian conquest were about to begin, Roosevelt might wish to hold up his plans to see how much progress was made, but that if he still wished to go ahead, Britain would support him. In the event, the telegram was dispatched without Cadogan's conciliatory conclusion. A copy was sent to Eden, who returned to London immediately. When two days later a telegram expressing Roosevelt's disappointment came, Eden sent a reply hoping that Roosevelt would not regard the previous telegram as a negative response. Chamberlain refused to send a covering telegram to this olive branch, and chided Eden that the Foreign Office was 'not sincere' in its efforts to reach a settlement with Germany and Italy.[129] Only with difficulty was Eden persuaded from resignation.[130]

On 25 January Eden had talks in Paris with Chautemps and Delbos,[131] who informed him that they did not object in principle to *de jure* recognition of the Italian conquest, but hoped that Spain would be part of the settlement. When Grandi told Eden on 10 February that the Italian Government was ready to open conversations on *de jure* recognition and would be prepared to discuss Spain, it seemed possible that agreement would be reached. However, not only did Eden regard this assurance with considerable scepticism, but a rapid deterioration in international affairs stiffened his resolve to gain something more than mere assurances from Italy. A recent recrudescence of attacks on shipping, and in particular the sinking of SS *Endymion* at the end of January, revived criticism of Italy.[132] Far more grave was the development of the Austrian crisis and the humiliation by Hitler in mid-February of the Austrian Chancellor, Kurt von Schuschnigg. As a result of these events, the divergence of attitude between the Prime Minister and Foreign Secretary became even plainer. While Chamberlain saw only the more need for rapprochement with Italy, Eden believed still more firmly in the necessity for a positive gesture of good faith, and felt that Mussolini's current anxiety for the future of Austria made this an opportune moment to press for the removal of Italian troops from Spain.

Undoubtedly Eden received much encouragement from opponents of Chamberlain, such as Lloyd George, to resign, and considerable abetment from Cadogan, Cranborne, J. H. Thomas and Harvey to challenge the Prime Minister in Cabinet. Certainly, it is true that 'Eden wanted to resign as much as Chamberlain wanted him to.'[133] The final clash came on the weekend of the 19–20 February. Despite a last-minute acceptance by Mussolini of the British Plan for withdrawal, Eden would not agree that Anglo-Italian conversations should start until withdrawal had actually begun. Twenty Ministers were present at the Cabinet meeting on 20 February. Excluding Chamberlain and Eden, fourteen supported the Prime Minister unequivocally, and four endorsed his policy with some reservation.[134] None backed Eden.[135] Abroad, the dictators greeted his resignation with triumph,[136] but for the democracies and for Russia, Eden's departure was a bitter blow.

BRITISH GOVERNMENT PRESSURE ON FRANCE

'Now at least they [the Anglo-Italian conversations] have a fair prospect of success.' With these words, Chamberlain concluded his diary entry on 19 February 1938. Success in the field of foreign policy was not to come so readily to Chamberlain. Although the Anglo-Italian agreement drawn up along the lines of the Cabinet decision of 19 February was signed in April, it was to prove politically impossible to ratify until the following December. In facing the Commons on 21 February, the Prime Minister had found it expedient to assure members that the Government regarded a settlement of the Spanish question as an essential feature of any agreement that might be arrived at with Italy, and that the situation in Spain during the conversations should not be materially altered by Italy, either by sending fresh reinforcements to Franco or by failing to implement the arrangements contemplated in the British Plan for withdrawal.[137] He was to remain shackled by these words for many months, despite assuring his colleagues on 2 March that it 'had never been on his mind as a *sine qua non* to an agreement that Italy should withdraw from Spain'.[138]

Meanwhile Lord Plymouth and Francis Hemming endeavoured to move forward with practical arrangements for the withdrawal scheme. On 8 February, a revised scheme was circulated to NIC representatives. It was estimated that withdrawal would begin roughly forty-five days from the commencement of counting by the commissions. But in order for the scheme to begin it was necessary for France to agree to close her frontier for the six weeks covering withdrawal in order to assure Italy that no further volunteers or aid were reaching the Republic. Petty quibbling as to numbers continued almost as a matter of course, but there were hopeful signs that a figure of 12,000 from each side would eventually prove acceptable to both Russia and Italy.[139] Thus all now depended on France, who continued to stick rigidly to the NIC resolution of 4 November 1937 which agreed to restoration of observation to concur with the withdrawal of volunteers. On 4 March, therefore, Sir Eric Phipps was asked to seek an interview with the French Foreign Minister and persuade him that if the NIA were to survive, it was necessary for France to close her frontier from the moment the commissions returned from Spain and for it to remain closed for sixty days, on the strict understanding that it would automatically be suspended unless within that period the scheme had begun to work.[140]

In Spain itself, however, the Republican army was hard-pressed in Aragon, where by the end of the month the Nationalist front had advanced perilously close to the Pyrennean border. If the Nationalists were to occupy all the territory south of the Franco-Spanish border the French would be faced with a third enemy front to contend with in case of war. Not surprisingly, reports of French activity in the Spanish arena therefore increased. On 13 March Léon Blum formed his second ministry, this time with the ardently Italophobe J. Paul-Boncour as his Foreign Minister. Daladier remained as Deputy Premier. Hopes of a more accommodating attitude on the part of the French were now dashed when the French Ministry for Foreign Affairs presented details of their requirements in return for the closing of the border. Restoration of control would begin twenty-five days after NIC adoption of the resolution for withdrawal based on the commissions' findings. This was to be automatically suspended if after forty days withdrawal had not begun.

News of the reinstatement of Blum was ill-received in the Foreign Office, but for the Spanish Government his appointment offered a glimmer of hope. Dr Juan Negrín, Spanish Government Premier since the resignation of Largo Caballero on 16 May 1937, immediately visited Blum and sympathetic ministers in Paris with a view to enlisting further French support. In return for French co-operation and aid, he offered to place Catalonia under the protection of France. This, Paul-Boncour told Phipps, he was prepared to accept, and admitted that the dispatch of French troops to Spain was contemplated. Phipps demanded an interview with Blum, and early next day on 17 May he spoke to Blum immediately before the council of war which had been arranged with General Gamelin and other military advisers to discuss the possibility of French intervention. Phipps managed to extract 'a regretful half-promise' that Blum would confine himself to a merely 'hypocritical' intervention in Spain. In the event the British Ambassador's plea was more than amply supported by the objections of the French military, and the project was abandoned.[141]

When giving Phipps his word that there would be no open infraction of the NIA (he refused to give an undertaking that no aid of any kind would be sent), Blum requested that a meeting be arranged between himself and the British Prime Minister and Foreign Secretary in order to discuss Spain and Czechoslovakia. The Foreign Office received the suggestion with horror. Registering his disapproval Orme Sargent wrote in a Foreign Office minute:

> M. Paul-Boncour at the Quai d'Orsay is a disaster, and an invitation to him would only strengthen his position, whereas it must be our sincere wish to see him out of office at the earliest possible moment. In fact, I should go so far as to say that anything we can do to weaken the present French Government and precipitate its fall would be in the British interest.

The French Government, he suggested, should be told 'as gently as possible' that no useful purpose would be served by such a meeting, but that if and when a French government was established on a broad national basis, the Foreign Office would be most glad to arrange a meeting. Cadogan and Halifax were in complete agreement with this view.[142]

Orme Sargent's minute was sent on to Phipps with a covering letter, which in view of the controversy which has grown up concerning earlier instances of British pressure on the French Government is worth quoting here:

> I don't think that you will disagree, but you may very well properly be shocked at the suggestion that we, or rather you, should do anything which might embarrass or weaken a French Government, even if it be in the hopes that it will, as a result, be replaced by a Government more adequate to the critical situation with which we are faced. But you need not – indeed you must not take my minute, or even the Secretary of State's approval thereof as representing in any way an instruction as regards this particular matter. Officially you have not seen it, or heard of it. But if the present Government falls and is speedily replaced by a Government *'de concentration nationale'*, with a strong, sensible and reasonable Minister of Foreign Affairs, we shall be pleased.[143]

The French Government was now, in any case, in very grave economic difficulties,[144] and the recent death of his wife had left Blum 'terribly broken'[145]. But, if the Government fell, who would replace Blum and Paul-Boncour? Here again British influence, according to Phipps, was felt:

> We were nearly cursed by having Paul-Boncour again at the Quai d'Orsay. The Socialists and Herriot wanted him to remain. I therefore had Daladier, the new Premier, and Paul Reynaud informed indirectly that it would be most unfortunate if Paul-Boncour were to remain, not only because of his mad hankering after intervention in Spain, but because it seemed highly desirable for France to get on better terms with Italy. Paul Reynaud was convinced by my message and used his influence with Daladier in the desired sense. Daladier himself was in full agreement but hesitated owing to inevitable considerations of electoral and political expediency. Finally, after an interview of over one hour with Paul-Boncour he did the right thing – or

rather the semi-right thing, for I should much have preferred Chautemps to Georges Bonnet who got it. However, we must be grateful for being spared Paul-Boncour, who was a positive danger to the peace of Europe.

I am always most particularly careful to avoid intervening in any way in French politics, but this time I felt it was my duty to take a certain risk, though a very small one as my messages were quite indirect and I can always disavow them.

Phipps went on to conclude this confession with the proposal that 'if Daladier does well, and Bonnet shows himself to be solid' the French ministers should be rewarded, as Blum had in vain requested, with an invitation to visit Halifax and Chamberlain. In the event Daladier and Bonnet received not only this, but the even greater accolade of an invitation to Windsor Castle.[146]

CLOSING THE FRENCH FRONTIER

The British Government had now snubbed Roosevelt, and had put considerable pressure on the French Government in pursuance of Chamberlain's Italian policy. Despite the rapidly deteriorating Czechoslovakian situation, which dominated all problems of foreign policy, and the signing of the Anglo-Italian Pact on 16 April, the British Government was still not free of the Spanish question. Moreover, after significant progress by the Spanish Nationalists in March, when it had seemed, as Ciano noted, that 'the collapse might not be far off',[147] the Republic was once more demonstrating astonishing resilience and fortitude. However, the latest War Office report indicated that large numbers of the newest type of aircraft, including bombers, were to be sent to Palma before the end of April, so it could be hoped that this latest setback might be soon redressed. If at this crucial moment the French frontier were also closed, the fate of the Republic would surely be sealed.

Only one voice was raised in protest in the Foreign Office at the short-sightedness of British policy towards Spain. Noting that the Anschluss of March had not ruptured the Berlin-Rome Axis, Laurence Collier recorded his fear that the coming year would see the domination of Europe by Greater Germany, and that Britain and France would be placed in a position of strategic inferiority. Whereas it would then be difficult to support France for geographic reasons, it was still relatively easy to support her in Spain in any measures she might take to prevent the country falling under German and Italian domination. France was the only great power which could enforce a cessation of the Spanish Civil War by military measures to which Germany and Italy could not reply in kind. It was, he argued, inconceivable that Hitler, if he could not get at Spain by sea, would risk an attack on the Maginot Line or a war with Britain. If he did not move, Britain could be sure that Italy would not move either. At least Britain should not try to stop the French from taking a different line and preventing the complete collapse of the Spanish Government by opening the French border to arms shipments.

> Yet this is what HMA at Paris has just been doing on instructions from London, thus providing the spectacle – surely unique in the whole history of British foreign policy – of a British Government doing its utmost to prevent a foreign government from taking action which would protect Britain's interests.

Although his memorandum was read by his colleagues with 'interest and benefit', it predictably influenced their views not one whit, despite his persuasive rider that the policy he advocated would also be vital to the Government's electoral chances. Mounsey riposted that Britain was in no better position than at the outset of the war to take direct action of any kind, being weakened by the war in the East. The premise that the risk involved was small was a matter of speculation. Vansittart, Plymouth and Cadogan all supported existing policy, the latter believing that whereas a Government victory in Spain would result in a bitterly divided country, a Nationalist victory would not necessarily do so.[148] The Foreign Office almost unanimously, therefore, supported Chamberlain's policy.

Since no settlement through the NIC seemed likely for the near future, the scheme for withdrawal being very complicated and expensive to organise, France was to be urged to a closer understanding with Italy in which Britain would play a part. Noting that although the Italians were still the worst offenders for breaches of the NIA, Mounsey suggested separate talks between France, Italy and Britain, and advocated that the French should close their border so that the Italians could be persuaded to withdraw unilaterally from Spain. With this in view the Anglo-

French conversations conducted on 28-29 April devoted roughly one-third of the time allocated to Spain and the rest to Czechoslovakia.[149] Léger, who attended the talks, played a strangely supportive role in persuading his government to adopt a more conciliatory attitude towards the Italians. Phipps interpreted his strategy as one of inducing the French to act more reasonably, in order to prove eventually to both French right-wing opinion and to British opinion generally that Italy had no intention of getting on better terms with France but only of separating her from Britain.[150] Daladier was persuaded during the talks not only to support Britain's recommendation at Geneva for a majority recognition of Italy's position in Abyssinia, but also to close the Franco-Spanish frontier on the day on which the commissions were reported to be in position to begin counting.

On 14 May, when despite all these efforts Mussolini responded with a viciously anti-French speech delivered at Genoa, it looked as though Léger's strategy would be rewarded.[151] Halifax, appalled by Mussolini's contemptuous attitude, declared, 'Anthony was right'.[152] Notwithstanding, Corbin was summoned to see Cadogan and chided on the amount of material still crossing the French border. Two days later, on the 19th, the French Ambassador was again harangued on the same subject. Desperation mounted as by the end of the week the Czechoslovakian crisis dominated all else. 'We must not go to war. We can't go to war,' wrote Cadogan.[153] On 3 June, prompted by public outrage at Franco's indiscriminate bombing of towns and shipping, Halifax saw Corbin in an effort to persuade him that the French should promise to close their frontier. Britain would then use this promise to put pressure on Italy to bring about an armistice in Spain, which was believed to be the only effective remedy for such atrocities.[154] This policy was not wholly acceptable to his colleagues. Both Strang and Roberts argued against it, fearing that it might bring down the French Government which would then be replaced by one less accommodating to British wishes than Daladier's. As a result of strong British pressure, however, the French frontier was now, in mid-June, finally closed.[155]

The gesture might at last have cleared the way ahead in Rome had not the French taken advantage of Halifax's misunderstanding of Cadogan's proposal allowing the important condition of 'substantial withdrawal' to be included as part of the proposed Spanish armistice. This had the effect of throwing the whole question back once more, much to Cadogan's exasperation, on to 'that blasted NIC'.[156] However, it is doubtful if anything could have come of an armistice proposal at a time when Franco was intensifying his campaign, and when the daily bombing of ships by Nationalists drew on Chamberlain's head the wrath of the House of Commons. 'I had to meet as savage a House as I have seen for a long time. Ll. G. fairly shook with passion,' he confided to his sister. Probably for the first time Chamberlain truly appreciated the place of the Spanish Civil War in foreign affairs, for he now acknowledged that here was 'the mess we must clear up next'.[157]

THE WITHDRAWAL OF VOLUNTEERS

On 5 July Spain headed the Cabinet agenda for the third week in succession. Summarising the situation regarding Spain, Halifax informed his colleagues that the major powers had reached agreement in the NIC on the question of withdrawal. The two Spanish parties would now be approached. However, he warned the Cabinet that the document on withdrawal as it stood 'offered every facility for any party seeking to make trouble'. This was the more likely since Britain had still not ratified the Anglo-Italian Agreement, despite the cessation of anti-British propaganda from Bari and the Italian withdrawal of troops from Libya.[158] In view of the probable delay in settlement at the NIC the British Government decided to reconsider the idea, first proposed in March,[159] of sending an intermediary commission to Spain. The commission, established in August, with a view to mediating and arranging an exchange of prisoners, was led by Field-Marshal Sir Philip Chetwode. When originally nominated for the post in March he had not been optimistic. 'It looks', he wrote, to R. A. Butler, 'as if Franco is going to win and there will be no question of an exchange of prisoners.'[160]

Chetwode's doubts were amply confirmed during the autumn months. First, Franco had been far from pleased to hear that the fate of Spain was to be settled by the great powers among themselves as a result of the Munich Agreement in September.[161] The suspicion that Spain was to be shunted to one side as part of Chamberlain's peace plans was in no way allayed by the arrival in Burgos of a mission headed by Francis Hemming, whose purpose was to smooth the way for the British Plan but whose presence was regarded by

Franco as further evidence of outside interference.[162] Moreover, Franco was particularly upset by reports in the popular British Press which suggested that Chetwode had reported in an unflattering manner on Franco's army whilst praising the Republican forces. Other reports that the powers were 'about to stop the war in Spain' made his task of mediation impossible.[163]

There was similar resistance to the overweening attitude of the powers in Republican Spain. On the question of Spanish pride, Roberts minuted:

> The test of the danger of a general war which had hitherto been lacking, and the absence of which had given the Spanish war an international importance out of all proportion to its real merits was afforded by last September. The proper conclusion seems to be that the Powers who did not fight over Czechoslovakia would be most unlikely to do so over Spain.[164]

Meanwhile, the Republican Government, as part of a last desperate effort to convince the democracies of its goodwill, its worthiness as an ally and of its strength and determination to win, arranged under the auspices of the League of Nations for its own unilateral withdrawal of foreign volunteers. The decision was announced by Negrín to the League of Nations on 21 September. Withdrawal, which went on over a period of months, began almost immediately. On 1 November a farewell parade for those who had been withdrawn from the front was addressed in emotional terms by Dolores Ibarruri, the communist better known as 'La Pasionaria'.[165] By 14 January 1939 the International Military Commissions set up by the League of Nations had verified 4,640 volunteers as withdrawn from Spanish Government territory (see Table 21).

Many were unable to return to their country of origin, and it was with some relief that it was learned that Mexico was prepared to take 1,500 of the stateless. It was expected that all foreign combatants, with the exception of the wounded, would have left the Republic by 15 February.[167] Some chagrin was expressed in the Foreign Office that the International Commission appeared unable to trace any Soviet volunteers. This was regarded as 'unfortunate, since the other side is firmly convinced that Soviet experts were present and distrust will increase in the absence of such'.[168] The disappearance of the fairly limited number of Russian experts was in all probability far more sinister than was imagined. Believed by

Table 21[66] *Nationality and numbers of volunteers withdrawn up to 14 January 1939*

Andorra	1	Iceland	2
Argentine	1	Italy	194
Austria	1	Luxemburg	13
Belgium	347	Mexico	1
Brazil	1	Netherlands	143
Bulgaria	2	Norway	56
Chile	4	Poland	283
Czechoslovakia	39	Puerto Rico	1
Denmark	115	Romania	2
Finland	27	Sweden	182
France	2141	Switzerland	80
Germany	46	Tangier	3
Greece	3	United Kingdom	407
Hungary	8	USA	548
		Yugoslavia	7
		No National Identity	11
		Total	4,640

Stalin to have been contaminated by their contact with the outside world, theirs was a far worse fate than deportation to Mexico or the concentration camps of southern France.[169]

In all, it has been estimated that there were some 35,000 volunteers fighting for the Republican cause, although probably not more than 15,000 at any one time.[170] Probably their greatest contributions were in the intangible areas of morale and of propaganda. Their presence played an important part in raising the spirits of the Republicans in November 1936, but also, by remaining a constant thorn in the side of the NIC and of the British Cabinet in particular, they kept the Spanish Government's cause in the public eye, even though ultimately this had no effect.

Despite Franco's unwillingness to co-operate with the British attempt at mediation, the Italian Government followed the Spanish Government's lead, withdrawing 10,000 Italian troops on 1 November. The extent to which this gesture was of any military significance is difficult to estimate. It seems likely that those withdrawn had served their allotted time in Spain anyway. The British War Office, which had watched the situation closely, made the following approximate summary of troops in Spain over the period February 1937 – October 1938:

1. Before Guadalajara: 70,000 organised into three volunteer divisions.
2. After Guadalajara: Organised Corps HQ, two divisions and three brigades, but of the latter 80 per cent were Spanish troops and 20 per cent Italians, officered by Italians.
3. Casualties, sickness and leave reduced these numbers to about 40,000 in the spring of 1938, and this is the figure quoted by the Italians at the time of signing of the Anglo-Italian Agreement.
4. After June 1938 there had been a notable increase in numbers: against a wastage of 200 there had been sent 5,600 reservists as well as a good deal of equipment.
5. Italian troops estimated to be in Spain in September 1938 were as follows:

Infantry	23,000
Artillery	7,000
Engineers	2,000
AVV Personnel*	1,000
Services	8,000

*Armoured Vehicle Volunteer

This gave an estimated number of Italians in Spain in September of 41,000, and if accurate belied Ciano's claim that in withdrawing 10,000 Italians, Italy's force in Spain would be reduced by half.

Besides these there remained in Spain an important proportion of the Italian Air Force. These were estimated as follows:

Machines

	Mainland	Balearics
Bombers	60	40
Fighters	100	30
Reconnaissance	20	
	180	70
Total	250	

Personnel	1,700	500
Total	2,200	

(and 2,000 civilian lorry drivers)[171]

In considering these figures the Cabinet was clearly conscious that technicians and weaponry counted for more than infantry, but despite this it was agreed that steps should be taken to bring the Anglo-Italian Agreement into force on the grounds that the condition Chamberlain had stipulated in a statement on 24 July had now come to pass, i.e. Spain had 'ceased to be a menace to the peace of Europe'.[172] Thus on 16 November Britain recognised Italy's conquest of Abyssinia and the way was clear for ratification of the Anglo-Italian Agreement and the Anglo-Italian conversations which had been the focus of Chamberlain's Mediterranean policy.

Meanwhile it was suspected that the French border was open again, and bombing of ships around Spain continued. But the Prime Minister's policies were no longer accepted unquestioningly. Spain was to be placed first on the agenda of the talks, the principle of which Halifax now suggested should be 'nothing for nothing', while Chamberlain reminded his colleagues that there should nevertheless be 'something for something', suggesting the Djibuti Railway as a suitable topic for discussion.[173] The extent of Chamberlain's deception by the Italian Government is revealed on almost any page of Ciano's diary and many noted the Prime Minister's gullibility with alarm. Certainly Franco-Italian relations were patched up to the extent that François-Poncet was received as Ambassador on 29 November. But this was a superficial and short-lived gesture intended only to tide relations over until after the British ministers' visit to Rome in the new year. Meanwhile, Mussolini advised Franco 'to proceed with caution until the war is virtually ended without accepting compromises or mediation of any kind'.[174]

The British Plan was, after all, never put into operation although much time and verbiage had been spent on it. Ultimately, as with every aspect of non-intervention, withdrawal came when it best suited those concerned. On 23 March 1937 Grandi was reported by Maisky as telling the Chairman's Sub-Committee: 'If you want my opinion, I'll say this, not one single Italian volunteer will leave Spain until Franco is victorious!'[175] In January 1938, following Chamberlain's visit to Rome, it was estimated that approximately 30,000 Italians were still in Spain, and the air force remained at the September estimate.[176] On 19 April 1939 the Cabinet learned that 2,500 Italians had landed at Cadiz between 22 and 25 March that year, and that a further 6,000 had arrived before the fall of Madrid on 29 March.[177] Thus Italian troops remained in Spain long after the ratification of the Anglo-Italian Agreement, after the January Anglo-Italian talks and indeed after the end of the Spanish Civil War, as Mussolini had always intended they should.

6 British Recognition of Franco

The complex question of volunteers was debated throughout the war, but although the British Government had played an important part in the endeavour to reach a solution, the responsibility for that problem had rested squarely with the NIC at least until the last months of the war. However, parallel to and connected with that topic ran the issue of the legal recognition of the rebels, and here it was not possible to hide behind the NIC, for responsibility for such a decision could rest only with the British Government.

In July 1936 that government had declared its intention of standing aloof from the Spanish conflict, although certainly Cabinet sympathy lay with the rebel cause and many decisions taken in July and August were actually damaging to the Spanish Government. Even so, the British Government continued to recognise the Republican Government as the *de jure* government of Spain until little over one month before the close of hostilities on 1 April 1939. Many other powers, both major and minor, recognised the Nationalist régime long before the end of the war. Yet the British Government felt unable to do so, even though by failing to recognise Franco she was left in April 1939 very far from having achieved the second of the Chiefs' of Staff main requirement of 'such relations with any Spanish Government which may emerge from this conflict as will ensure benevolent neutrality in the event of our being engaged in a European war'. Indeed, the abysmal state of Anglo-Spanish relations in 1939 was, as will be demonstrated, to present the Chiefs of Staff with a well-nigh insoluble dilemma of strategy.[1]

It is evident that the British Government throughout this period sought to establish links of one kind or another with the Nationalists. But were these links worth while, and what of Anglo-Republican relations meanwhile? As mentioned, almost the entire Diplomatic Corps was in residence at San Sebastion during the summer months, and in 1936, on the outbreak of hostilities, the majority moved across the border to continue their mission from France. The British Ambassador was no exception and left for Zaraus on 26 July before crossing into France on 1 August. The Madrid Embassy was left in the care of Acting Vice-Consul Milanes, and so it remained until the return to Madrid on 16 August of Mr Ogilvie Forbes, who then became and remained until April 1937 the British Chargé d'Affaires. The last Republican Government with which Sir Henry Chilton had direct dealings of any kind was that of Casares Quiroga, which ended on 18 July 1936.[2]

The fact that Chilton appeared to make no effort to return to Madrid, and was not ordered to do so, was very much resented by the Spanish Government, the more so since Ogilvie Forbes had found no difficulty in reaching the capital. In addition it was soon realised that the British Ambassador was in communication with the rebels, and this was an added affront. Through Señor Castro, their liaison officer with the Diplomatic Corps, the Spanish Government therefore informed the British Government that heads of missions could act as such only in the territory to which they were accredited. From then on, therefore, they dealt exclusively with Ogilvie Forbes.

Foreign Office reaction to the Republican rejection of Chilton, is interesting for its calm acceptance of the bizarre situation which ensued, with Sir Henry Chilton continuing to hold his title and position of Ambassador to the Spanish Republic, although never acting in that capacity.[3] Thus while officially accredited to the Spanish Government he became the *de facto* Ambassador to the Franco régime, personally dealing almost exclusively with Anglo-Nationalist relations, although his office remained the clearing-house for reports to Britain from consulates throughout the country. It was remarked by the German Chargé at Salamanca, Dr Karl Schwendermann, that notes and telephone messages came from Chilton almost every day.[4] Indeed, when Claude Bowers, the American Ambassador, reported that everything Chilton did was '. . . intended to cripple the Government and serve the Insurgents',[5] his accusation was probably nearer the truth than even he imagined.

On 18 August there was some discussion in the Foreign Office as to the Appointment of an official Agent to the rebel authorities. The idea was rejected on the grounds that it was too early, and that an adequate channel of communication existed through the Marquis

Merry del Val, then living in Britain, and Sir Henry Chilton in
Hendaye.[6] Actually of more importance than Sir Henry was A. J.
Pack, Commercial Secretary at the British Embassy, who in the
period up to the appointment of Sir Robert Hodgson as British
Agent to Nationalist Spain in November 1937, acted as intermediary between Salemanca and Hendaye. Two other useful
channels to the Nationalists were used. The first was through the
British Ambassador to Portugal, Sir Charles Wingfield. Though he
could not act officially, he was instructed to maintain informal
relations with the rebels.[7] Later Cmdr. Alan Hillgarth was able to
build invaluable links with the Nationalist forces.

In comparison with these active, if unofficial, channels of
communication with the rebels, the degree and manner of communication with the existing Republican Government seems
somewhat strained and grudging. Perhaps the Popular Front
Government was not well represented by Senor López Oliván, the
Ambassador in London at the outbreak of war, although unlike
colleagues in Berlin, Rome and Paris he had at least stayed at his
post. He was, by this act of loyalty, trapped in Britain, and knew
only too well that he could expect scant sympathy from the rebels in
the event of victory. Yet his sympathies were not notably pro-
Republican either. Indeed, he told a Foreign Office official that
neither side could be said to represent democracy and liberty. It
would, he suggested, be wrong to suppose that a régime of the right
would necessarily be close in foreign policy to Germany and Italy.
On 24 August following news of the fate of his brother-in-law in
Madrid's model prison, the Ambassador asked to be relieved of his
post.[8]

His successor, Pablo de Azcárate y Flores, was a man more truly
representative of embattled Republican Spain. The appointment
was greeted with moderate approval in the Foreign Office, but
elsewhere the new Ambassador found considerable reserve, and
even, in some quarters, rudeness. When, for example, Lord Cecil
tried to present Churchill to the new Ambassador, the former
turned away muttering 'blood, blood'.[9] There is no evidence that on
any occasion on which Azcárate was received by the Foreign
Secretary, he was given the slightest hope or encouragement to
convey to his government.

It is scarcely surprising that neither side in Spain was satisfied
with Britain's makeshift diplomatic arrangements. Although the
coolness between Britain and Republican Government did not

assuage resentment in Burgos, Britain's continued recognition of the Republic and failure to give any degree of recognition to Franco made the British increasingly unpopular during the first months of the war. Unlike the Republic, Nationalist Spain had nothing to lose diplomatically, and was the more ready to put pressure on Britain whenever possible.

But of all questions of Anglo-Spanish relations which faced the British Government that of when, and in what degree to recognise the Nationalist régime was undoubtedly the most complex, bounded as it was not only by what was politically possible, but also by the limits and ambiguities of international law. There are many degrees of recognition which one country may afford another, but here those that concerned the British Government, the question of belligerent rights, and the question of *de jure* recognition, are considered.[10]

The limits which international law imposed on possible courses of action open to the British Government were, in August 1936, to prove an additional reason for British support of the NIA. For the Republican blockade and Franco's threat to bomb Tangier made it imperative that the question of an award of belligerent rights be considered, since such a step was the normal means of affording protection to merchant shipping. An award of belligerent rights would have allowed either Spanish party to stop and search merchant ships with impunity. Without such rights merchant shipping could expect full military protection at sea. Similarly, on land, rights of search and possible requisition would exist. In return the awarding country could expect a certain consideration in mutual transactions and compensation for damage and loss.

Examining the situation, Sir William Malkin, Legal Adviser to the Foreign Office, warned that the Spanish Civil War had created a legal situation of great complexity, and indeed the position was 'not altogether definite'. Legal authorities[11] based their analyses on the leading precedent of the American Civil War, which unfortunately did not provide an exact analogy as the insurgents in that instance had been endeavouring to set up an independent state, and not, as in this case, to conquer the entire country.[12] Moreover, according to the authority favoured by the Foreign Office, a grant of belligerent rights was given as a matter of 'pure grace' by the grantor. There was no legal obligation,[13] although it was admitted that legal opinion was fairly evenly divided on this point.

However, since it was necessary to adopt a definite and public attitude to the hostilities in Spain, Malkin set out the conditions under which an award of belligerent rights could be made. These were:

1. A serious revolt, i.e. a war. This was considered to have been fulfilled.
2. Possession of a considerable portion of the land, also achieved.
3. An identifiable government. Malkin regarded this point as less certain.[14]
4. Hostilities conducted in a regular manner. Here too, Malkin was doubtful, but suggested that the rebels were probably no worse than the legal government, for example in the matter of the shooting of prisoners. Much depended on the question of humanity and the impossibility of treating a large percentage of the population as criminals.

If the Government decided to award belligerency there were two main grounds on which it might be made. A state had every right to recognise belligerency as a measure of self-protection if (a) an effective blockade were set up or (b) if it possessed territory contiguous to the area in question – in this case in Gibraltar, or in regard to Britain's shared responsibility in Tangier. However, the first of these conditions was held not to be fulfilled as the Republican navy was not thought capable of setting up an effective blockade. Furthermore, the Admiralty was at this stage adamantly against an award of belligerent rights, as they had no wish to allow the Republican navy rights of search over British ships.[15]

It was suggested, however, that if the British Government did not wish to take such a positive and irreversible step as an award of belligerency was bound to be, an alternative solution was available. A declaration of neutrality, which was favoured in some sections of the Foreign Office, would amount to the same thing as an award of belligerency, minuted Malkin, since 'neutrality can only exist in law on the assumption of there being two belligerents'. He suggested instead that 'an attitude of simple non-intervention on the other hand would not necessarily involve recognition of the insurgents as belligerents . . . it depends on what is to be covered by the term non-intervention'.[16] Here then, given the uncertain Spanish situation, was one more reason for British adherence to the NIA.

By the end of September the rebel forces had made extensive gains. In the Foreign Office Roberts proposed that since all the conditions for recognition were now fulfilled, the Government should make such a gesture. Once again the subject was debated from all angles. It was suggested that a proclamation of neutrality should be made, and this was so far accepted that the document was drawn up and the Dominions circulated. Nothing came of this, however, for several reasons. New Zealand was then, and remained throughout the Civil War, adamantly against any suggestion of recognition in any degree.[17] With trouble brewing in the Far East Britain was in no position to disregard the attitude of a country which could (and had in the past) field a splendid fighting force in her defence. France, too, was trenchantly opposed to any rapprochment with the Nationalists. Equally, Sir William Malkin was against the proclamation because he believed that the appropriate moment for such a step would have been two months earlier, if at all.

At the beginning of November, when the Spanish Government withdrew from Madrid to Valencia as the capital seemed about to fall, the French took the very positive step of moving their Chargé to Valencia. Eden assured the Cabinet that he would try to keep the French in line with British policy as far as possible.[18] But by mid-November it was clear that the French would not on this occasion be so easily led. The First Lord called for a Cabinet decision on recognition on its merits and not one which would follow the lead of the French, and his colleagues agreed to recognise Franco's belligerency on the fall of Madrid.[19] Less than one week later, Germany and Italy recognised Franco,[20] and the Nationalists issued their most forceful blockade warning to date.

In theory the Merchant Shipping Act of that December tightened up existing legislation on the carriage of arms, thus giving the Nationalist navy less need to stop and examine British shipping bound for Spain. There is little doubt, however, that an award of belligerent rights would have solved the many practical difficulties that continued to arise. Certainly, such an award might have been given according to existing precedent, had the provisions of international law been the sole criterion by which the situation was judged. As the Nationalist blockades intensified and were extended in the new year, failure to recognise the belligerency of both parties in Spain from the beginning was much regretted.

Early in February 1937 Sir Henry Chilton was approached by the Nationalist Conde de Albiz,[21] who suggested that Britain 'would do well' to appoint her own representative to Nationalist Spain.

Inevitably the suggestion that belligerent rights should be awarded instead was again made. Rejecting the idea once more, though agreeing that negotiations on those lines should continue, Eric Beckett[22] described very clearly the method by which Britain had so far, and would meanwhile, keep on good terms with the Nationalists:

> Having taken the steps we have, we shall now continue to refuse to recognise belligerent rights. We shall therefore have, in doing whatever we do, to avoid using the actual expression of recognising the status of a belligerent government, but short of using the consecrated legal expression with its belligerent rights association, we may well explain our position in terms which otherwise amount to the same thing. Such an explanation of the position would in fact only be a statement of the point we have now reached by what we have already done.

The explanation to be offered would of course be that of Britain's support of non-intervention:

> We still will not recognise either side as having belligerent rights, not because this is the logical deduction . . . but because we declare in this struggle we shall not do so, and we regard the Non-Intervention Agreement and the provision about carrying arms in ships as a substitute for the present struggle.[23]

However, in April the Nationalist blockade intensified. Beckett now reminded his colleagues that he had warned them that only recognition of belligerency would solve shipping problems, but conceded that to adopt such a course at so late a stage would, although legally possible, now be humiliating for the Government. It was politically impossible, he argued, both internally and externally. Externally it would look as though Britain were frightened; internally it would be to admit a complete change of policy.[24]

Thus it was that in the first quarter of 1937 the British Government became increasingly dependent upon the NIA as a plausible and acceptable explanation for her otherwise inexplicable policy. After the Government's humiliating retreat from its endeavour to avoid protecting British shipping during the Bilbao blockade, the situation continued uneasily throughout the summer.

But in July the threatened breakdown of the NIC caused by the withdrawal of Germany and Italy from the Naval Patrol Scheme, was solved by the unfortunate expedient of linking the inherently different problems of volunteers and belligerent rights. Belligerent rights thus became endowed in Nationalist eyes with a political importance not justified by practical reality, since the Admiralty had long since returned to the Nelsonian practice of turning a blind eye.

Belligerent rights had ceased to be a practical expedient and the question now become entirely politicised. Note has been taken of the cynicism of the dictator powers in using belligerent rights as a delaying tactic in the NIC.[25] The German Chargé d'Affaires in Britain revealed the artificiality of NIC negotiations in a dispatch to the Wilhelmstrasse:

> It proved a good move on our part to throw the question of belligerent rights into the discussions again and again without our really getting into an awkward situation publicly.[26]

It should be remembered, however, that Britain, too, found protractions of this kind suited her own purposes very well. On 30 June Halifax suggested to the Cabinet that 'the right course was to play for time, keeping in view the grant of belligerent rights as a possibility'.[27] But if the situation in the NIC provided a plausible reason for not granting belligerent rights some other means of balancing Britain's relations with both sides in Spain had to be found. The Foreign Office turned, therefore, once more to the idea first broached in February that year, of appointing an Agent to Burgos.

THE PROPOSED APPOINTMENT OF THE BRITISH AGENT

In March 1937 secret preparations for the appointment of a British Agent to Burgos reached an advanced stage. The British representative, Sir Robert Hodgson,[28] had been selected, and it seemed likely that the British would be acting in concert with the French who were reported to be about to make a similar move.[29] However, at the last moment the project was shelved. At first, it had seemed the ideal moment to take what was bound to be an unpopular step, the House of Commons being for the time fairly quiet.[30] There were more positive reasons. Both the War Office General Staff and the Air Staff had expressed concern that Britain lacked military observers on the Nationalist side, and were thus deprived of information as to the most recent developments in land and air fighting. While no official diplomatic links existed between Britain and the Nationalists, it was unlikely that Franco would receive military observers. Moreover, the appointment of an Agent, Eden assured his cabinet colleagues, could be defended on the grounds of commercial interests, which at that time were receiving much attention.[31]

This was probably the least of the considerations which prompted the Government to approve the appointment. Negotiations were by now going relatively smoothly between Burgos and Hendaye, conducted as they were by the capable A. J. Pack. The appointment of an Agent would not only cut across his own negotiations but create the anomaly of a person of ministerial rank at Burgos while Valencia was left in charge of a representative of inferior rank.

In the event, Parliament and the press, which had been relatively quiet on Spain, erupted again, provoked by Grandi's declaration to his non-intervention colleagues that Italian volunteers would be withdrawn only after Franco's final victory. Leaked to the press by the Russian Ambassador, the information brought sharp protests. Chamberlain complained that he had no fewer than twenty-five Parliamentary Questions addressed to him, and some of these were deliberately 'calculated to irritate S. Mussolini'.[32] In addition to this, on 25 March the New Zealand Government protested once again that they were 'firmly and unalterably opposed to any action which, either directly or indirectly could be interpreted as, or tend towards, recognition of any administration in Spain other than that of the lawfully constituted Government'. That day the Cabinet met and decided to postpone the appointment of the Agent.[33]

Throughout the ensuing months, Spain was kept in the public eye, first by the blockade of Bilbao, then by the tragic events of Guernica, the bombing of Italian and German warships, reprisals against Almeria, the alleged torpedoing of the *Leipzig*, and finally the breakdown of the NIC negotiations. In April professional opinions differed as to the progress of the war. In the Cabinet on 7 April, Eden reported that Ogilvie Forbes had suggested to him that 'time was on the side of the [Spanish] Government'. Although the First Lord countered by asserting Admiral Backhouse's opinion that 'the Valencia Government had almost ceased to exist as control was

exercised by committees',[34] the former view was the one repeated to
the Imperial Conference in July.[35] Similarly, if the systematic
destruction of Guernica indicated a new ruthlessness on the part of
Franco, and a frightening commitment to the Nationalist cause on
the part of Germany, this was to some extent politically balanced by
the degree of sympathy the appalling event aroused for Spanish
Republicans. The British Government therefore steered a discreetly
balanced course for some while.

However, the Nationalist capture of Bilbao on 19 June influenced
British Government attitudes to the extent that a new look was
taken at the idea of appointing an Agent to the Nationalist side.
Over the past two and a half months Anglo-Nationalist relations
had been decidedly cool, Franco resenting continued British
recognition of the Republican Government at a time when he was
denied even the lesser step of recognition of belligerent status. In
mid-June, however, the Duke of Alba, Franco's unofficial representative in London, told Cranborne that despite all, 'there was
nothing the General desired so much as good relations with
England', and revealed that 'relations between Salamanca and
Rome were not too comforatble'.[36] Cranborne therefore produced a
memorandum arguing the case for the appointment of a British
Agent to Nationalist Spain. Such a step was now essential, he
suggested, in view of Britain's Imperial position:

> These implications have always been present in our minds, but
> they have not been sharply defined. A nation torn by revolution
> presents no immediate menace to any other power. While
> conditions remained chaotic, we had no reason for anxiety. That
> phase of the Spanish conflict is however now over. It has ceased to
> be a revolution – it has become a civil war. There are two Spanish
> Governments, each with its internal adminstration and its own
> foreign policy. The foreign policies of both these Governments
> must directly concern us, but in the nature of things it is the
> foreign policy of General Franco which must cause us the most
> serious preoccupation. For it is his Government that controls that
> area of Spanish territory that dominates the Straits of Gibraltar
> on both sides, and that abuts on Gibraltar itself. The western
> entrance into the Mediterranean is a vital interest to Great
> Britain. It must be a main purpose of British policy to secure it.

There were, he suggested, two directions towards which a

modification of British policy might be directed. First, Britain could throw her weight in on the side of the Republic. But this Cranborne believed impossible, since it would, he claimed, 'split England from top to bottom'. It would destroy the current unity which was one of Britain's strengths. A milder version of this would be to bring non-intervention to an end and declare willingness to supply arms to either side. It was, however, not certain that this would bring the benefit to the Republican Government that was generally supposed, he argued, since the Republicans were receiving more than the Nationalists (This had been true of the early summer but the position was changing.)[37] Alternatively Britain could set about cultivating more friendly relations with Salamanca. While recognition of belligerency and of *de jure* status might be unacceptable, there would be several advantages in the appointment of an Agent, who would 'come to occupy a position of increasing influence', dissipating the myth that Britain had been biased against Franco throughout the conflict. Cranborne believed that the appointment could still be 'defended in the House of Commons on the score of British interests'.

Sir George Mounsey approved Cranborne's memorandum, and Eden, too, pronounced himself 'much impressed' and willing to appoint an Agent to Franco.[38] Sir Henry Chilton was now instructed to negotiate an exchange of agents which, whilst not strictly a new measure of official recognition, would increase the international status of General Franco's government and might be acceptable to him even in the absence of a grant of belligerent rights. As a result it was learned in mid-August that orders had been issued to the Nationalist press to cease the bitter campaign which had raged against Britain in the past.[39]

But once again, plans for this limited degree of recognition were thwarted, this time by the serious situation arising in the Mediterranean as a result of Italian submarine activity. In vain Cadogan argued that it was still the most opportune time:

as we are, for the moment, not daily badgered about specific cases in the House of Commons. When the House meets again we shall be strongly pressed to take retaliatory action against General Franco and the atmosphere will again become unfavourable for the appointment . . . This is the crucial moment.

For once, however, Cadogan was effectively overruled by Vansittart, who wanted the decision postponed until after the Nyon Conference which he hoped would result in a decision favourable to both Britain and 'Valencia'. 'Franco is a pirate – through his allies. There would be an outcry if we took steps towards recognition at the height of the piracy trouble.'[40]

By the end of August Eden himself was against the appointment for political reasons. Chief of these, he suggested, was the fall of Santander, which had been 'a considerable blow to Valencia' and marked the 'beginning of the end'. He continued:

> However that may be, it is clearly not to our interest that the end should come quickly, in as much as a complete and early victory for Franco would greatly increase the prestige of Italy especially in view of Mussolini's exchange of messages with Franco and the hardly concealed assistance of the Italian Navy to the Nationalists.[41]

Once more, therefore, the appointment of a British Agent was shelved.

After so many delays, it was doubtless with considerable relief that the British Government finally felt able, following Franco's release of seven British ships, to announce on 16 November 1937 the appointment of Sir Robert Hodgson as Commercial Agent to the Nationalist authorities. At the same time it was arranged that Mr John Leche, the British Chargé d'Affaires to the Republican Government, which that autumn moved to Barcelona, should be given the personal rank of Minister Plenipotentiary in Spain.[42] No one was deceived by the fact that in theory Sir Robert had neither official status nor any diplomatic privileges. His title meant that he replaced A. J. Pack, who was withdrawn. 'It does not look like a question of merely sending trade agents,' commented Attlee, 'it looks much more like the opening of diplomatic relations prior to recognition.' The appointment amounted, in effect, to *de facto* recognition[43] and had the effect of increasing the Opposition's determination that no further concessions should be made and of adding bitterness to the rancour already aroused by the Civil War.

In return Britain officially acknowledged the 'unofficial' appointment of the Duke of Alba, on 24 November. His position, as one historian has noted, was clearly defined under British law when in March 1938 the London County Council Motor Licence Department was asked by the Foreign Office to exempt the Duke of Alba's secretary from a driving examination on the grounds of diplomatic immunity. It was stated at the time that the British Government had agreed to the Spaniards 'receiving privileges and facilities on the same scale as members of the conventional diplomatic missions in London'.[44] In Spain, where Sir Robert Hodgson finally arrived on 16 December, a similar situation pertained: '. . . full diplomatic privileges were in fact accorded to me by a generous Nationalist Government despite Mr Eden's disclaimer.'[45]

Thus Britain maintained an uneasy balance between two acknowledged governments in Spain. The hope that the appointment of an Agent to Franco would improve Anglo-Nationalist relations was, however, vain. 'In Nationalist circles', recalled Sir Robert Hodgson, 'we were *mal vus*.'[46] By making the appointment the British Government had in fact gained nothing, for Franco now set his sights on formal recognition of belligerent rights, scorning the very considerable step the British Government had already taken in his favour. Throughout the following year the number of governments recognising the Nationalists increased, so that by November 1938 eleven countries had granted *de jure* recognition, thirteen had granted *de facto* recognition, and two others had appointed Commercial Agents.[47] In addition Chile and Portugal had appointed Commercial Agents.

Table 22 Countries affording recognition to the Nationalist administration by November 1938[47]

De jure *recognition*		De facto *recognition*	
Germany	Manchukuo	Czechoslovakia	Norway
Albania	Nicaragua	Bulgaria	Yugoslavia
Guatemala	Portugal	Greece	Switzerland
Hungary	Salvador	Holland	Turkey
Italy	Vatican	Denmark	United Kingdom
Japan		Finland	Uruguay
			Venezuela

MODERATING INFLUENCES

Why, despite her poor standing with the Nationalist authorities, did Britain feel unable to take any further step towards recognition until the final phases of the war?

Clearly the British Government had tried very hard over the preceding sixteen months to accommodate Franco's sensibilities, but these efforts had been hampered at every turn by what the Cabinet and Foreign Office loosely referred to as 'political' factors. It is, however, difficult to assess exactly either the nature of such considerations, or the extent of their influence in the formulation of Anglo-Spanish policy. In terms of external pressures, it is true that publicly the Popular Front Government in France was against an award of belligerent rights. But on several occasions, for example in the autumn of 1936, in the spring of 1937 and again that autumn, France asked to be kept informed of British intentions regarding recognition with a view to taking similar steps herself. Indeed, on one occasion in March 1937 France was believed to be about to anticipate British action in this sphere. Moreover, it is difficult to believe that the British Government, which was so easily able to put pressure on France in the matter of non-intervention and the closing of the French border in June 1938, would have accepted any restraint from France in the matter of recognition.

As regards the USA, Chamberlain showed himself unwilling to become dependent on that nation, which in any case continued with its strict isolationist policy.[48] Of the Dominions only New Zealand regularly took positive steps in support of the Spanish Republic by vetoing any step towards recognition of the Nationalists, although hers was a relatively influential voice.[49] One other major external body which might have been expected to act as a brake on pro-Nationalist policy was the League of Nations, but this organ of international opinion was by now largely disregarded by the British Government and spoke, if at all, in weak and vacillating tones. It is true that the League gave Republican Spain an international platform from which to air her grievances, and at times this gave rise to some embarrassment, but the British Government response was to point firmly to the NIA as her officially adopted method of dealing with Spanish affairs.[50] Spain's presence at Geneva as a semi-permanent member of the League Council was an irritant, none the less, to the British Government, and one which the latter hoped soon to remove.

In 1937 Spain, together with Chile and Turkey, was due to retire as á non-permanent member of the League Council. She therefore applied for a declaration of re-eligibility and for re-election as she had done successfully in 1928, 1931 and 1934. But to some, including Britain, Spain was no longer considered a congenial

member of the League. The Foreign Office, with Lord Cranborne
alone dissenting, supported instead the proposed election of
Belgium to a semi-permanent seat.[51]

There remained, of course, ardent British supporters of the
League, but these were a decreasing band. At government level
repeated appeals by the Spanish Republic to the League of Nations
received scant attention. As Lord Cecil noted:

> The Council was very poorly attended. Indeed, from this time
> [December 1936] forward the tendency of our Government to
> avoid bringing to the League any important international
> question was accelerated on the ground that in the absence of
> Germany, Italy and Japan no vigorous action by the League
> could be looked for.[52]

An additional difficulty was that the League could not be other than
a reflection of European attitudes and these were deeply divided on
the Spanish issue. Thus Negrín's resolution calling for an end to
non-intervention, and for the League Council to examine the
question of Spain, was vetoed by Portugal and Albania on 2
October 1937, with fourteen more countries abstaining. Only the
USSR and Mexico supported the resolution.[53] As Eden explained
to the House of Commons: 'There are, discreditable though the
honourable gentlemen opposite no doubt think it, a great many
nations, members of the League, who want General Franco to
win.'[54] In terms, therefore, neither of ability nor of attitude did the
League act as a check to British Government attitudes to Spain.

As to internal considerations, these are more difficult to assess.
Certainly from the Cabinet Conclusions it seems clear that 'public
opinion', as it was broadly called, was proffered rather mechani-
cally for or against propositions. What was actually meant by
'public opinion' in the context of Cabinet Conclusions is not always
plain, but there is little evidence that it had much influence on
overall policy. Two examples will perhaps suffice. The first concerns
what was internationally the most notorious event of the Civil War:
the bombing of Guernica. This incident has been the subject of
recent detailed study[55] and much passionate debate. Here, what is
important is that the intensity of public feeling aroused by the aerial
attack on defenceless men, women and children of a small market
town brought no echo of response from the British Government. It is
true that this was not an issue of direct concern to Britain. It did,

however, serve to stimulate widespread anti-German and anti-Franco attitudes. Yet even on the question of seeking a ban on the bombing of open towns the Government was loath to take rigorous action. Their attitude can best be illustrated by Lord Plymouth's limp comment to the NIC that 'His Majesty's Government has come to the conclusion that the method most likely to be efficacious is to ask the parties in Spain to abstain from bombardment from the air.'[56] For despite strong evidence from their own representative that the attack had indeed been made by German aeroplanes dropping a new type of German incendiary bomb,[57] the Government had no intention of offering any sop to British public opinion if it might endanger Anglo-German relations. Meanwhile, Germany accumulated in Spain experience which would be of considerable value to her in any future conflict.

The second and, since it affected British interests, the more striking example, concerns the attacks on British shipping during the last six months of 1938. Again, lack of action can be explained in terms of the exigencies of Anglo-German relations, but in this instance even Chamberlain, as correspondence with his sister indicates, was shocked by the degree of protest (which he described as savage) that Government inaction produced in the House of Commons.[58] Even so, no adjustment of policy took place. In part the Government's invulnerability lay in the protection afforded by adherence to non-intervention, which obviated any further positive action. The opposition on the other hand needed to present positive and convincing alternatives, and this they were never able to do.

Certainly as regards parliamentary opinion the Government did their best to ensure that unpopular decisions were taken during the parliamentary recess. But in the case of the suspension of the Anglo-Spanish Payments Agreement and of the appointment of the Agent to Nationalist Spain, as on other occasions, this proved impossible. Yet the Government suffered no insupportable opposition on these issues. This is not, however, to minimise the very considerable efforts of those who at the time endeavoured to keep the plight of Spain constantly before Parliament. To this end, for example, the all-party Parliamentary Committee for Spain was formed.[59] It proved resoundingly ineffectual. 'It didn't in fact accomplish much,' recalls the Rt. Hon. George Strauss, one of its most active members. 'Indeed I doubt whether it was ever anticipated that it would.'[60]

As to the national press, the Government's equanimity is even more remarkable. In general it was regarded as a reasonably tame creature, and one which could be manipulated without too much difficulty when necessary. Almost always the press responded well to Government directives such as that given by Eden in August to the Foreign Office 'to inspire our press to emphasise our wholehearted support of the French attitude more vigorously.'[61] Often the Government received unlooked-for support, even from the left-wing press.[62] Certainly *The Times* was brought to heel easily enough after complaints from Germany as to that paper's coverage of the Guernica story, which pointed initially to German responsibility,[63] and there are many other examples of Foreign Office or Cabinet intervention to be found in the archives.[64] Very occasionally *The Times* saw fit to ignore the guidance of the Foreign Office Press Department, and did so on the occasion of Lord Halifax's visit to Germany in November 1937.[65] But this was exceptional.[66]

The most notable instance of contemporary restraint by the press concerned events leading up to the abdication of Edward VIII.[67] Indeed, not long after, Ribbentrop was described by Sir Eric Phipps, then still Ambassador in Berlin, as 'depressed at the power of the British Government to mould public opinion'.[68] An even more striking example of press discipline was the elimination from the text of an interview between a *Daily Herald* reporter and the Duke of Windsor, of all reference to an alleged statement by the Duke that 'if the Labour Party wished and were in a position to offer it he would be prepared to be President of the English Republic'.[69] Naturally, outspoken and critical articles were the staple of the left-wing press. Indeed, the *Daily Herald* with a circulation of 2 million was regarded as 'a very clever propaganda newspaper'.[70] But there is little evidence that this or other papers were feared for specific articles on Government policy. Later, in 1938, the press became less compliant, and it was noted that the rôle of 'candid friend' was increasingly adopted.[71] Occasionally articles on Spain did succeed in penetrating Cabinet complacency,[72] but in general the Government did not feel threatened. The same is not true, however, of the foreign press, which was followed carefully by the Foreign Office. Articles in *Il Popolo di Roma*, for example, were frequently written by Mussolini himself and consequently aroused great interest.

Turning to other channels of communication, a similar picture emerges. Although the BBC was very careful to balance reports and talks on Spain, it was inevitably accused by supporters of both sides of bias,[73] a fact which might indicate true impartiality. Nevertheless, despite claims of disinterestedness the BBC was regarded by the Conservative Research Department as having 'a definite Left-wing bias'. So much so that it was suggested that a new Director-General should be appointed and other changes of staff made.[74] Certainly, a degree of control appears to have been exercised by the Government over broadcasting in regard both to the amount and to the content of the material broadcast. On 30 July 1936 Mr Walker of the News Section of the BBC assured the Foreign Office that 'if the BBC in fact carried a statement concerning the Consulate at Ceuta without consulting the Foreign Office, it was entirely an oversight and every care would be taken to avoid a recurrence.'[75] The following spring when negotiations with the insurgents for the appointment of an Agent were first under way, it was suggested in Cabinet that the sheer bulk of Spanish topics broadcast tended to keep the conflict before the public and that the BBC should therefore be asked to limit these.[76] Reduction of time spent on Spain, however, would have amounted to a serious form of censorship, denying the public information and discussion of a topic many considered to be of vital importance to Britain.

Similarly, in the absence of widespread television ownership 20 million members of the public[77] received their most graphic accounts of current affairs from newsreel shown in local cinemas. But there was little to be feared by the Conservative Party here, for Maj. Sir Joseph Ball, Head of the Conservative Research Department, had cultivated close personal contacts with the leaders of the British film industry, and was satisfied that he could 'count on them for full support to a reasonable degree'.[78] Here the readership of the *Daily Mail*, with a circulation of 1,579,000 in 1937,[79] joined viewers of British Movietone, for both were controlled by Lord Rothermere, whose newscasters invariably dubbed the Republican forces 'Reds' and the Nationalists 'anti-Reds'.[80] But the chief theme for all British newsreel companies was one of anti-war. 'Civil war in all its naked horror influences the whole of Spain,' thundered British Paramount.[81]

In this theme too lies one explanation for the comparative impotence of the Labour and trades union movements, for many members of these bodies were also staunch supporters of the Rev. Dick Sheppard's Peace Pledge Union.[82] Equally, the left's often equivocal attitude to Spain derived in part from the same ideological roots as the right. Speaking to Eden in August 1936, Arthur Greenwood let slip, to the discomfiture of his colleagues, that he too 'thought it possible that the outcome of this dispute would be a communist dictatorship in Spain'.[83]

Having hesitated initially to take firm action or even to display a united front against British Government policy, it became increasingly difficult to do so once non-intervention had become established. Once the Labour Party had endorsed non-intervention, albeit with reservations, at their Edinburgh Conference in September 1936,[84] no amount of calls for 'arms for Spain' nor torrents of Left Book Club tracts could convince the Government that left-wing opinion on Spain held any terrors for them. In fact, as the French Ambassador noted, the British Labour Party appeared to be 'not much interested' in Spain.[85] This remark is perhaps borne out by the remarkably little space afforded to this topic in his memoirs by the Leader of the Opposition, Clement Attlee,[86] despite his impassioned speeches to the House. Even the TUC was noted by the Cabinet for its 'very reasonable' attitude.[87]

For all its incompetence and lethargy the NIC had in this respect fulfilled its unpublicised aim rather better than its proclaimed purpose of preventing international strife. For although it inspired dislike and dissatisfaction, the very shambling vagueness of the NIC, as well as its veneer of international respectability, tended to sedate internal opposition and take 'the steam out of press insinuations which excite public opinion'.[88] This is not to argue that the Government did not watch domestic reaction to the Spanish question very carefully, for they did. Sir John Simon, the Home Secretary, warned the Cabinet in December 1936 that 'the Spanish Civil War is getting troublesome from a domestic point of view'.[89] It seems likely that in the matter of the appointment of an Agent, public opinion contributed a delaying effect and later helped prevent an award of belligerent rights to Franco. But in regard to both these aspects of British policy the loss of prestige that would have been involved in completely reversing a firmly adopted policy before the whole world constituted a far greater brake on Government pro-Nationalism. 'We have', noted Sir George Mounsay in April 1937, 'effectively burned our boats.'[90]

RECOGNITION OF FRANCO

While the Cabinet in the first half of 1938, despite slight misgivings of some of its members, demonstrated no signs of hesitation in its policy towards Spain, in the Foreign Office some indications of a change of attitude of the British representatives in Spain began to appear. This was in part a reflection of changes in Spain itself, and these were, from the Republican side, most striking in the almost Pauline conversion of the British representative, Mr John Leche. He admitted freely that at first he had believed that 'victory by the Reds would be in every way a disaster'. However, after the advent of Indalecio Prieto, War Minister from 1937,[91] his views had mellowed. He now believed there to be 'very few Russian elements'.[92]

> I believe (he wrote) that a complete victory by Franco would be disastrous for the peace of Europe – a similar victory by Barcelona might be equally disastrous. If Alvarez del Vayo and Négrin were to disappear we should probably have a representative republican and socialist government. Such a government would be prepared to negotiate.[93]

But despite Leche's derogatory dismissal of Negrín, political realities were fully recognised by the Spanish Premier and he no longer needed communist support as much as the communists needed him. From March 1938 Russian aid, which had in any case dropped dramatically after the Nyon Agreement, continued to decline after a short build-up at the beginning of the year.[94] The Republican Government had always been most anxious to gain the good offices of the democracies, and it was partly for their benefit that in April 1938 he issued the Thirteen Points, or aims of his government. These included: independence from foreign influence; a democratic republic elected by universal suffrage; respect for regional and civil liberties; freedom of worship; guarantees for private property; agrarian reform; social reform; support for the League; and a full amnesty to all those willing to co-operate in the reconstruction of Spain.[95]

The purpose of this declaration *vis-à-vis* international opinion was twofold. First it was to convince the democracies of the moderation of the Republican Government, and second, to convince them of the possibility of a negotiated peace. In June 1938 the latter was an objective which Vansittart strongly supported. He was not convinced that a victory for Franco was inevitable, and pointed out that in the last war the attitude of Spain to Britain had been very unsatisfactory, and the same classes hostile to Britain were now Franco's staunchest supporters.[96] Although at that time Vansittart's warning was dismissed, by the autumn there were many more supporters for his views.

Meanwhile a 'settlement of the Spanish question' was essential if the hoped-for ratification of the Anglo-Italian Agreement were to be achieved. Such a settlement would come either through a clear victory for one side or another – and in the summer of 1938, after a reversal for the Nationalists at the River Ebro, this still seemed far away[97] – or through a negotiated settlement. The latter had the advantage of seeming to offer some positive effort on the part of the British Government towards a solution without actually anta-gonising either side. This was a solution favoured not only by the French,[98] but also by Chamberlain who hoped to emulate his stepbrother Austen Chamberlain's success as a peacemaker. Thus it was that an international commission first mooted in the spring[99] and headed by Field-Marshall Sir Philip Chetwode arrived in Spain in September, with a view to negotiating an exchange of prisoners and mediating between the two parties.

Interestingly, Chetwode's appointment had initially been re-sisted by the Republicans on the grounds that as a Conservative and a military man he could not but be pro-Nationalist.[100] But like Leche and Stevenson he gave, and was widely reported as giving, a very different picture of the situation in Spain from the one expected. He was reported by the press as believing Franco's army to be 'ill-organised and inefficient' whereas the Republican army was 'so good that given equal numbers and good material it could smash Franco in a few months'.[101] Although Chetwode deprecated the advertisement of his views and the way in which they were expressed, his report to the Foreign Office was, in essence, very much on those lines.

His first impression of the Republican leaders was:

> . . . big men there are, really big men with brains, and the performance they have put up against Franco, helped as he has been by the Italians and Germans, is little short of marvellous. They started with literally nothing in the way of warlike equipment. Now they are fairly well provided as regards rifles, machine-guns and field artillery, but lack sufficient aeroplanes, tanks and other modern advantages.[102]

Indeed, Republican chances of holding out were now estimated to be fairly good. The military front was by then so shortened that troops could be concentrated on the remaining lines, destroying Nationalist hopes of an early breakthrough.

Thus, at first, the prospect of a negotiated peace seemed fairly bright.[103] Both sides were believed by the Foreign Office to be far closer politically than could ever have been imagined in 1936 or even 1937. Negrín not only had avowed his intention of living on good terms with Italy, but was reported to be prepared to repudiate his communist supporters if the democracies would aid the Republic.[104] Even more astonishing, perhaps, was the willingness he expressed to consider the restoration of the monarchy – a scheme which attracted a certain amount of attention in the Foreign Office,[105] where it was realised that there was little to distinguish the Falangist social reform programme from Negrín's own policies, and even the war aims of the two parties had much in common.[106]

Noting with surprise the atmosphere of moderation in Republican Spain, the new British Chargé, Ralph Skrine Stevenson, reported:

> The first thing that strikes an observer entering Government Spain is that the epithet 'red' has been vastly overworked. It is a magic word that has been a godsend to the Nationalist Propaganda Department. It conjures up the picture of an atmosphere of perpetual revolution, of brandished fists, of hammers and sickles, of constant incantation of the 'Internationale' and of mob law.[107]

During the last year, the Republican Government had adapted radically. War-weariness in Spain, the diversion of Russian attention to the Far East and indeed to her own borders, encouraged Republican thoughts of peace, although not, Leche thought, 'peace at any price'.[108]

It had seemed as though similar goodwill existed on the Nationalist side, too, for Franco made no objection to the appointment of Francis Hemming, Secretary of the Non-Intervention Committee, as head of a commission to investigate the problem of withdrawal of volunteers in order to expedite, if need be, a grant of belligerent rights to Franco. Ratification of the Anglo-Italian Agreement was unthinkable while British ships were being bombed by the Nationalist navy, which was believed in Britain to receive assistance from Italy. If volunteers were withdrawn, then under the British Plan accepted by the NIC belligerent rights could be awarded to Franco and one more obstacle towards Anglo-Italian rapprochement removed. After the Munich Conference in September, at which Mussolini had made no secret of his weariness of the Spanish problem and Hitler had disclaimed all territorial ambitions, the time had seemed ripe for an international commission, and the concept of a one led by Hemming was supported by five of the major NIC powers, Britain, France, Italy, Germany and Portugal. Russia alone had objected.[109]

From Hodgson's reports it is all too clear what went wrong:

> Burgos did not take kindly to the manner in which the approach was made to them by the five Powers. They were asked whether they were prepared to discuss matters with the General Secretary of the NIC and suddenly found themselves confronted with a numerous delegation. At that particular moment the idea that the Munich Agreement was likely to be followed by an attempt of the Powers to impose peace on Spain by mediation had almost assumed a mania. They are quite convinced of their own righteousness and ability to win, provided they get that which they have a right to – belligerent rights. They do not consider themselves called upon to make concessions.[110]

Certainly belligerent rights had now become as much an obsession with Nationalists of all kinds as they were already with the Nationalist navy:

> They do not know what belligerent rights are – what, for instance, would be contraband – but the two words have become a sort of talisman to cure all ills, make all paths straight . . . The Republican fleet in being is not nearly so great a deterrent as the helpless feeling produced by the absence of belligerent rights.[111]

Hodgson was not alone in his assessment of the damage done by the presumptions of the great powers in thinking to arrange the fate of Spain. Chetwode, too, complained of the way in which the press of Europe discussed the powers' decision to 'stop the war in Spain'.[112] On 10 November he was received by Franco, but was able to make little progress in the exchange of prisoners. The Republican Government had arranged to suspend all death sentences pronounced before 1 September 1938 on a basis of reciprocity. Franco on the other hand refused to give any such undertaking, claiming that his were common-law prisoners, whereas those whose sentences had been commuted by the Government were political. He also claimed that 33 per cent of those condemned in his territory normally received clemency. However, at that time Chetwode believed that large numbers of prisoners, many of whom were prisoners of war, had been executed.[113] Yet, lest negotiations at Burgos should be hampered, the Republic was asked not to publicise its own clemency.[114] Comparison of Republican liberality with Nationalist brutality was to be avoided at all costs if the effect of the commission as an exercise in public relations in Britain itself was not to be entirely lost. However, the success or failure of the commission was soon to become irrelevant in post-Munich Europe.

In the summer, relative abundance of food had temporarily helped Republican morale. With the onset of winter, the food shortage in Republican territory gave the relatively well-fed Nationalists an additional advantage. In Catalonia there was a marked increase in scurvy and rickets. Birth-weight of infants was down by an average of 15 ounces. Ralph Stevenson noted, too, the 'pinched faces and uncanny quietness of the children'.[115] As Republicans starved, a terrible propaganda campaign was waged against Barcelona. Nationalist aeroplanes bombarded the hungry population of the city with small loaves wrapped in brown paper bags bearing the inscription:

Toda es mentira en las propagandas rojas.
Este es el pan de cada dia en España de Franco.[116]
(There is no truth in red propaganda.
This is the daily bread ration in Franco's Spain.)

In October Negrín asked France and Britain for aid, suggesting that if it were forthcoming he 'could and would suppress the Communist Party in a week'. The arms he specified were: 500,000 rifles, 12,000 machine-guns, 1,600 field guns, 200 light and meeium tanks, 300 bombers and 300 fighters. With these he could, he claimed, finish the war by April.[117] The aid was not forthcoming, and any hopes that it would be were dashed when, in mid-November, the Anglo-Italian Agreement was ratified and arrangements went ahead for the Prime Minister and Foreign Secretary to visit Rome in the new year.

War-weariness now gripped the Republic, although Negrín declared himself to be determined to continue at least until Franco could be persuaded to announce a reasonably liberal programme and a measure of mercy for his opponents. But, although the Premier himself was described as 'as combative as ever', dissensions within the Republican Government grew. In December it was reported that the Government had 'had a transport aeroplane standing by for months past to take them to safety whenever they felt the moment had come'.[118]

Nevertheless, before the departure for Rome of Chamberlain and Halifax the Foreign Office went through the motions of reviewing Anglo-Spanish policy. Now that even the Cabinet accepted that the outcome of a Republican victory was no longer likely to result in a 'communist régime', the advantages of a compromise solution increased in attraction, and Walter Roberts recommended that the British Government should seek a compromise if no military decision were reached in the near future. The outlook for an armistice was not good, but he thought it worth asking Mussolini to use his influence with Franco to advise on local autonomy for the Basques and Catalans. Similarly Mussolini might agree to approach the Papacy with a view to reconciliation with the Republic.[119] These suggestions were never more than remote possibilities. On returning from Rome the Prime Minister, who described Mussolini as having 'a strong sense of humour and an attractive smile', told the Cabinet that Italian philosophy was dictated by the belief that General Franco would pull off a quick success. It was admitted that in some quarters it would be felt that there was 'no reason why the French should be bluffed out of action which they had a perfect right to take and that a continuance of the war in Spain would weaken Italy', but this view was not held by the Cabinet.[120]

Yet it seems likely that Halifax, at least, was not as convinced as his chief, for at his request Coulson drew up a memorandum on the pros and cons of revising policy in Spain, examining once more whether or not Britain should abandon non-intervention. But the arguments had not changed. It was recognised at last that non-intervention 'probably benefits Franco', and that the Spanish Republic had now sent away all her volunteers, and that to scrap non-intervention would 'probably benefit the Spanish Government'. Yet if that were done a grant of belligerent rights would have to be made.

From an international point of view there were other criteria to be considered. The very costly scheme would come to an end, and there would be no more 'bickering about broken promises or bad faith'. The danger was that the French and Portuguese would open their frontiers and there would be an immediate escalation of tension. From the British point of view, the Opposition would welcome an end to non-intervention but would attack the attendant award of belligerent rights. Nothing would therefore be gained. There remained the question of short-term help to the Spanish Republic, but again this would bring retaliation with all its dangers. As to giving positive aid to Franco, though this would be welcomed by some interests, the French would not co-operate except under considerable pressure, and this would inevitably lead to a rift. Coulson therefore concluded that a reversal of policy was a dangerous way of securing Franco's victory and it would be better to let matters continue, as Franco appeared to be winning.[121]

Meanwhile, from Spain both Stevenson and Hodgson counselled caution and a compromise solution. Stevenson suggested that the British Government should publicly recognise the political evolution of the Republican Government, and should acknowledge that the danger of a communist Spain, if it had ever existed, was now a thing of the past. Moreover, with the Republic's slight bias towards the democracies an ultimate decision in favour of the Republic would, he argued, be in the interests of Britain. His views were dismissed by the British Chargé d'Affaires at Hendaye, Owen O'Malley, who predictably believed that early recognition of Franco was essential if Britain were to obtain 'an ally and play a large part in the reconstruction of Spain'.[122] By now Hodgson, who was in a better position to judge than the Chargé, was by no means sure that this was any longer possible and expressed his foreboding that Italy and Germany would extract payment for their services to Spain at the end of the war. Foreign Office opinion, however, was still fairly solidly in support of the views of O'Malley,[123] although both Sir Alexander Cadogan and Vansittart admitted to doubts on the wisdom of British Government policy.[124]

Suddenly, with a decisive advance by General Yagüe, Nationalist troops entered Barcelona on 26 January, and the end of the war did indeed seem to be in sight. As they advanced the Nationalists took possession of arms and military equipment worth some 200 million gold pesetas. This, according to Major Edmund Mahoney, Assistant Military Attaché at Burgos, included 800 lorries loaded with arms and war material; 1,000 new machine-guns still in their boxes; 600 railway wagons loaded with war material; 70 pieces of artillery unused at the front; 15 million litres of petrol; 100

aeroplanes in their crates; and material for 200 tanks. Much of it was material sent by France in answer to Negrín's previous plea for arms, but had arrived too late to be used. 'French policy *vis-à-vis* Spain', commented Vansittart, 'has been a tragedy of errors'.[125]

Apparently undaunted, on 2 February Negrín pleaded for arms in one last bid to save the Republic, claiming that if he could procure 60,000 more rifles and 2,000–3,000 more machine-guns he could hold out indefinitely in north Catalonia, but without them it could be only a matter of weeks, even of days. Two days later, Stevenson, who was in the border town of Amélie-les-Bains, received a message from the President of the Republic, Manuel Azaña, claiming that Negrín had tried to prevent him from seeing the British representative, and that he was now at complete variance with his premier. He begged Britain and France to intervene in a mediatory capacity.[126]

On 5 February, Azaña, Companys and Aguirre, the Catalan and Basque leaders together with other Republican ministers, crossed into France. On 7 February, Negrín himself admitted defeat and informed Stevenson that he would agree to a cessation of hostilities on condition of a formal declaration by General Franco that Spain would be completely independent; that the Spanish people would be free to choose their own form of government; and that there would be no reprisals, and political and military leaders would be evacuated (these were estimated at several thousands). If these conditions were not met, then the Government would continue until crushed.[127]

The situation on the Franco-Spanish border was now one of chaos, with an estimated 5,000 refugees streaming across the border every hour.[128] Telegraph facilities were also affected, and the Foreign Office did not receive Stevenson's account of the week's happenings until 13 February. Meanwhile, Franco had announced his intention to proceed with 'the greatest of clemency' towards those who had committed no crimes.[129] This was, of course, as the British Cabinet recognised,[130] a statement of the greatest ambiguity, since Franco himself was to be the arbiter of what constituted a crime.

On examining the Republican peace proposals, Montagu Pollock minuted: 'Although HMG do not wish to be drawn into the role of mediator, the three conditions laid down by Dr Negrín are ones with which they cannot fail to sympathise.'[131] Here, however, he was mistaken, for not all shared his view. John Coulson, for example, described the proposals as 'blackmail': 'If we support the Spanish Government proposals with General Franco, we get into a position of making ourselves responsible for them, if not, we are responsible for their continued resistance.' Yet after much consideration, and discussions on 13 and 14 February with Azcárate, Hodgson was instructed to convey Negrín's conditions to General Franco.[132] The reply, if reply it was – for it was not clear from the corrupt text of the telegram whether it was intended as an answer or was merely quoted from a public declaration – was unrelenting: 'Nationalist Spain had won the war'. Unconditional surrender was demanded.[133]

Diplomatic activity now reached a peak. There had been, and remained, one very cogent reason for Britain to delay recognition of Franco and to press the Republic's peace formula, as Halifax had explained to his Cabinet colleagues:

> . . . if we could avoid the political misrepresentation which would attend early recognition of General Franco's Government without incurring any serious delay, we should do so. If it should prove possible to persuade the Republican Government to stop fighting of their own volition, this would greatly ease the difficulties in the way of recognition.[134]

Already, the Cabinet learned, the French were in consultation with General Franco and proposed sending a representative, M. Léon Béraud, to Burgos to conduct negotiations. If his proposals were accepted, the simultaneous recognition by France and Britain would follow. Halifax's proposal to persuade Franco to refrain from reprisals in accordance with the Republican demands met with approval from the Chancellor, who believed it would strengthen the Government's hand when it came to recognition. However, the Cabinet agreed to recognise Franco in the near future, if possible in accordance with the Spanish Government's proposals, but 'if the Spanish Government authorities proved obdurate and negotiations were prolonged it might be necessary for recognition of General Franco's Government to precede a cessation of hostilities.'[135] There was, in any case, no question of awaiting the fall of Madrid, for Franco had let it be known that he did not intend to enter that city until he was in a position to provision its inhabitants.[136]

On 16 February, the day following the Cabinet meeting, Halifax saw Azcárate who informed him that the only condition his

Government now insisted upon was the last of the three, i.e. that there should be no reprisals. A telegram was drafted to this effect and discussed with Alvarez del Vayo, the Spanish Foreign Minister who was currently in Paris. He believed that so important a decision must be put to the Prime Minister, and duly tried to locate Negrín.[137] However, in view of the French negotiations, time was short, and Halifax warned Azcárate that definite consent from Negrín to send the telegram must be received by the date of the next Cabinet meeting fixed for 22 February. In the event Negrín could not be found,[138] and his confirmatory reply was not received until 25 February.[139]

The British Cabinet had now Franco's firm demand for unconditional surrender, but equally had his protestation that he would act with clemency. With the exception of Negrín who could not be located, major Republican political figures had left Spain. The Spanish capital was still bravely defended, but it was known that separate negotiations between Madrid and Burgos with a view to a negotiated peace had been under way since the end of January.[140] Sickened by the defeatism of many members of the Republican Government, Col. Casado, Commander of the Army of the Centre in Madrid, was determined to secure his own settlement with Burgos,[141] and his activities further fragmented the remaining authority of the Republic. Moreover, the French negotiations by Béraud were now under way. On 20 February, the Spanish Ambassador, despairing of an early answer from Negrín, had said that 'as he could not assure us that the action which we proposed to take would have the support of his Government, the best course would be that we should act on our own initiative.[142]

For all these reasons, therefore, a telegram was dispatched to the British Ambassador in Paris indicating that Britain wished to recognise the Nationalist Government without delay, and in any case no later than 24 February.[143] In the event the French replied that they could not recognise Franco by the 24th, and asked for a postponement of British recognition until 27th. To this the British Government agreed, despite the embarrassment of a 'leak' in Paris of their intentions. Thus on 27 February the British Government was at last able to grant to General Franco full recognition, although a grant of belligerent rights, as such, was never made.

Almost immediately the machinery of the NIC began to be dismantled. As early as January the Portuguese had made known their intention to cease to contribute their share of the expense of

maintaining British observers on the Portuguese frontier.[144] From 1
February the respective contributions of the powers had been
reduced from £5,000 per month to £1,250 per month.[145] Some
members had already left the committee, and the Chairman of the
Board, Admiral Van Dulm, had resigned his post after disagreement with Hemming in November 1938. Disbandment of the
Observation Scheme began on 3 March 1939. In fact, although
observers had remained at their posts, only the Gibraltar frontier
had been actively manned since the summer of 1937. The final
meeting of the NIC was held on 20 April 1939, but was attended by
only twenty-one countries. At that meeting a resolution was
adopted releasing the governments represented on the Non-
Intervention Committee from their obligations. It then remained
only to distribute the residual funds.[146]

EPILOGUE

Ultimately the recognition of Franco long favoured by the British
Government was an essentially pragmatic move, for there was by
February 1939 little alternative. France was eager to recognise, and
America, too, was considering her position. It is impossible to say
what effect earlier recognition would have had on Anglo-Spanish
relations during the coming years, but the difficulties encountered
by British diplomats resulting from the tardiness of the concession
have been well documented.[147]

Although in theory Franco remained neutral throughout the
Second World War, this did not preclude his sending the 'Blue
Division' of 47,000 Falangists to fight for Hitler on the Russian
front.[148] More serious for the Allies, however, was the inevitable
insecurity to which the uncertainty of Spanish policy during the
continued presence of German and Italian advisers gave rise. This
was precisely the kind of position against which the Chiefs of Staff
had warned in August 1936. Then it had been said that Britain
should remain on friendly or at worst neutral terms with whichever
power emerged victorious. Thus, by pursuing a policy of non-
intervention which was on balance favourable to a Nationalist
victory, the British Government had achieved in three years only
the lesser of the strategic objectives set by the Chiefs of Staff.

Foreign policy may be formulated on the basis of many
considerations, including, for example, economic, political, social

or strategic factors, and usually will be an amalgam of several such. From the first outbreak of war in Spain, there were many from all points of the political spectrum who argued that where policy towards Spain was concerned, strategic considerations should rank uppermost, and that the gate to the Mediterranean at Gibraltar and the lines of communication between southern France and North Africa should be kept open. From a purely British point of view, it was unfortunate that the strategic case, which was an impressive one, should have been clouded by political and ideological pressures from both left and right. Having read and interpreted the Chiefs' of Staff recommendations in accordance with a non-interventionary policy, the strategic issues of Spanish policy were rarely considered *per se* by the Cabinet. That Spain should have excited emotions was found distressing and even slightly puzzling, especially in March 1938 when diplomatic attention was focused on Czechoslovakia.[149] Yet however emotional or instinctive preoccupation with Spain may have been, it also made strategic sense, for Spain, bounded as it was by two British allies, could far more easily be defended and provided, therefore, a much more logical point of confrontation than Czechoslovakia.

Myopia on the subject of Spain was not confined to the Cabinet but extended to the Foreign Office as well. Only in the last months of the Spanish Civil War did Cadogan admit that were it possible he would then have 'plumped for a Barcelona victory'.[150] Even Vansittart, whose views on policy towards Italy and Germany were relatively straightforward, had not fully grasped the strategic issues involved in the Spanish Civil War until mid-1938.[151] In January 1939 he wrote to Halifax expressing his deep concern at the results which policy towards Spain was producing. That month Daladier had refused the Republican Government arms on the grounds that it 'was impossible owing to the attitude of HMG'. The French Premier's remark, suggested Vansittart, was ominous. He reminded his colleague that although the Prime Minister had denied in the House of Commons that any pressure had been put on the French Government to close their frontier in June 1938, documentary evidence existed that the Government, through Phipps, had done just that. More recently Halifax had telegraphed from Rome a record of his advice to the Italians to 'refrain from advertising more than necessary the help they were giving Franco'. This would be taken, Vansittart believed, as 'an invitation *à la valse*'. He continued: 'The whole course of our policy on non-intervention has in reality, as we all know, worked in an entirely one-sided manner, and has been putting a premium on Franco's victory.' He now could 'conceive of nothing more certain to make our already very precarious position well nigh untenable in the future'.[152] If British policy, which had so clearly been aimed at a Nationalist victory, did not turn out to have been in Britain's interests or even in the interests of France, lies or wilful misrepresentations to the House of Commons would bring the Government into disrepute. Belatedly, Vansittart was moving towards the position taken by Laurence Collier, who as early as December 1936 had argued that not only was British policy towards Spain wrong on strategic grounds, but it would ultimately alienate the electorate.[153]

But how grave was the strategic danger? One of the most respected military strategists in both military and civilian circles was Capt. Basil Liddell Hart. From 1936 on, at every possible opportunity, in lectures to the Staff College and in the articles he wrote regularly for *The Times* as their military correspondent, Liddell Hart pressed the view that a victory for Franco in which Italy or Germany had any part would be a disaster for the democracies. Throughout this period his constant theme was: 'It is folly for us to allow any sympathies we may have for one side or the other in the Spanish conflict to blind us to strategic dangers which imperil the British Empire, as well as France.'[154]

For those who shared his views, questions asked in the House of Commons on the positioning of heavy howitzers on concrete platforms within range of Gibraltar were disquieting. It was alleged that these guns had been positioned under German supervision, although at the time this was denied by Eden. The House of Commons was assured that the matter received 'constant attention',[155] but this is a statement the historian cannot yet verify satisfactorily as Gibraltar remains an area of sensitivity for the British Government.

The Spanish Civil War ended on 1 April 1939, and only then did Cabinet and Foreign Office appear to become aware of the full import of their policy towards Spain, of the advantages which had thereby accrued to Germany, and the commensurate disadvantages which Britain now faced. Yet the dictators had made no secret of their interest in a Nationalist victory[156] nor of the military and strategic benefits they had gained. Indeed, in June 1938 General von Reichenau, the Commander of the Fourth Army at Leipzig, had addressed Nazi leaders on just this subject. Claiming that

Germany had been strengthened by her intervention, Reichenau described Spain as a military staff college. Nor, he claimed, was the Spanish war a second-class war, but a test of strength of a modern kind. On the basis of experience in Spain an entirely new air arm had been built, although in 1936 aviation had, he averred, been Germany's Achilles' heel. Other lessons had been gained in infantry, and in the uses of motor vehicles. In addition, Spain had indicated new ways of organising and employing Intelligence. Last but not least, Germany held 'a favourable position at one of the crucial points of the Mediterranean basin'.[157]

Although the General's speech was by no means an overstatement of the situation, the general consensus in the Foreign Office was that the address had been an 'exercise in propaganda rather than a statement of policy'. It was also remarked that German popularity was on the wane in Spain.[158] Certainly this latter point was true. But it would not prove easy for Franco to dislodge his allies. Moreover, it did not mean that the British would prove any more popular, as British representatives, Sir Maurice Peterson[159] and Sir Samuel Hoare[160] were later to testify. The British Government had always hoped that economic necessity would drive Spain to seek aid for reconstruction from Britain, and in the spring and summer of 1939 endeavours to improve commercial relations with a view to strengthening ties with Spain were continued.

As early as May, however, British hopes suffered a serious setback. With a deteriorating international situation, British Government options in seeking allies were very limited. Faced with the expansionist policies of Germany, the Chiefs of Staff were asked to report on 'the balance of strategic value in war as between Spain as an enemy and Russia as an ally'.[161] That it was ever necessary to face such a choice was the direct result of British policy towards Spain over the previous three years. Franco's whole aim had been to rid Spain of communism, and on 26 March 1939 Spain adhered to the Anti-Comintern Pact. If Britain now opted for Russia as an ally, her chances of reconciliation with Franco would be very slim indeed.

Although it was conceded that the Spaniards were war-weary and could be put under considerable pressure if need be by a blockade, the disadvantages to Britain and France of the entry of Spain into the war as an enemy were listed thus:

1. The naval facilities at Gibraltar might be made largely or even wholly unusable by land and air bombardment, and as a result our control of the Straits would be threatened.

2. German and Italian submarines and aircraft operating from Spanish territory including the Balearic and Canary Islands would add greatly to the difficulties of protecting our own sea communications in the Atlantic, and French communications between North Africa and France, the more so if the Meditterranean route were already closed.

3. Air attack could be brought to bear on the French bases in North Africa, the use of which by allied naval forces, if Gibraltar were not available, would be essential for the control of the western Mediterranean. Without the use of these bases it would be difficult to interrupt Italian trade from the Atlantic.

4. Furthermore, the important French armament industries in the south of France at Toulouse, the mouth of the Gironde, and at Tarbes would be menaced by air attack from Spain. In view of the shortage of their fighter aircraft, the French take a serious view of this possibility.

5. The Biscayan ports which would be used by the British Field Force and French formations from Africa would be within range of air attack from northern Spain.

6. A French offensive from Tunisia against Libya would be delayed until French communications had been secured by the removal of the threat from Spanish Morocco.[162]

These were precisely the dangers which many, including Liddell Hart and Mme Geneviève Tabouis[163] had been publicising for years. Constrained by political considerations from following a pro-Franco policy, the British Government refused to follow a pro-Republican one.[164] It was maintained by the Foreign Office that such a course would 'split England from top to bottom', yet it has since been admitted that the policy of non-intervention did precisely that anyway.[165] It is of course understood that the National Government of Britain would never have sent arms to the Spanish Government. Yet had Britain simply maintained the unilateral policy of non-intervention which she at first adopted in July 1936, and refrained from putting pressure on France, the outcome of the Civil War might well have been very different. Mussolini and Hitler would have been less inclined to pursue their initial backing of Franco, and it is unlikely that they would have become as deeply committed to a Nationalist victory as happened in November 1936. In that event a Republican victory would have been possible. But even failing an outright victory, it is likely that the Republic could have held out until World War II began, or have at least come to a favourable compromise settlement.[166]

British policy was not directed from economic interest, except in the very broadest sense of a logical wish to see capitalism triumph over communism, and the improvement of trade and commerce with the Nationalist Government was above all a political objective. However, the re-negotiation of the Anglo-Spanish Payments Agreement of 1936 was as positive and tacit an indication of the British Government attitude towards the Nationalist cause as the sending of an Agent to Nationalist Spain at the end of 1937, or of full recognition of Franco in 1939. So enthusiastic a pursuit of the re-establishment of economic relations with Franco was an indication of the Government's belief in the political expediency of her policy, not a measure of economic necessity. Because the Republic with Soviet and French help was able to put up such strong resistance, the outcome of the war was never sufficiently certain for the British Government to overlook the Chiefs' of Staff warning that it was necessary to remain on good, or at least neutral, terms with whichever side emerged victorious, and their support of the NIC represented an acknowledgment of this. But by turning a blind eye both to the intervention of the dictators and to the need for firm protection of British shipping to Spain the British Government aided Franco as decisively as if it had sent arms to him. By working actively for the policy of multilateral non-intervention, by shoring up the NIC throughout its inglorious existence, and by applying acute pressure to the French Government to conform to British policy, a strategic position of potential danger was created at a time when Britain was at her most vulnerable.

Appendix A Senior Officials of the Foreign Office, 1936–38[1]

Appointed

* Rt. Hon. Anthony Eden, MC, MP (Secretary of State for Foreign Affairs)   22 Dec. 1935

Sir Robert Gilbert Vansittart, GCMG, KCB, MVO (Permanent Under-Secretary of State)   1 Jan. 1930

* Viscount Cranborne, ·MP (Parliamentary Under-Secretary of State)   5 Aug. 1935

Rt. Hon. the Earl of Plymouth (Parliamentary Under-Secretary of State)   1 Sept. 1936

Capt. Rt. Hon. Euan Wallace, MC, MP (Additional Parliamentary Under-Secretary of State)   28 Nov. 1935

* Halifax's appointment as Foreign Secretary announced 25 February 1938.
* R. A. Butler's appointment as Parliamentary Under-Secretary announced 25 February 1938.

Deputy Under-Secretaries of State

Hon. Sir Alexander M. G. Cadogan, KCMG, CB   1 Oct. 1936

Sir Lancelot Oliphant, KCMG, CB (Superintending Under-Secretary, Eastern Department)   1 Mar.

216

Appointed

Assistant Under-Secretaries of State

Sir George Augustus Mounsey, KCMG, CB,
  OBE   15 July 1929
Sir Orme Garton Sargent, KCMG, CB
  (Superintending Under-Secretary, Central
  Department)   14 Aug. 1933
Sir Robert Leslie Craigie, KCMG, CB   15 Jan. 1935
Charles Howard Smith, CMG (Principal
  Establishment Officer)   22 Aug. 1933
Sir Frederick G. A. Butler, KCMG, CB
  (Finance Officer)   22 Aug.

Sir Herbert William Malkin, GCMG, CB,
  KC (Legal Adviser)   1 Oct. 1929
William Eric Beckett, CMG (Second Legal
  Adviser)   1 Oct.
Gerald Gray Fitzmaurice (Third Legal
Adviser)   6 Nov.
Montague Shearman, OBE (Claims Adviser)   1 Oct.

Counsellors (in order of appointment to Counsellors' posts)
Charles William Orde, CMG   15 July 1929
George Nevile Maltby Bland, CMG   14 Nov.
Ronald Ion Campbell, CB, CMG   19 May 1930
George William Rendel, CMG   1 Oct.
William Strang, CMG   1 July 1932
Laurence Collier, CMG   1 Nov.
David John Montagu-Douglas-Scott, CMG   14 Apr. 1933
Owen St. Clair O'Malley, CMG   2 Aug.
Reginald Wildig Allen Leeper, CMG, CBE   22 Aug.
Frank Trelawny Arthur Ashton-Gwatkin,
  CMG   17 July 1934
Oliver Charles Harvey (Private Secretary to
  the Secretary of State)   21 Jan. 1936
Walter St. Clair Howland Roberts, MC
  (Acting)   2 Oct.
Ralph Clarmont Skrine Stevenson (Acting)   1 Jan. 1937

The League of Nations and Western Department

Departments and Superintending Under-Secretaries	Clerks	Distribution of business	Head
	D. F. Howard, MC	League of Nations	W. St. C. Roberts MC (Who succeeded Sir Horace Seymour in September 1936)
Hon. Sir A. Cadogan, KCMG, CB	W. H. Montagu-Pollock R. M. Makins C. A. E. Shuckburgh A. E. Lambert	Portugal, Spain, Morocco, New Hebrides	
Sir G. Mounsey, KCMG, CB	I. P. Garran D. D. Maclean C. H. Johnston	General	
	A. F. Orchard (Economic Relations) H. M. G. Jebb A. E. L. Parnis* F. T. Campion	Economic Relations	F. T. A. Ashton-Gwatkin, CMG

* Of the Consular Service.

Appendix B Spanish Cabinet formed on 4 September 1936[2]

Prime Minister and Minister of War	Francisco Largo Caballero (Socialist)
Minister of State	Julio Alvarez del Vayo (Socialist)
Minister of Marine and Air	Indalecio Prieto Tuero (Socialist)
Minister of Interior	Angel Galarza Gago (Socialist)
Minister of Finance	Juan Negrin Lopez (Socialist)
Minister of Agriculture	Vicente Uribe Galdeano (Communist)
Minister of Public Instruction	Jesus Hernandez Tomas (Communist)
Minister of Public Works	Manuel de Iyujo* (Basque nationalist)
Minister of Justice	Mariano Ruiz Funes (Republican Left)
Minister of Industry and Commerce	Anastasio de Gracia (Socialist)
Minister of Communications	Bernardo Giner de los Rios (Republican Union)
Minister of Labour	José Tomás y Piera (Esquerra de Cataluna)
Minister without Portfolio	Hosé Giral y Pereira (Republican Left)

* Appointed on 25th September.

Appendix C British Consular Representation in Spain 15 June 1937[3]

Barcelona	Consul-General	N. King, KCMG (1937)
Gandia	Vice-Consul	F. Romaguera
Palma	Consul	Lt.-Cmdr A. Hillgarth, RN (retd), OBE
San Feliu de Guixols	Acting Vice-Consul	J. Boada
Tarragona	Vice-Consul	I. Navarro
Bilbao (fell to Nationalists, 19 June 1937)	Consul	R. C. Stevenson (left 15 June 1937)
San Sebastian	Acting Vice-Consul	E. M. Golding
Santander (fell to Nationalists, 23 August 1937	Consul	T. Bates, OBE (but under instructions to leave)
Madrid	Acting Consul	J. H. Milanes, MVO
Malaga	Acting Consul	J. G. Clissold, OBE
Almeria and Adra	Vice-Consul	M. R. Harrison
Cartagena	Pro-Consul in charge	W. Leverkus
Linares	Vice-Consul	H. C. Holberton
Seville	Consul	F. G. Coultas
Algeciras	Vice-Consul	E. G. Beckingsale
Cadiz	Acting Vice-Consul	R. A. Black
Huelva	Vice-Consul	Capt. J. Morrison
Jerez de la Frontera	Vice-Consul	Capt. G. D. Williams, MC
La Linea	Vice-Consul	Capt. A. J. Patron

Corunna	Acting Consul	H. Guyatt, MBE
Vigo	Acting Vice-Consul	P. Cairns
Gijon (fell to Nationalists, 21 October 1937)	Acting Vice-Consul	J. Lovelace
Valencia	Consul	W. J. Sullivan

Appendix D Dates of Adherence of Countries to Non-Intervention Agreement[4]

	Date of reply to French Government	Effective date of measures
Albania	31 August	
Austria	28 August	
Belgium	21 August	Licensing system introduced 19 August. Effective presumably from 21 August.
Bulgaria	27 August	Decree of 31 August.
Czechoslovakia	22 August	
Denmark	21 August	21 August.
Estonia	3 September	10 September.
Finland	31 August	Arms embargo in force 31 August. Aircraft legislation to be introduced.
France	15 August	15 August.
Germany	27 August	Measures announced 24 August.
Greece	27 August	
Hungary	31 August	
Irish Free State	25 August	
Italy	21 August	28 August.
Latvia	27 August	
Lithuania	28 August	Licence system introduced 27 August; in force 28 August.
Luxemburg	2 September	
Netherlands	24 August	24 August.
Norway	26 August	
Poland	27 August	Measures in force from outset of Civil War.

	Date of Reply to French Government	Effective date of measures
Portugal	21 August	27 August.
Romania	18 August	Published in *Gazette* 5 September.
Sweden	20 August	
Switzerland		Measures 14 and 21 August.
Turkey	28 August	28 August.
USSR	23 August	28 August.
United Kingdom	15 August	
Yugoslavia	23 August	Embargo in force in practice from about 6 September, pending promulgation of decrees.

Appendix E Outline of Main Work of the Technical Advisory Sub-Committees[5]

Technical Advisory Sub-Committee No. 1
To report on the supervision of aircraft
entering Spain by air   November 1936

Technical Advisory Sub-Committee No. 2
To report on the technical aspects of the
proposal for the establishment of a system of supervision over the land and sea
frontiers of Spain and the Spanish
dependencies   December 1936

Technical Advisory Sub-Committee No. 3
To report on:
The problem of the entry of foreign nationals into Spain for the purpose of taking
service in the civil war   December 1936
Methods of securing the supervision of the
application of the Non-Intervention Agreement in the case of vessels proceeding
to Spain and the Spanish dependencies   January 1937
The international supervision of the fron-
tiers of the countries limitrophe to Spain   January 1937
Possible modifications in the naval obser-
vation system   June 1937
Review of the suggestions for restoring and
strengthening the Observation Scheme
contained in the Van Dulm-Hemming
Report   December 1937

The question whether the Naval Patrol
System should be restored, and the proposal for the stationing of neutral officers
in Spanish ports

December 1937

Review of the suggestions for restoring and
strengthening the Observation Scheme
contained in the Van Dulm-Hemming
Report

February 1938

Technical Advisory Sub-Committee No. 4

To report on the possibility of extending the
Non-Intervention Agreement to cover
the supply of financial aid to either of the
parties in Spain

January 1937

Technical Advisory Sub-Committee No. 5

To report on the grant in certain circumstances of belligerent rights to the two
parties in Spain

November 1937

Technical Advisory Sub-Committee No. 6

To report on measures necessary for the
extension of the Non-Intervention Agreement in order to include in the plan
the withdrawal of foreign volunteers
from Spain

November 1937

Committee of Jurists

To report on the import into members'
respective countries of Spanish capital
assets

April 1937

Appendix F List of Instances of Mussolini's Public Congratulations to Franco[6]

1. On the occasion of the entry of General Franco's forces into Bilbao in June 1937, Mussolini sent a telegram to Franco in the course of which he stated: 'I wish to express to Your Excellency my warmest felicitations on the great enterprise which has reunited for the country of Spain one of its noblest provinces and which marks a gigantic step forward towards the full triumph of the National cause.'

2. In August 1937 on the fall of Santander.

3. In October 1937, on the first anniversary of General Franco's assumption of the headship of the state, Mussolini addressed to him a telegram which included the following sentence: 'In the name of Fascist Italy which has followed with passionate solidarity these heroic events, I add the most fervent wishes for the complete triumph of the Nationalist Spanish cause as personified by Your Excellency.'

4. In his speech delivered at Genoa on 14 May 1938, Mussolini said: 'They [the French] desire the victory of Barcelona, we on the other hand desire, and mean to see, the victory of Franco.'

5. In conversation with Lord Perth on 20 June 1938, Count Ciano said: 'Franco trusted Signor Mussolini and Signor Mussolini would stand by him.' He also said that once Mussolini had given his friendship he would stand by his friend to the last resort.

6. In July 1938, on the occasion of the second anniversary of the Spanish National Movement Mussolini stated in a telegram to General Franco: 'Fascist Italy is proud of having contributed . . . to your victory over the destructive forces of Spain and Europe.'

7. When the 10,000 Italian legionaries left Spain on 15 October 1938 Mussolini sent a telegram to General Franco stating: 'I wish to assure you that Fascist Italy remains and will remain in brotherly sympathy with you, and fervently desiring your victory.'

Appendix G Committee of Imperial Defence, Chiefs' of Staff Sub-committee Report[7]: Balance of Strategical Value in War as between Spain as an Enemy and Russia as an Ally

We have been asked to give our views as a matter of great urgency on the balance of strategical value in war as between Spain as an enemy and Russia as an ally.

   2. We make our report in the following form:
- (a) Disadvantages to Great Britain and France of the entry of Spain into the war as an enemy.
- (b) The advantages to Great Britain and France of an alliance with Russia.
- (c) Other aspects.
- (d) Conclusions.

Spain

   3. If Spain was allied in war to Germany and Italy, the following strategic disadvantages would ensue for Great Britain and France.

   4. The naval facilities at Gibraltar might be made largely or even wholly unusable by land and air bombardment, and as a result our control of the Straits would be threatened.

   5. German and Italian submarines and aircraft operating from Spanish territory, including the Balearic and Canary Islands, would add greatly to the difficulties of protecting our own sea

communications in the Atlantic, and French communications between North Africa and France, the more so if the Mediterranean route were already closed.

6. Air attack could be brought to bear on the French bases in North Africa, the use of which by allied naval forces, if Gibraltar were not available, would be essential for the control of the Western Mediterranean. Without the use of these bases it would be difficult to interrupt Italian trade from the Atlantic.

7. For France the entry of Spain into the war would entail the defence of a third land frontier with a consequent dissipation of her resources.

8. Furthermore, the important French armament industries in the South of France at Toulouse, the mouth of the Gironde, and at Tarbes could be menaced by air attack from Spain. In view of the shortage of their fighter aircraft, the French take a serious view of this possibility.

9. The Biscayan ports which would be used by the British Field Force and by French formations from Africa would be within range of air attack from Northern Spain.

10. A French offensive from Tunisia against Libya would be delayed until French communications had been secured by the removal of the threat from Spanish Morocco.

11. If Spain were hostile, she could quickly overrun Portugal and we should not be able to use Lisbon as a base.

12. The strategic disadvantages summarised in the preceding paragraphs are formidable. It must, however, be borne in mind, with particular reference to the neutralisation of Gibraltar (para. 4) and the threat to the Franco-Spanish frontier (para. 7), that the Spaniards are war weary and in process of demobilisation, and would probably have little stomach for serious fighting; that they would be subjected to a rigorous blockade (subject to the extent to which the allied naval forces are able effectively to maintain control of the Western Mediterranean); that their resources in war material, particularly in the matter of oil fuelage are strictly limited; and that their manufacturing capacity is meagre. In these circumstances the disadvantages which we have enumerated may not be nearly so serious as they might appear to be at first sight; nor would they be of long duration, if our blockade is successful.

Russia

13. The military value of Russia has recently been the subject of

consideration in FP (36) 82, where the conclusion was reached:

(a) The Russian Navy in the Baltic would:
   (i) contain considerable German naval strength;
   (ii) interfere to some extent with the supply to Germany of Swedish iron ore;
   (iii) provide ports in the Baltic for our use if required.

(b) The Russian Navy in the Far East would:
   be an added deterrent to Japan from undertaking any large-scale operations against Australia, New Zealand or Singapore.

(c) The Russian Army in the West:
   (i) would not be in a position to afford material support to Poland;
   (ii) would not be in a position to maintain in Romania or in Turkey any military effort of a size which would have a material effect on the situation;
   (iii) is likely to resist a German advance through the Baltic States;
   (iv) would contain substantial German forces in the Eastern theatre in the event of Poland and Romania being overrun.

(d) The Russian Army in the Far East:
   would exercise a containing influence on Japan and might be of some assistance to China.

(e) The Russian Air Force in the West could:
   (i) produce a limited threat against Germany and Italy from advanced air bases in Poland, Romania or Turkey if these countries consented to aircraft operating from their territories;
   (ii) contain on the German eastern frontier more German air defence units than would otherwise be allotted for that purpose;
   (iii) be of some assistance in strengthening the air defences of Poland.

(f) The Russian Air Forces east of Baikal would have a restraining influence on the Japanese, contain some Japanese air forces and might afford valuable assistance to China.

(g) Russia could not assist us or our allies to any considerable extent by the supply of war material, but her co-operation would be invaluable in denying Russian sources of raw material to Germany.

14. As regards the naval situation, the advantages are greatly minimised by the fact that the Russian Baltic Ports are limited to the Gulf of Finland and are ice-free only for half the year. It is only during this period therefore that a proportion of the German naval strength would be contained.

15. The value of a Russian Alliance as far as concerns direct assistance, by land or air, to Poland and Romania is likely to be slight. The Polish and Romanian requirements of war material might be met without a military alliance.

Other Aspects

16. If there is no alliance with Russia it is essential to retain sufficiently friendly relations with her to ensure not only that the chances of Turkish co-operation with us are not prejudiced but also that Russian resources are denied to Germany.

17. We cannot overlook the danger which would result from a rapprochement between Germany and Russia – an aim which has been in the minds of the German General Staff for many years. A combination of the German capacity for organisation with the material and man-power resources of Russia would not only eliminate all hope of saving Poland and Romania, but would have repercussion throughout Europe and in India, the serious nature of which it would be difficult to exaggerate.

18. We are not in a position to assess the degree of reliance that could be placed on any Russian undertaking. But we would point out that the dangerous military consequences which would ensue if after we had contracted an alliance with Russia and made our dispositions accordingly, she were to withdraw from her obligations at the last moment.

Conclusion

19. To sum up, the active enmity of Spain, and the exploration by Germany and Italy of the geographical position of Spain and her dependencies would weaken our position in the Western Mediterranean and threaten our Atlantic communications.

On the other hand, the war weariness of the Spaniards, the inadequacy of their reserves of war material, and their lack of manufacturing capacity, would progressively reduce the extent of the dangers to which we would be liable in the opening stages of the war.

20. The active and whole-hearted assistance of Russia as our ally would be of great value, particularly in containing substantial enemy forces and in supplying war material to our other allies in Eastern Europe. In the latter respect, however, her contribution might be as readily forthcoming if she remained neutral.

21. Assuming that if Russia is not with us she is at least neutral, we consider that from the military point of view, the advantages of an alliance with Russia would not offset the disadvantages of the open hostility of Spain.

On the other hand the greatest danger to which the British Empire could be exposed would be a combination of Russia and Axis Powers. If, therefore, the Cabinet consider that there is a possibility of Russia joining the Axis Powers, either as a result of the failure of the present negotiations or for any other reason an entirely new problem would arise. We would request that in that event we should be fully informed of all the political implications, and be given an opportunity of reconsidering the military position afresh.

(Signed) C. L. N. NEWALL
            GORT
            A. B. CUNNINGHAM, DCNS (for CNS)
Richmond Terrace, S.W.1.,
  10th May, 1939.

Notes

NOTES TO CHAPTER 1

1. FO 371/20537 W10422/62/41, note for the Secretary of State by Charles Howard Smith, Assistant Under-Secretary, 1 September 1936.
2. By the Locarno Treaties of 1925, France, Germany and Belgium recognised the inviolability of the Franco-German and Belgo-German frontiers, and acknowledged as signatories the existence of the demilitarised zone of the Rhineland. Britain and France guaranteed this treaty. Other guarantees were given under Franco-Polish and Franco-Czech treaties.
3. In 1936 some 10 per cent of the working population continued unemployed, and subject to the 1931 means test. The Public Order Act in March had checked the power of quasi-military groups such as Moseley's Blackshirts. The great Jarrow march was yet to come.
   Despite the withdrawal in June of the economic sanctions imposed on Italy following her invasion of Abyssinia in October 1935, Britain's failure to recognise the Italian conquest was to embitter Anglo-Italian relations for the next two-and-a-half years.
4. The military rebellion which began in Spanish Morocco was followed the next day, 18 July, by insurrections in metropolitan Spain. See Luis Bolín, *Spain: The Vital Years* (London: Cassell, 1967) chs 1–5.
5. The Cabinet Conclusions now in the Public Record Office and cited hence forth as CAB/23. Here, CAB 23/85, 6, 9 and 16 July 1936.
6. The Spanish election brought sixteen communist deputies to the Cortes, but none was in the Cabinet until after the military rising (see appendix B). Similarly, in France, seventy-two communists were elected in the polls of May 1936, but again, none served in the Cabinet.
7. See ch. 3, pp. 72–3, for details of this agreement.
8. *Acción Popular* formed the core of CEDA, the right-wing Catholic party of which José María Gil Robles y Quinones was the leader, and *El Debate* its journal.
9. Foreign Office Confidential Prints 1936, henceforth FO 425. Here, FO 425/413 W342/62/41, Chilton to Eden, 7 January 1936.
10. FO 425/413 W343, W344, W1013/62/41.
11. *Ibid.*, W1639/62/41, Chilton to Eden, 21 February 1936. Francisco Largo Caballero, socialist and Secretary-General of the UGT, the socialist trades union.
12. Claude Bowers, *My Mission to Spain* (London: Gollancz, 1954) p. 291.
13. FO 425/413 W1639/62/41.
14. The Baldwin Papers, Cambridge University Library, vol. 124, F2 series B,

letter to Baldwin, 13 April 1936; henceforth Baldwin.
15. FO 425/413 W2105/62/41, 3 March 1936.
16. See also Ramón Tamames, *Estructura Económica de España* (Madrid: Gomez, 1965) p. 731, n. 10.
17. Foreign Office General Correspondence, FO 371/20522 W5718, W5521, W743 and W5365/62/41.
18. FO 425/413 W5670/62/41.
19. Sir George Mounsey was the Superintending Under-Secretary of the Western and League Department and in this capacity held responsibility for Spanish matters (see appendix A).
20. FO 371/20522 W5670/62/41. But see Luis Bolín, *op. cit.*, pp. 246–7.
21. FO 371/20522 W6400/62/41.
22. Parliamentary Debates of the House of Commons (henceforth HCD), vol. 314, cols. 1643–4.
23. FO 425/413 W2868/62/41, 21 March 1936.
24. *Ibid.*, W5256/62/41, 5 June 1936.
25. Hugh Thomas, *The Spanish Civil War* (Pelican, 1977) pp. 167, 204.
26. FO 371/20529 W8335/62/41. Indeed, the French Premier, Blum, was assured by Jimenes de Asua, a Spanish socialist, on 18 July 1936: '*O, la situation est excellente, nous sommes très satisfaits.*' *Les Événements survenus en France, 1933–1945*, vol. I, p. 213.
27. See also Arthur Loveday, *World War in Spain* (London: Murray, 1939) pp. 55–8, 103; K. W. Watkins, *Britain Divided: the effect of the Spanish Civil War on British Political Opinion* (London: Nelson, 1963) p. 41.
28. FO 371/20522 W4919/62/41, 29 May 1936.
29. Frank Ashton-Gwatkin, *The British Foreign Service* (Syracuse University Press, 1954) p. 52.
30. *Ibid.*, p. 26. 'A definite abuse arose from the Treasury ruling that an officer could not retire before he was sixty, except for reasons of health, without forfeiting his pension. The Service is hard on its officers, and a fair number of them are finished before they are sixty. There are no longer many, if any, easy posts into which a harmless incompetent can be tucked away.' Sir Henry Chilton (1877–1954) was appointed Ambassador to Spain 1 October 1935.
31. FO 575/413 W585/62/41, 10 January 1936.
32. FO 371/20526 W7648/62/41.
33. FO 371/205 W7995/62/41.
34. *Ibid.*, W8121/62/41, report from Chilton, 10 August.
35. FO 371/20535 W9698/62/41 28 August 1936; FO 371/20531 W8995/62/41 14 August 1936.
36. FO 371/20525 W7450/62/41, from Zarauz, 1 August 1936.
37. Julio Alvarez del Vayo, *Freedom's Battle* (London: Heinemann, 1940) p. 244; also FO 371/20540 W12125/62/41.
38. Sir Geoffrey Thompson, *Front Line Diplomat* (London: Hutchinson, 1959) pp. 117–20. Thompson joined Forbes in Valencia (the Spanish Government seat after December 1936) at the beginning of February 1937, remaining in Spain until July 1938.
39. FO 371/20530 W8547/62/41; FO 371/20531 W8758/62/41.
40. FO 371/20536 W9985/62/41, 28 August 1936.
41. See appendix B for list of ministers in that government.

42. FO 371/20536 W9541/62/41, W9606, and W9686/62/41.
43. FO 371/20536 W10298/62/41; FO 371/20537 W10729/62/41. Professor Lindemann, also present at the dinner, remembered no such conversation, but Spender's view is supported generally by John Langdon-Davies in *Behind the Barricades* (London: Secker & Warburg, 1936) p. 97. In a letter to the present writer, Mr Spender confirms the remarks made in his article in the *News Chronicle*, although he now regards his use of them as a 'breach of privacy'. For an analysis of the provocative rôle of the right in Spain in events leading up to the October Revolution of 1934, see Paul Preston, 'Spain's October Revolution and the Rightist Grasp for Power', *Journal of Contemporary History*, vol. 10, no. 4, October 1975.
44. Lord Avon, *The Eden Memoirs: Facing the Dictators* (London: Cassell, 1962) p. 400 (henceforth Eden); also FO 371/20536 W9733/62/41, report, 21 August (received 26) 1936.
45. FO 371/20530 W8509/62/41, 8 August 1936.
46. FO 371/20524 W7064/62/41, 28 July 1936.
47. FO 371/20525 W7642/62/41, 4 August 1936.
48. FO 371/20546 W15357/62/41. Capacity of the Embassy was estimated at 150 persons, FO 371/20523 W6841/62/41.
49. Ivan Maisky, *Who Helped Hitler?* (London: Hutchinson, 1964) pp. 21–5.
50. David Avery, *Not on Queen Victoria's Birthday* (London: Collins, 1974). See ch. 17 for an account of the first impact of the rebellion on the company, and the evacuation of women and children; FO 371/20523 W6831/62/41, FO 371/20522 W6531/62/41, from Senior Naval Officer Gibraltar, 20 July. It should be said that Algeciras suffered badly from bombing in the first days of the rebellion; FO 371/20523 W6621/62/41 from Acting Consul Vaughan at Barcelona; and W6831/62/41 from Rio Tinto, 23 July 1936.
51. In the first week of August the Foreign Office gave instructions for as many sub-consulates as possible to be closed. All subordinates who chose to remain did so at their own risk (FO 371/20533 W9039/62/41). See appendix C for list of consular officers.
52. Eden, p. 393.
53. Thomas Jones (ed.), *Diary with Letters* (London: Oxford University Press, 1954) pp. 229–30.
54. Viscount Halifax, *Fullness of Days* (London: Collins, 1957) p. 193.
55. The others were Sir John Simon, 1931–5, and Ramsay Macdonald, 1924.
56. Eden, pp. 319 and 383.
57. John Harvey (ed.), *The Diplomatic Diaries of Oliver Harvey* (London: Collins, 1970); henceforth Harvey. 'Halifax is idle and pernickety,' p. 51.
58. The meeting which took place on 2 September was, strictly speaking, a meeting of ministers and not a Cabinet meeting. The first plenary Cabinet session took place on 14 October 1936 (CAB 23/85).
59. Maisky, *op. cit.*, p. 45. But Sarita, Lady Vansittart is emphatic that her husband 'felt very strongly against the Communist cruelty followed by the subsequent reprisals in that terrible time'. Letter to the writer, 20 February 1975.
60. The Vansittart Papers, 1/17, 10 September 1936; henceforth VNST.
61. David Dilkes (ed.), *The Diaries of Sir Alexander Cadogan, 1938–45* (London: Cassell, 1971) p. 12; henceforth Cadogan. His appointment was not officially

gazetted until 1 October 1936, but he was much in evidence in the Foreign Office throughout the summer.

62. See appendix A.

63. Ian Colvin, *Vansittart in Office* (London: Gollancz, 1965) p. 92.

64. '. . . specialising in the political aspects of the Civil War', Shuckburgh was considered 'indispensable' when his new Head of Department, Walter Roberts, replaced Horace Seymour in September 1936 (FO 371/20576 W11343/9549/41).

65. FO 371/20522 W6529/62/41, report from Consul at Vigo, 18 July, received 20 July.

66. HCD, vol. 315, col. 41.

67. FO 371/20522 W6544, W6529, W6534, and W6569/62/41. The reconstituted government included José Giral as Prime Minister, Augusto Barcía as Minister of the Interior and Pablo Azcárate y Florez as Minister of State.

68. FO 371/20524 W7064/62/41.

69. Kenneth Edwards, *The Grey Diplomatists* (London: Rich & Cowan, 1938) p. 246. By 27 July, 5,000–9,000 British and French refugees were streaming across the borders into France and Gibraltar (HCD, vol. 315, col. 1073).

70. Hugh Thomas, *op. cit.*, pp. 226–7. Also Brian Crozier, *Franco: A Biographical History* (London: Eyre & Spottiswoode, 1967) p. 192 and, for Franco's call to arms, p. 522, appendix 5.

71. FO 371/20523 W6747/62/41, W6758/62/41.

72. FO 371/20523 W6753/62/41.

73. FO 371/20523 W6754/62/41 and W6747/62/41.

74. FO 371/20523 W6754, W6768/62/41.

75. FO 371/20523 W6777/62/41.

76. CAB 23/85.

77. The Statute of Tangier, 1923, was signed by Britain, France and Italy. By that statute Tangier became an international zone ministered by a Control Committee. As such it was automatically neutral (FO 371/20523 W6591/62/41). See also Brian Crozier, *op. cit.*, p. 193.

78. FO 371/20523 W6628/62/41 and W6839/62/41.

79. The most detailed recent study is David Carlton's 'Eden, Blum and the Origins of Non-intervention', *Journal of Contemporary History*, vol. 6, no. 3, 1971.

80. *Événements*, p. 215.

81. Lewis Namier, *Europe in Decay, 1936–1940* (London: Macmillan, 1950) pp. 14–15.

82. *Événements*, p. 215.

83. *Documents Diplomatiques Français*, 1932–9, 2ᵉ. Série (1939–9), tome IV, no. 126; henceforth DDF.

84. CAB 23/85, 16 July.

85. Pierre Renouvin, 'La Politique extérieure, du Premier Ministre Léon Blum', in Edouard Bonnefous, *Histoire politique exteneur de la Troisième République* (Paris: Presses Universitaires de France, 1965) vol. VI, appendix iv, p. 400. I am indebted to Dr Neville Waites of the Department of French Studies, Reading University, for drawing my attention to this source.

86. Carlton, *op. cit.*, p. 28.

87. *Événements*, p. 216, Eden, p. 406.

88. According to the *News Chronicle*, 25 July 1936, their resignation was triggered by the news of the dispatch to Spain of four aircraft.

89. Léon Blum, *L'Oeuvre de Léon Blum, 1934–1937*, (Paris: Albin Michel, 1954–7) vol. IV, part I, p. 417.

90. D. W. Pike, *Les Français et la guerre d'Espagne, 1936–1939*, (Paris: Presses Universitaires de France, 1975) pp. 36–46, for an excellent survey of the French press.

91. *Daily Telegraph*, 24 July 1936; Joel Colton, *Léon Blum: Humanist in Politics* (New York: Knopf, 1966) p. 237.

92. *Événements*, p. 217.

93. FO 371/20525 W6978/62/41, Clerk, 26 July 1936. While a licence would be required for war material, this would not apply, he reported, to commercial aircraft. Later three more aircraft arrived, to bring the total in gold to £742,000.

94. FO 371/20523 W6758/62/41.

95. Thomas Jones, *op. cit.*, p. 231.

96. CAB 23/85, 29 July 1936.

97. CAB 23/85, 29 July 1936.

98. FO 371/20528 W799/62/41.

99. FO 371/20525 W7492/62/41.

100. HCD, vol. 315, cols. 1071–2.

101. FO 371/20525 W7400/62/41, minute by H. S. Seymour, 29 July 1936.

102. FO 371/20524 W7188, W7204/62/41, 27 July 1936. For seaplane episode, FO 371/20526 W7702/62/41.

103. FO 371/20524 W6960/62/41, 25 July 1936, Clerk.

104. FO 371/20524 W7453/62/41.

105. FO 371/20526 W7007/62/41, dispatch from Mr Dodd, British Chargé d'Affaires, 27 July.

106. *Événements*, p. 217.

107. FO 371/20525 W7445/62/41, tel. 5.30 p.m., 31 July.

108. FO 361/19858/200 C5170/1/17, 29 July 1936.

109. FO 371/20526 W7649/62/41, Foreign Office minute, 1 August 1936.

110. HCD, vol. 315, col. 1971, 31 July 1936.

111. DDF, tome III, no. 52, 31 July 1936.

112. *Événements*, p. 218.

113. FO 371/20526 W7504/62/41, 2 August 1936.

114. FO 371/20527 W7777/62/41.

115. DDF, tome III, no. 71, 19 July – 19 November 1936.

116. FO 371/20527 W7748/62/41.

117. *Événements*, p. 218. Sir Maurice Hankey was Secretary to the Cabinet 1918–38, and Secretary to the Committee of Imperial Defence 1912–38.

118. FO 371/20527 W7781/62/41.

119. *Événements*, p. 218; Carlton, p. 49.

120. Lawrence E. Pratt, *East of Malta, West of Suez* (Cambridge University Press, 1975) p. 43, n. 35.

121. FO 371/20520 W8341/62/41, Foreign Office minutes, 11 August.

122. See below, pp. 170–2.

123. CAB 23/85, Conclusions for meetings in July.

124. FO 371/20527 W7809/62/41, 2 August. It is not clear when Eden himself saw

these papers, though some were read while he was on holiday in Yorkshire. Eden, p. 406.

125. FO 371/20525 W7491/62/41, 30 July 1936.
126. FO 371/20528 W7964/62/41. Clerk's report to the Foreign Office.
127. FO 371/20527 W7887/62/41.
128. FO 371/20528 W7964/62/41.
129. See below, p. 171.
130. DDF, tome III, p. 108, note of conversation with the British Ambassador on 7 August 1936.
131. FO 371/20528 W7964/62/41.
132. FO 371/19858 C6126/1/17, 28 August 1936.
133. Geoffery Warner, 'France and Non-Intervention in Spain, July and August 1936', *International Affairs*, vol. 38, no. 2, 1962, p. 211.
134. Carlton, pp. 52–4.
135. Sir Walter Citrine and Mr William Gillies were, respectively, Secretary of the Trades Union Congress 1926–45, and International Secretary of the Labour Party.
136. FO 371/19858 C6126/1/17.
137. FO 371/20527 W7918/62/41, 7–10 August, 1936.
138. Eden, p. 403.
139. FO 371/20529 W8321/62/41, Sir George Clerk, 11 August 1936.
140. *Daily Herald*, 10 August; FO 371/20530 W8416/62/41. Halifax wrote in person to reproach Strabolgi.
141. FO 371/20534 W9331/62/41; Eden, p. 405.
142. FO 371/20573 W9965/9549/41, minute by Mounsey, 26 August 1936. Others present at the second meeting were Lord Halifax and Lord Cranborne.
143. FO 371/20579 W13010/62/41, 1–7 October 1936. Mr Paul Mason, Private Secretary to Viscount Cranborne.
144. FO 371/20533 W9182/62/41; FO 371/20529 W8331/62/41
145. FO 371/20528 W8075/62/41.
146. Manuel Azaña y Díaz (1880–1940). Decree of 25 April 1931 brought in as an economy measure for an army with an exceptionally high officer ratio.
147. FO 371/20530 W8538/62/41, August 1936:
148. FO 371/20528 W8188/62/41.
149. FO 371/20530 W8809/62/41, 14 August 1936. The Spanish Ambassador himself admitted things were ' . . . not going too well for the Government forces', and that he thought very highly of the force Franco had so far been able to transport (FO 371/20529 W8331/61/41, interview between Lopez Oliván and Halifax on 10 August 1936).
150. FO 371/20534 W9331/62/41.
151. FO 371/20531 W8700/62/41.
152. FO 371/20534 W9331/62/41, 13 August 1936.
153. Ismay to Cadogan, FO 371/20535 W9708/62/41; Cabinet Paper FP (36) 10, CAB 27/626; FO 371/20573 W9885/9549/41.
154. The Non-Intervention Agreement and the part played by other European powers is examined in ch. 2.
155. FO 371/20573 W9717/9549/41, Foreign Office minutes 19–21 August 1936.
156. Geneviève Tabouis, *Blackmail or War* (Penguin Special, 1938) p. 58, claimed that under a secret treaty with Spanish monarchists, 'Italy obtained the right

in case of war, to establish and maintain the military base in the Balearic Islands', and '. . . to prohibit the passage of French troops on her territory'. This was a constant theme. See also Pertinax in *Echo de Paris*, 31 July 1936, in similar vein, and FO 371/20525 W7453/62/41.

157. David Cattell, *Soviet Diplomacy and the Spanish Civil War* (University of California, 1957) p. 6. Comparatively little information was reported from Russia by the British Ambassador, Lord Chilston, and what there was tended to be based on *Izvestia* and *Pravda*; but see chapter below on intervention, and FO 371/20530 W8628/62/41 for Chilston's report of 10 August indicating '. . . any threat to France is a threat to the Soviet Union'.

158. The Chiefs of Staff Sub-committee of the Committee of Imperial Defence consisted of: Admiral Sir Ernle Chatfield, General Sir Archibald Montgomery-Massingberd and Air Chief Marshal Sir Edward Ellington, with Sir Maurice Hankey as Secretary.

159. CAB 53/28, 24 August 1936. The report was signed by E. L. Ellington, C. J. Deverell, and C. E. Kennedy-Purvis (ACNS for CNS).

160. Denis Mack Smith, *Mussolini as a Military Leader*, Stenton Lecture, Reading University, 1973 (Reading University Press, 1974), p. 6. There is no doubt that the Chiefs of Staff had been much humiliated by the Abyssinian affair.

161. CAB 27/622, 25 August.

162. Jules Moch, *Rencontres avec Léon Blum* (Paris: Plon, 1970) p. 195.

163. FO 371/20573/9549/41, 20 August 1936.

NOTES TO CHAPTER 2

1. DDF, tome III, no. 75, 4 August 1936; DDF no. 65, Delbos to François-Poncet, 3 August 1936.

2. DDF, no. 83, 5 August 1936. For dates of adhesion of various governments see appendix D.

3. DDF, no. 127. The question of American attitudes is dealt with in R. Traina, *American Diplomacy in the Spanish Civil War* (Indiana University Press, 1968). But American policy in this field only rarely impinged on that of Britain.

4. The best analysis of legal aspects of the Non-Intervention Agreement and Committee remains that of N. J. Padelford's *International Law and Diplomacy in the Spanish Civil Strife*, (New York: Macmillan, 1939).

5. DDF, tome III, no. 83, 5 August 1936, and no. 150, 15 August 1936.

6. Padelford, *op. cit.*, p. 57.

7. FO 371/20532 W8929/62/41, Foreign Office minute, 15 August 1936. 'As the French Government have now decided not to exchange similar notes with all the other governments party to the Non-Intervention Agreement,' declared the FO, 'we see no point in regarding our exchange, of notes with them as a formal agreement for treaty purposes.'

8. Padelford, *op. cit.*, p. 65.

9. CAB 62/2. The CAB/62 category includes original memoranda of the NIC.

10. CAB 62/2.

11. CAB 62/41.

12. CAB 62/2.

13. FO 849/1, 9 October 1936, fifth meeting of NIC.

14. See appendix D for full list of dates of adherence.
15. DDF, tome III, nos. 199 and 226; FO 371/20530 W8597/62/41, Clerk, 13 August 1936.
16. Eden, p. 402; FO 371/20529 W8597/62/41, Delbos to Clerk, 13 August 1936; Foreign Policy Committee, CAB 27/622, 25 August 1936; CAB 23/85, meeting of ministers, 2 September 1936.
17. FO 371/20574 W10398/9549/41, telegram 4 September 1936 to Basil Newton, British Minister in Berlin, 1935–7, in answer to inquiry from Dr Hans Heinrich Dieckhoff, Acting State Secretary, August 1936–April 1937.
18. Documents on German Foreign Policy (henceforth GD); here GD 72, 4 September 1936.
19. FO 371/75 W10805/9549/41, Foreign Office minute.
20. The 2nd Earl of Plymouth, *b.* 1889; Parliamentary Under-Secretary of State at the Foreign Office, 1 September 1936.
21. Francis Hemming's own NIC papers, mainly duplicates, are held by Corpus Christi College, Oxford.
22. FO 371/20584 W15094/9549/41, 17 November 1936.
23. FO 371/20576 W1112/9549/41, Foreign Office minute.
24. See appendix E.
25. Padelford, *op. cit.*, p. 6.
26. FO 849/1, 28 September, annexe C.
27. FO 849/1, fourth meeting of NIC. See also Padelford, *op. cit.*, p. 70.
28. CAB 62/1.
29. GD 246.
30. FO 849/1, fifth and sixth meetings of NIC, 9 October 1936.
31. But see below, p. 60.
32. FO 371/20580 W13672/9549/41, 12 October.
33. CAB 23/85.
34. FO 849/1, seventh meeting of NIC.
35. FO 371/20584 W15341/9549/41, Foreign Office minutes, 16–17 October 1936. But see Hugh Thomas, *op. cit.*, pp. 440–7.
36. FO 371/20582 W14308/9549/41, Foreign Office minutes.
37. FO 849/1, twentieth meeting, 5 May 1937.
38. FO 371/20584 W15624/9545/41, Foreign Office minutes, 16 November 1936.
39. GD 127. The Spanish Republican forces were to be designated 'Spanish Bolshevists'. The British Government continued to refer to Franco's forces until mid-1937 as the 'insurgents'.
40. CAB 62/69. See appendix E for list of dates and functions.
41. FO 371/20586 W16559/9545/41, Foreign Office minutes, 23–25 November 1936; FO 371/20582 W14335/9459/41, Foreign Office minutes, 26 October 1936.
42. CAB 62/69.
43. See Angel Viñas, *El Oro Español en la Guerra Civil* (Madrid: Instituto de Estudios Fiscales, Ministerio de Hacienda, 1976) p. 28.
44. FO 849, vols. 31–40.
45. FO 371/21319 W1085/7/41.
46. FO 371/20590 W18649/9549/41, Spanish Government reply, 21 December 1936. FO 371/20590 W18609/9549/41, insurgent reply, 19 December 1936.

47. FO 849/7, fifteenth meeting of Chairman's Technical Advisory Sub-committee No. 3, 4 March 1937.
48. FO 849/1, 24 March 1937, fourth meeting, Annexe C, Portuguese note to France; FO 371/21326 fol. 65.
49. GDs 50, annexe, p. 51 (3) and 252, p. 283.
50. FO 849/1, fifth meeting, 9 October 1936.
51. FO 849/28, Chairman's Sub-Committee, 18 February 1937.
52. FO 371/21321 W2109/7/41, minutes on the second report of the Technical Advisory Sub-Committee No. 3 regarding supervision, 25–29 January 1937. Cahan, alternatively spelt Kagan.
53. See below, p. 58.
54. FO 849/7, Annexe, p. 124. The International Council for Non-Intervention in Spain was incorporated on 20 April 1937, subject to the provisions of the Companies Act 1929, section 14 (FO 849/15). NIS (36) 764, para. 11.
55. FO 371/21321 W2109/7/41, second report of Technical Advisory Sub-Committee No. 3.
56. FO 371/21326; FO 849/1, 24 March 1937.
57. FO 371/21321 W2109/7/41; also FO 849/7 and CAB 62. See map on p. 00. The naval powers were reported ready to commence duties as from 13 March 1937 (FO 849/1, sixteenth meeting NIC, 8 March 1937).
58. FO 849/28.
59. FO 849/28.
60. FO 371/21320 W1101/7/41. All did eventually contribute, even if only nominally.
61. CAB 62/34.
62. FO 849/1, twenty-fourth meeting of NIC, 9 July 1937.
63. FO 849/1, letter read at fourteenth meeting, 28 December 1936.
64. See below, p. 138.
65. FO 849/1, 28 May 1937, twenty-second meeting.
66. FO 849/27, 31 May 1937.
67. FO 849/1, 16 July 1937, twenty-seventh meeting.
68. FO 849/1.
69. War Office, notes on the supply of arms to Spain (FO 371/21395 (April) and FO 371/21336 (May)).
70. FO 371/21336, report from the administrative offices of British Observers, Lisbon.
71. FO 849/1, twenty-fifth meeting, 9 July 1937.
72. The dictators recognised Franco's Nationalist Government on 18 November 1936. For discussion of this and the British attitude, see below, ch. 6.
73. FO 849/1, twenty-fourth meeting, a.m., 9 July 1937.
74. FO 849/1, twenty-sixth meeting, 16 July 1937.
75. For full definition of 'belligerency' see below, p. 107.
76. CAB 27/622, Foreign Policy Committee, 1 July 1937.
77. FO 371/21323 W2865/7/41, 16 February 1937, minute by Sir George Mounsey.
78. See below, ch. 5.

NOTES TO CHAPTER 3

 1. This theme occurs frequently, but see for example, FO 371/21346 W19006/7/41, or FO 371/20519 W14919/62/41. Foreign observers also remarked on this assumption: 'The British', reported the American Ambassador, Norman Davis, 'were convinced that within two years of a Franco victory, the General would be eating out of British hands.' See Richard Traina, *op. cit.*, p. 128.
 2. FO 371/20569 W10320/4719/41. This document, entitled 'British capital invested in Spain: estimate', does not appear to have been kept, but it seems likely that it concerned the request sent to Lazards for such an estimate. See below p. 66 n. 1; also Angel Viñas, *La Alemania Nazi y el 18 de Julio* (Madrid: Alianza Universidad, 1974) p. 220, n. 64.
 3. FO 371/21381 W3004/40/41, letter and report from Mr G. K. Logie of Lazards, 9 February 1937.
 4. FO 371/23536 F9888/9378/10.
 5. Sir Richard Kindersley, 'British Overseas Investments in 1935 and 1936', *Economic Journal*, vol. XLVII, December 1937. But see also *The Economist*, vol. CXXIX (1937), 20 November 1937, pp. 359–66.
 6. Herbert Feis, *The Spanish Story* (New York: Norton, 1966) p. 269. Five tankers bound for Spain were diverted to the rebels, and supplies were continued throughout the Civil War.
 7. FO 371/20529 W8326/62/41, 11 August 1936.
 8. FO 371/21381 W3004/40/41. This list did not specify the Orconera Iron Company, which was British, had a capital of £2,000,000, and was situated in Republican (Basque) territory (FO 371/20713). The Barcelona Traction and Light Company was registered in Canada and had ceased to have a London office after 1921 (Companies Registration Office, F 1148 D).
 9. FO 371/20536 W10422/62/41, note for the Secretary of State by, 1 September 1936.
10. FO 371/20518 W8779/62/41 and W9143/62/41, 20 August, 1936.
11. FO 371/20518 W11923/62/41.
12. It had been rumoured in the first weeks of the rebellion that the Basques were considering an alliance with the rebels in return for which the Basques would be granted autonomy (FO 371/20526 W7516 and W7519/62/41). Basque autonomy was granted by the Republic, however, in October 1936.
13. FO 371/20570 W14126/62/41.
14. FO 371/21404 W20413/15464/41. Katherine, Duchess of Atholl, *Searchlight on Spain* (Penguin Special, 1938) p. 163.
15. Sir Geoffrey Thompson, *op. cit.*, p. 121.
16. FO 371/22673 W3145/457/41.
17. FO 371/22673 W3145/457/41.
18. FO 371/24144 and 24149 W11874; estimate by Committee of British Ship Owners trading to Spain, The *Manchester Guardian*, 9 January 1939; FO 371/24249 W1337.
19. GDs 783, 784 and 809.
20. HCD vol. 331, cols. 649 and 1503, 1505, 7 and 14 February 1938.
21. FO 371/22670 W4595/354/41, Joaquim Juliá, British Commercial Secretariat, Barcelona, 25 March 1938.

22. Table 3, FO 371/20565, based on figures submitted by the Board of Trade. See also table 4.
23. Elizabeth Monroe, *The Mediterranean in Politics*, (London: Oxford University Press, 1938) p. 12. Between 9 and 14 per cent of British imports came via Suez.
24. Tamames, *op. cit.*, p. 559; FO 371/20518 W14719/62/41.
25. Here, I am grateful to Teresa Lawlor of Reading University for allowing me to read her unpublished M.A. dissertation, *An Economic Perspective of the Spanish Civil War* (1973).
26. FO 371/20518 W14719/62/41, 30 October–9 November 1936, report and minutes on the Anglo-Spanish Payments Agreement. See also Cmd. 5058, 6 January 1936.
27. FO 371/20518 W12335/62/41, minutes on meeting at the Treasury, 24 September 1936.
28. Tamames, *op. cit.*, p. 115, table 5.
29. FO 371/20518 W14719/62/41.
30. *Ibid.*
31. FO 371/20540, minutes, 30 September–13 October 1936; see below, ch. 6.
32. FO 371/20519 W15436 and W15700/62/41.
33. Juan de la Cierva acted as an agent for the Nationalist authorities.
34. Juan de la Cierva had previously seen Mounsey on 2 September and indicated Franco's sense of grievance at the continuation of the Anglo-Spanish Payments Agreement (FO 371/20519 W14818/62/41).
35. *The Times*, 2 February 1937.
36. FO 371/21319 W963/7/41.
37. FO 371/22633 W766/83/41.
38. FO 371/20519 W14919/62/41, formal request from HM Consul at Bilbao.
39. See table 4; also Viñas, *op. cit.*, p. 219.
40. Based on *International Trade Statistics, 1938* (League of Nations, 1939) pp. 280 and 302.
41. FO 371/20518 W3090/62/41.
42. FO 371/20519 W1588/62/41, 11 November 1936.
43. *Annual Statement of Trade of the United Kingdom, 1939* (London: HMSO, 1941) vol. IV, p. 274.
44. See below, ch. 6., p. 191.
45. See table 7, p. 9.
46. Based on HMSO *Annual Statement of the Trade of the United Kingdom with British and Foreign Countries in 1939 and compared with the Years 1935–1938*, vol. I.
47. See, for example, Hugh Thomas, *op. cit.*, p. 448; and the comprehensive study by Angel Viñas, *El Oro Espagnol en la Guerra Civil* (Madrid: Instituto de Estudios Fiscales, Ministerio de Hacienda, 1977).
48. FO 371/21320 W1427/7/41, memorandum and minutes, 12–13 January 1937.
49. FO 371/22685.
50. FO 371/22681, report issued from Frankfurt, 2 April 1938.
51. Glenn Harper, *German Economic Policy in Spain* (The Hague: Monton, 1967) Angel Viñas, *La Alamania et et 18 de Julio*
52. FO 371/20569 W10637/62/41, memorandum, 21 July 1937.
53. I am indebted, here, to the generous advice of both Professor David Williams,

resident geologist with Rio Tinto in Spain, 1928–32, and consultant geologist to that company, 1946–70; and Dr Alan Bromley of the Camborne School of Mines, Cornwall. See also S. G. Checkland, *The Mines of Tharsis*, (London: Allen & Unwin, 1967) p. 23, and David Avery, *op. cit.*

54. *Annual Statement of Trade, op. cit.* See table 9.
55. *Annual Statement, op. cit.*, 1939, vol. II, p. 409.
56. FO 371/22673 W15896/386/41.
57. FO 371/20713 C472/18; Viñas, *op. cit.*, pp. 240–2.
58. FO 371/20569 W10637/62/41.
59. FO 371/21306 W5969.
60. FO 371/20569 W10631/4719/41.
61. FO 371/20518 W8779/62/41, 17 August 1936.
62. FO 371/20569 W10741/4719/41.
63. Now Lord Gladwyn, H. M. G. Jebb was then assistant in the economic section of the Spanish Office of the Western and League Department.
64. The best published account of this remains that of Glen Harper, *op. cit.* There is also a comprehensive account in an unpublished MA dissertation by Norman Cooper of Reading University, *Nazi Germany and the Spanish Conflict* (1973).
65. FO 371/20713 C472/13/18.
66. The French, reported to have only three months supply left (FO 371/20570 W11480), were short of pyrites, despite having taken considerably more in 1936 than in 1935. See table 10, p. 83.
67. FO 371/21381 W3237/40/41, Chilton, Hendaye, 11 February 1937.
68. FO 371/21304 W2368 and W2465, 29 January–1 February 1937.
69. CAB 24/268, CP82, pp. 3–11, Geddes to Vansittart, 24 February 1937.
70. CAB 24/268 C.P.82 (37), 1 March 1937.
71. CAB 23/87, 3 March 1937; CAB 24/268, C.P.80, 3 March 1937, note by Sir Samuel Hoare.
72. The Templewood Papers, Cambridge University Library (henceforth Templewood); here IX, iii.
73. *L'Oeuvre*, 9 March 1937.
74. Templewood, IX, ii, 17 March 1937.
75. CAB 23/87, 3, 10 and 17 March 1937. This promise was to be repeated in June 1937.
76. *Financial News*, 25 April 1936, Rio Tinto Annual Report.
77. *Ibid.*, 20 April 1937, Rio Tinto Annual Report.
78. FO 371/22673 W15896 and W15897/386/41, 21–30 November 1938.
79. Halifax to Geddes, 8 December 1938. France was obliged to import pyrites from Italy, which had considerably increased her imports although she herself was normally a pyrites producer.
80. FO 371/20713 C246/13/18.
81. FO 371/21263 W1550/514/28, 7 October 1936; FO 371/20713/13/18, 9 January 1937.
82. FO 371/20713 C472/13/18, Industrial Intelligence Centre, 13 January 1937.
83. FO 371/20713 C246/13/18.
84. CAB 23/87, 27 January 1937; FO 371/21263 W2900/514/28, 3 February 1937.
85. CAB 24/268 C.P.90, 10 March 1937.

86. FO 371/21306 W5418/3/41, report from Chilton, Hendaye, 10 March 1937.
87. FO 371/21306 W5418/3/41, minutes.
88. *Ibid.*
89. FO 371/21307 W7328 and W7341, Army Council and Board of Trade minutes, 14 April 1937.
90. See below, ch. 6.
91. FO 371/20713 C472/13/18.
92. FO 371/21298; also CAB 27/626 F.P.(36) 35, Cabinet Committee on Foreign Policy, memorandum by Lord Cranborne.
93. FO 371/21298. It was never Germany's intention to cut off Britain permanently from the produce of the iron ore mines of the north (GD392).
94. CAB 24/271 CP 207, meeting of ministers, 2 September 1937, and FO 371/21299.
95. FO 371/21298 W14857. Cardiff received its first cargo of iron ore at the end of August (*The Times*, 28 August 1937).
96. Based on figures supplied to the Foreign Office by the exiled Basque Government (FO 371/22682). See table 13.
97. FO 371/22682. Table 13 taken from *Gaceta del Norte*, 24 January and 15 May 1938.
98. *Daily Telegraph*, 27 July 1937; *The Times*, 24 and 28 August 1937; Fo 371/22681 W7525/1142/41, report by Sir Robert Hodgson, 3 June 1938; GD591, 634, 655, 682.
99. FO 371/22691 W13997.
100. HCD vol. 346, col. 1681.
101. Robert Blake, 'Baldwin and the Right' in John Raymond (ed.), *The Baldwin Age* (London: Eyre & Spottiswood, 1960) p. 34. In 1919 Baldwin had presented one-fifth of his fortune to the Treasury.
102. This paragraph is drawn from Simon Haxey, *Tory M.P.* (London: Gollancz, 1939) pp. 109–10, 159, 216–17 and 220.
103. FO 849/1, e.g. 26 and 28 May 1937. Wallace described the attacks on Italian ships by the Republic as an 'intolerable outrage'.
104. *The Times*, 27 January 1937. Anthony Eden became a director of Rio Tinto in 1946 (Companies House, *loc. cit*).
105. Ivan Maisky, *Spanish Notebooks* (London: Hutchinson, 1966) p. 138.
106. Haxey, *op. cit.*, p. 35.
107. Blake, *op. cit.*, p. 27. See also Keith Middlemas and John Barnes, *Baldwin: a Biography*, (London: Weidenfeld & Nicolson, 1969) p. 25.
108. For example, a parliamentary question submitted by Capt. Ramsay for 8 February 1937 read:

> To ask the Secretary of State for Foreign Affairs, whether his attention has been drawn to the fact that the latest information goes to prove that the present régime of the left in Spain represents not only the minority of the country at the elections but a minority financed and directed by Moscow for many years; and whether His Majesty's Government recognises these facts as now established and are prepared to reconsider their recognition of that régime as the legitimate government of Spain.

> Advising on the draft reply, Montagu Pollock noted that the Popular Front had won the previous election by 'a substanital margin', and that the Spanish Government contained only one communist (FO 371/21284

W2799). In fact, two communists joined the Spanish cabinet for the first time in September 1936. See Hugh Thomas, *op. cit.*, p. 345.

109. The Neville Chamberlain Papers, Birmingham University Library (henceforth NC; here NC 7/1/29/40, Margesson to Chamberlain, 1 August 1936; and NC 8/24/1, March 1937.

110. Companies House, Rio Tinto Zinc, 7132, vol. 6a.

111. *The Economist*, 24 October 1936, vol. 125; and 13 February 1937, vol. 126.

112. Both the Alcoy and Gandia Railway and Harbour Company and the Stanhope Shipping Company expressed themselves well pleased with their treatment in Republican Spain (*The Times*, 24 and 28 March 1938).

113. See above, p. 69.

114. *Financial Times*, 6 January 1938.

NOTES TO CHAPTER 4

1. Admiral Sir A. Ernle Chatfield, *The Navy and Defence: The Autobiography of Admiral of the Fleet Lord Chatfield*, vol. 2, *It Might Happen Again* (London: Heinemann, 1942) p. 92.

2. CAB 27/606, Committee on the Position of the Fleet in the Mediterranean, Admiralty minutes, 14 May 1936.

3. CAB 27/639, Committee on the Protection of British Shipping (Spain), 28 April 1937.

4. Eden, *op. cit.*, p. 413.

5. *Jane's Fighting Ships*, Francis McMurtrie (ed.), (London: Sampson Low & Co., 1936), notes on Naval Treaties, appendix ix.

6. Admiralty Papers: P.R.O, henceforward ADM. 167/94, Admiralty Board memorandum, 21 July 1936.

7. Jane's *op. cit.* Totals for Britain given in their source differ very slightly from Admiralty figures, which would have been more up-to-date.

8. CAB 27/606, Committee on the Position of the Fleet in the Mediterranean, 19 May 1936.

9. Lawrence R. Pratt, *East of Malta, West of Suez: Britain's Mediterranean Crises, 1936–1939*, (Cambridge University Press, 1975) p. 9.

10. CAB 27/606.

11. David Dilkes (ed.), *The Diaries of Sir Alexander Cadogan, 1938–1945* (London: Cassell, 1971) p. 15.

12. Eden, p. 436.

13. FO 371/23 W6778/62/41.

14. FO 371/20525 W7235/62/41.

15. FO 371/21296 W12901/1/41.

16. Chatfield, *op. cit.*

17. Vice-Admiral Sir William James, *The Sky Was Always Blue* (London: Methuen 1951) p. 187; FO 371/21385.

18. FO 371/20527 W7755/62/41.

19. Chatfield, *op. cit.*, The work was not always arduous. In aid of better relations, football matches were arranged between the Navy and local Basque teams (FO 371/20528 W8092/62/41).

20. Approximately two-thirds of Nationalist naval officers lost their lives during

the Spanish Civil War, the majority of losses occurring in the first three months.

21. Hugh Thomas, *op. cit.*, p. 192.
22. FO 371/20551, fol. 57.
23. FO 371/20529 W8356, W8365/62/41.
24. GD 48, telegram from Dieckhoff of the German Foreign Ministry, 20 August 1936.
25. FO 371/20586 W1652/9549/41.
26. FO 371/20533 W9182/62/41.
27. FO 371/20534 W9264/62/41, 21 August 1936.
28. FO 371/20534, fol. 186, 16 August 1936.
29. FO 371/20586 W1639/9549/41, War Office note on the supply of arms to Spain, 23 November 1936.
30. CAB 23/86, 4 November 1936.
31. FO 371/21281. But compare the more recent figures of Alcofar Nassaes, *Las Fuezas Navales en la Guerra Civil Española* (Barcelona: Dopes, 1971) pp. 15–16.
32. CAB 23/86, 7 and 18 November 1936.
33. PREM 1/359, 20 November 1936.
34. *Ibid.*, Letter to Baldwin from Lord Runciman, President of the Board of Trade, 21 November 1936.
35. Eden, p. 413.
36. Prime Minister's files P.R.O. henceforth PREM 1/366, draft of the Merchant Shipping (Carriage of munitions to Spain) Bill.
37. CP 335 (36), Spain: the Balearics.
38. CP 6 (37), and Eden, pp. 433–4; FO 371/21/21282.
39. Eden, p. 435.
40. Templewood, xi, iii, notes on *General Politics*, January 1937.
41. CAB 23/87, 8 January 1937.
42. Templewood, *loc. cit.*, 'Irresponsibility of FO.
43. Kenneth Edwards, *op. cit.*, p. 257.
44. GD 156, telegram from Von Hassell, German Ambassador to Italy, 17 December 1936.
45. FO 371/21351.
46. FO 371/21352.
47. HCD, vol. 321, cols. 7–9, 1 March 1937; col. 993, 9 March 1937.
48. FO 371/21351.
49. FO 371/21352.
50. FO 371/21352.
51. Chatfield, *op. cit.*, p. 92.
52. FO 371/21352.
53. ADM 116/3512, MO 2155/37.
54. FO 371/21288.
55. FO 371/21352.
56. CAB 23/88, 7 April 1937; CAB 27/639, Committee on the Protection of British Shipping (Spain), 7 April 1937.
57. ADM 116/3512 MO 2155/37.
58. FO 371/21352.
59. CAB 23/88, 11 April 1937.
60. FO 371/21352.

61. *Ibid.*
62. HCD, vol. 322, cols. 1029–1142, 14 April 1937.
63. ADM 116/3514 M2521.
64. FO 371/21355.
65. FO 371/21352; ADM 116/3521; CAB 27/639; Almirante Juan Cervera Valderrama, *Memorias de Guerra* (Madrid: Editora Nacional, 1968) pp. 145–6.
66. CAB 27/639, 28 April 1937.
67. CAB 27/639, fourth meeting, testimony of Admiral Blake who therefore recommended that ships should call at La Pallice rather than St. Jean-de-Luz. Shortly after this Chilton was sent on 'extended' leave.
68. See below, p. 87.
69. James, *op. cit.*, p. 184.
70. The most recent published work on this is the article by Peter Gretton, 'The Nyon Conference – the naval aspect', in the *English Historical Review*, vol. XC, no. CCCLIV, January 1975, pp. 103–12.
71. Winston S. Churchill, *The Second World War vol. 1, The Gathering Storm* Cassell, London 1948 p. 171.
72. FO 371/21359, report, 24 July 1937.
73. *Ibid.*
74. Juan Cervera Valderrama, *op. cit.*, pp. 224–5.
75. Between August 1936 and September 1937 the following had suffered attack of one type or another: HMSs *Blanche, Royal Oak, Gypsy, Hawk* (twice), *Gallant, Hunter* and *Havock* (ADM 116/3534).
76. Gretton, *op. cit.*, p. 105.
77. HCD, vol. 326, cols. 2572–4, 22 July 1937.
78. FO 371/21299 W15803/1/41, report of interview between Chilton and Sangroniz, Chief of Nationalist Diplomatic Cabinet at Salamanca. The moderately anglophile Sangroniz claimed Duff Cooper's remarks in the House had 'done much good'.
79. Eden, pp. 457–8.
80. ADM 116/3522; FO 371/21359 W16584/1/41.
81. Eden, p. 459.
82. ADM 116/3522.
83. See below, p. 140.
84. ADM 116/3522, record of telephone conversation between Chatfield and Cunningham.
85. Ciano placed the responsibility for this attack on the Italian submarine *Iride*. (Malcolm Muggeridge (ed.) *Ciano's Diary, 1937–1938* (London: Methuen, 1952 p. 8).
86. FO 371/21359.
87. FO 371 87. FO 371/21359.
88. ADM 116/3522.
89. FO 371/21359, meeting of ministers, 2 September 1937.
90. FO 371/21359, 5 September 1937.
91. *Ibid.*, see also Gretton, *op. cit.*, p. 106.
92. *Ibid.*, GD 413.
93. CAB 23/89, 8 September 1937.
94. John E. Dreifort 'The French Popular Front and the Franco-Soviet Part,

1936–37': A Dilemma in Foreign Policy', *Journal et Contemporary History*, vol. II, 1976, p. 223.

95. ADM 116/3522. The Soviet ship *Timiriasev* was sunk on 31 August, and the *Balgoev* on 1st September.

96. CAB 23/89, 8 September.

97. FO 371/21344 W17243/7/41, 11 September 1937.

98. See Gretton *op. cit.*, pp. 107–8.

99. Ciano, *op. cit.*, p. 15, 21 September 1937.

100. PREM 1/360, Eden to Chamberlain, 14 September 1937.

101. Gretton, *op. cit.*, p. 9.

102. Ciano, *op. cit.*, p. 13, 15 September 1937.

103. FO 371/21363 W20533/23/41, minutes, 3 November 1937.

104. *Ibid.*, W20863/23/41, report from Consul-General Knight, Tunis, 2 November 1937.

105. *Ibid.*, W20533/23/41.

106. Eden, pp. 463–4.

107. Churchill, *op. cit.*, pp. 207–10.

108. FO 371/21300 W17174/1/41, minutes by Sir George Mounsey, 17 September 1937.

109. FO 371/22633.

110. Eden, p. 469.

111. CAB 27/623, Cabinet Committee on Foreign Policy.

112. On 4 February 1938 Hitler assumed supreme command of the armed forces. Schuschnigg, the Austrian Chancellor, was forced to accept the Nazi Seyss-Inquart as his Minister of Security.

113. CAB 27/623, Foreign Policy Committee; CAB 23/92, 2 and 9 February 1938.

114. See Chapter 5.

115. *Ibid.*, for circumstances of Eden's resignation.

116. CAB 23/96, 9 November 1938.

117. CAB 23/96, 30 November 1938.

118. In mid-November the Nationalists crossed the Ebro to begin the Catalonian campaign.

119. FO 371/22656 W14985/86/41.

120. NC 2/25, *A few political notes on foreign agreements re our duties*.

121. Successor to John Leche, Ralph Clarmond Skrine Stevenson was appointed Chargé d'Affaires at Barcelona with local rank of Minister in October 1938.

122. FO 371/22685.

123. CAB 27/639.

124. FO 371/2261 W13626/83/41.

125. FO 371/22627 W8723/29/41, Foreign Office minutes on a memorandum by Vansittart, 27 June – 11 July 1938. Later the Cabinet did, however, agree against strong Admiralty opposition to contribute to funds for an international and impartial scheme of relief. The gesture came to nothing as Franco refused to allow facilities for the work to go ahead (FO 371/22615 W15965/99/41, 2 December 1938).

126. CAB 23/93, 1 June and 5 July 1938.

127. By November 1936 220 voyages of evacuation had been made by the British navy, 75,724 miles had been covered, and 11,195 refugees evacuated at an approximate cost of £40,000 (HCD vol. 317, col. 847).

128. FO 371/21291 W8661/1/41, minutes on a report on Guernica by the British Consul, R. C. Stevenson, 28 April 1937.
129. Stephen Roskill, *Naval Policy Between the Wars*, vol. II, *1930–1939* (London: Collins, 1976) p. 388.

NOTES TO CHAPTER 5

1. The term 'volunteer' is used here for convenience, and because it was the term generally used by the NIC. It was adopted by that body, again partly for convenience but also as a euphemism acceptable to the dictators.
2. Real improvement did not come until 1937. See Jason Gurney, *Crusade in Spain* (London: Faber, 1974) pp. 91–3, and George Orwell, *Homage to Catalomia* (Penguin, 1971).
3. John Coverdale, *Italian Intervention in the Spanish Civil War* (Princeton University Press, 1975) p. 175. The number of Italian ground forces shipped to Spain had reached almost 49,000 by mid-February.
4. HCD, vol. 317, col. 1923.
5. FO 849/1, sixth meeting NIC.
6. FO 371/20583 W14663/9549/41, minute on Admiralty report, 27 October 1936.
7. FO 371/20580 W13764/9549/41. Azcárate and Eden were already well acquainted from their work at Geneva, but despite a certain degree of friendliness, Azcárate did not believe Eden to be well disposed towards the Republic (Pablo Azcárate, *Mi Embajada en Londres Durante la Guerra Civil Española*, (Barcelona: Ariel, 1976) p. 39).
8. FO 371/20581 W14328/9549/41, Foreign Office memo, 26 November 1936.
9. FO 371/20576 W11219/9549/41, Foreign Office minute on report from HMS *Antelope*, 13 September 1936; FO 371/20581 W14208/9549/41, report by Sir E. Monson, Riga, 22 October 1936.
10. FO 371/20584 W1543/9549/41.
11. FO 371/20586 W16391/9549/41, minute by Roberts, 23 November 1936.
12. FO 371/20586 W16391/9549/41, War Office note on the supply of arms to Spain, 23 November 1936.
13. FO 371/20586 W16391/9549/41.
14 Eden, p. 400, conversation with Senhor Armindo Monteiro, Portuguese Foreign Secretary, 20 July 1936.
15. FO 371/20573 W9906/9549/41, 22 August 1936, Monteiro to Sir Charles Wingfield, British Ambassador to Portugal.
16. FO 371/20576 W10853/, 21 September 1936.
17. See above, ch. 2, pp. 59–60.
18. FO 371/20584 W15121/9549/41, minutes on letter from Miss E. F. Rathbone to Anthony Eden alleging violation of the NIA, 2 November 1936. See also Glyn Stone, 'The Official British Attitude to the Anglo-Portuguese Alliance, 1919–45', in the *Journal of Contemporary History*, vol. 10, no. 4, October 1975, p. 738.
19. FO 371/20584 W15121/9549/41, 2 November 1936.
20. Sir Robert Hodgson, *Spain Resurgent* (London: Hutchinson, 1953) p.70.
21. Ricardo de la Cierva y de Hoces, 'The Nationalist Army in the Spanish Civil

War', in Raymond Carr (ed.), *The Republic and the Civil War in Spain* (London: Macmillan, 1971) p. 206.

22. FO 371/20586 W16391/9549/41, War Office note on the supply of arms to Spain, 23 November 1936.
23. FO 371/20586 W1639/9549/41, minutes on War Office report, 23 November 1936.
24. FO 371/20588 W17100/9549/41.
25. FO 371/20588 W18025/9549/41. It has been estimated that only 43 per cent of 48,000 Italian who served in Spain were regular troops (Coverdale, *op. cit.*, p. 181).
26. FO 371/20584 W15289/9549/41, Lt-Cmdr. (later Capt.) Alan Hillgarth, Chief of British Naval Intelligence, Eastern Theatre, 1944–6.
27. FO 371/20588 W17521/9549/41.
28. FO 371/20588 W18182/9549/41.
29. FO 371/20586 W16815/9549/41.
30. D. W. Pike, *Conjecture, Propaganda, and Deceit in the Spanish Civil War* (Californian Institute of International Studies, 1968) p. 89.
31. FO 371/20590 W18689/9549/41, 18 December 1936. Admiral Godefroy's rank was roughly equivalent to that of the British Assistant Chief of Naval Staff.
32. Eden had already confided to his diary his ambition to do just that: 'I do not want even to appear to follow Hitler and Mussolini at the moment, but would prefer to "show a tooth" in the Mediterranean' (Eden, p. 413).
33. FO 371/20587 W17441/9549/41, minutes on a dispatch from Hillgarth, 10 December 1936.
34. The Consul-General at Milan speculated as to whether uniforms supplied to Italians were made in Spain or Italy. In either case considerable foresight was implied (FO 371/20588 W17498/41).
35. CP 355(36); CAB 53/29; FO371/20588 W18182/9549/41, memorandum by Eden, 14 December 1936.
36. Georges Bernanos, *A Diary of My Times* (London: Boriswood, 1938) pp. 101–6. Bernanos estimated assassinations in the island to have numbered at least 3,000 in the first seven months of the Civil War.
37. CP 355(36), *loc. cit.*
38. There was, however, no definite indication of how far the French were prepared to go to prevent the occupation of Majorca, and the British regarded the occupation of the Balearics as suggested by the French as being too extreme.
39. CAB 23/86, 16 December.
40. Eden, pp. 430–1.
41. FO 371/20589 W18270/9549/41, Hillgarth, Majorca, 17 December 1936.
42. For the text of the agreement see Eden, p. 431.
43. Eden, p. 441.
44. CAB 27/628 CP6(37), memoranda of the Foreign Policy Committee; FO 371/21282, memorandum by Secretary of State, 8 January 1937.
45. FO 859/4, tenth meeting of NIC, 4 December 1936; see also GD 35, 10 August 1936.
46. FO 371/21296 W12902/41.
47. GDs 157 and 158. Total forces in Spain probably never exceeded 15,000 at

any time (FO 371/21296 W12902/1/41).

48. FO 371/20593 W18699/11115/41, seventeenth meeting of the Chairman's Sub-committee, 22 December 1936.
49. FO 371/20590 W18814/9549/41. Appeal sent on 26 December 1936.
50. FO 371/20590 W18827/9549/41, Drummond, Rome, 26 December 1936; FO 371/20590 W18826/9549/41, Chilston, Moscow, 27 December 1936; FO 371/20590 W1017/7/41, Phipps, Berlin, 4 January 1937.
51. FO 371/21319 W1017/7/41.
52. The Foreign Enlistment Act, 1870, made it an offence punishable by fine or imprisonment for any British subject to accept or agree to accept any commission or engagement in the military or naval service of either party in a civil war.
53. FO 371/20589 W18567/9549/41.
54. FO 371/20587 W17160/9549/41.
55. FO 371/10589 W18227/9549/41.
56. Accounts by individual volunteers are legion. See, for example, Esmond Romilly, *Boadilla* (London: Macdonald, 1971) p. 18, and for a good general survey see Andreu Castells, *Las Brigadas Internacionales de la Guerra de Espana* (Barcelona: Ariel, 1974).
57. FO 371/20589 W18227/9549/41.
58. FO 371/21319 W737/7/41.
59. FO 371/21317 W7/7/41.
60. FO 371/21320 W1271/7/41.
61. FO 371/20588 W17975/9549/41, Madrid, 12 December 1936; and W1857/9549/41; FO 371/20583 W14849/9549/41, signal from HMS *Grafton*, 1 November 1936.
62. FO 371/21320 W1271/7/41. It was stressed that these figures were incomplete, but were not an exaggeration. Those in the reception camps formed only a small proportion of the total. Delperrie de Bayac, *Les Brigades internationales* (Paris: Fayard, 1968) chs 5–7.
63. FO 371/20587 W17160/9549/41, 3 December 1936, minute by Shuckburgh; FO 371/10590 W18793/9549/41, Foreign Office minutes, 24–31 December 1936. See also *The Times* leading article, 10 February 1976.
64. FO 371/20590 W18970/9549/41, Foreign Office minutes, 23 December 1936–8 January 1937.
65. CAB 23/87.
66. *The Times*, 11 January 1937.
67. FO 849/1, eighteenth Meeting of NIC, 12 March 1937.
68. Correspondence with the Director of Public Prosecutions, 23 March–3 May 1976. Between 1936 and 1939 eleven cases were referred to the DPP, but no action taken.
68a. FO 371/21330, 21395 and 21336, for War Office reports of March, April and May 1937 respectively.
69. Letter from William Alexander, Commander of the British Battalion of the International Brigade, printed in *The Times* in reply to article by Louis Blom-Cooper on Foreign Enlistment Act, 7 (February 1976). Mr Alexander estimates that out of 2,015 Britons who went to Spain, at least 1,600 left after January 1937, and that new volunteers continued to arrive until the end of July 1938; FO 371/21340 W13090/7/41.

70. FO 371/21326 W4675/7/41, secret report, 8 March 1937.

71. FO 371/21326 W5046/7/41.

72. FO 849/1, nineteenth meeting of the NIC, 24 March 1937. See also FO 849/41, notes from the Spanish Government to the United Kingdom, France, Russia and the League of Nations; here, 'Documents seized at Guadalajara from Italian units'.

73. FO 371/21330 W6947/7/41.

74. Ivan Maisky, *Spanish Notebooks* (London: Hutchinson, 1966) p. 125.

75. FO 849/28, forty-fifth meeting of the Chairman's Sub-committee, 15 April 1937.

76. FO 849/40, Committee of Jurists, on which were represented the United Kingdom, Czechoslovakia, France, Germany, Italy, Portugal and the USSR.

77. FO 849/40. At the last meeting of the Committee of Jurists on 17 April, Hemming informed representatives that it was impossible to follow the movement of Spanish gold as the German representative had desired, since the Bank of Spain had ceased to issue statements of its gold holdings from 18 July 1936. See above, p. 51.

78. *Ibid.*, fifty-second meeting, 24 May 1936.

79. FO 849/28, fifty-fourth meeting of Chairman's Sub-Committee, 21 June 1937. Discussion of the 8th Report of the Technical Advisory Sub-committee for the Withdrawal of Volunteers.

80. GDs 287–97, 310–46. Grandi and Ribbentrop resumed their places at the NIC on 18 June 1937.

81. CAB 27/622, meeting of the Foreign Policy Committee, 21 June 1937.

82. The Government of Léon Blum was replaced on 22 June 1937 by a government led by Camille Chautemps. Blum became Vice-President of the Council and Delbos remained Foreign Secretary.

83. CAB 27/622, 21 June 1937.

84. See above, ch. 2. Germany and Italy had 37 observation officers each in the Sea Observation Scheme. These were withdrawn but it was hoped to recruit replacements. German and Italian ships continued to pick up observers (FO 849/28, fifty-fifth meeting of Chairman's Sub-Committee, 29 June 1937).

85. Gordon Craig, 'The German Foreign Office', in *The Diplomats*, Gordon Craig and Felix Gilbert (eds.), (New York: Atheneum, 1965) p. 431.

86. CAB 27/622, 1 July 1937, appendices I and II, telegram from Phipps, and communication from the French Embassy.

87. *Ibid.*, 28 June 1937.

88. FO 371/21338 W12406/7/41, 25 June 1937.

89. FO 371/21341 W13125/7/41.

90. Keith Feiling, *Life of Neville Chamberlain* (London: Macmillan, 1970) p. 299.

91. FO 371/21340 W13090/41.

92. However, Eden did know that Grandi had given the Prime Minister a letter from Mussolini (Feiling, p. 333, and NC 2/24A, diary).

93. CAB 27/622, 1 July 1937.

94. FO 849/1, twenty-fourth and twenty-fifth meetings, 9 July; twenty-sixth and twenty-seventh meetings, 16 July 1937.

95. Maisky, *Spanish Notebooks*, p. 33.

96. John Harvey (ed.), *The Diplomatic Diaries of Oliver Harvey, 1937–1940* (London: Collins, 1970) p. 412.

97. CAB 23/89. During the early summer supplies of arms from Russia had been stepped up (see for example War Office note, 7 June 1937, FO 371/21336 W11182/7/41), but this source of aid had been effectively cut off by the pre-Nyon submarine activity. The Spanish Government purchased old arms from Bolivia in September, but by then Italian aid was building up again (FO 371/21346).

98. FO 371/21345 W18484/7/41.

99. FO 371/21345 W18200, 18395/7/41; GD 427; Eden, p. 474.

100. This was proposed by the Greek Minister in Paris. Delbos used the suggestion to impress on Eden the extent of disaffection among the Balkan states (FO 371/21345 W18476/7/41).

101. FO 371/21345, Green Paper W18656/15813/G/1937; FO 371/21346 W19006/7/41, 4 October 1937.

102. *Ibid.*

103. CAB/89, Cabinet meeting, 8 September 1937, called to discuss the situation in the Far East and in the Mediterranean.

104. FO 371/21346. Only one of five ships which had set out from Russia actually arrived in Spain.

105. FO 371/21345 W18695/7/41. See also De Bayac, *op. cit.*, p. 322. The decree ordering amalgamation of the Brigades with the Spanish army was given on 27 September 1937.

106. FO 371/21346 W18849/7/41.

107. FO 371/21345 W18696, W18710/7/41, and FO 371/21346 W18736/7/41m 6–8 October 1937.

107a. CAB 23/89.

107b. FO 849/33.

107c. The Phipps Papers (henceforth PHPP), (Churchill College, Cambridge); here PHPP 1/19, 20 October 1937.

108. FO 849/33, sixty-four to sixty-eigth meetings.

109. FO 371/21347 W19876/7/41, telegram to Lord Chilston, 27 October 1937.

110. Russian and British Intelligence were in accord on this point. The War Office report for October noted Italian 'movements of troops and munitions on a considerable scale' up to the middle of October (FO 371/21395 W10648/2397/41).

111. FO 371/21347 W19912/7/41, Chilston, 29 October 1937.

112. CAB 23/90, 17 December 1937.

113. See table 20.

114. FO 371/21395 W20648/2397/41.

115. FO 371/21350 W21867/7/41.

116. FO 371/21350 W22028/7/41, minutes 21 October–1 December 1937.

117. CAB 56/5 and 6, Joint Intelligence Sub-committee, Spain (closed).

118. CAB 53/8, Chiefs of Staff memoranda, 22 December 1937, 226th meeting of Chiefs of Staff.

119. Ciano, *op. cit.*, 2 November (Eden '. . . is trying to land us a good kick on the shines') p. 27; FO 371/21347 W1994/7/41. Quotations from *Popolo di Roma*, 23 October 1937.

120. FO 371/21345 W19177/7/41.

121. Harvey, *op. cit.*, p. 56, diary entry, 3 November 1937.
122. *Ibid.*, p. 57 and appendix G.
123. Eden, p. 517.
124. FO 371/21338 W12204/7/41, Foreign Office minutes on a telegram from Sir Neville Henderson, British Ambassador in Berlin, 24 June 1937.
125. Eden, pp. 540–6.
126. NC1/17/7, 2 February 1938.
127. NC1/17/5, 16 December 1937.
128. Cadogan, *op. cit.*, pp. 32–3.
129. For a more detailed account of these events see Harvey, *op. cit.*, pp. 76–9. Unfortunately, the summaries for the meetings of the Foreign Policy Committee on 19, 21, and 29 January 1938 are missing (CAB 27/622).
130. NC 2/24 A, diary entry for 19–27 February 1938, and quoted by Iain Macleod in *Neville Chamberlain* (London: Muller, 1961) pp. 211–17.
131. On 14 January the French Government was defeated, but re-formed with the Chautemps-Daladier partnership as before. Daladier replaced Blum as Deputy Prime Minister.
132. HCD, vol. 331, cols. 38–40, 1 February 1938.
133. Maurice Cowling, *The Impact of Hitler* (Cambridge University Press, 1975) p. 174.
134. These were: Malcolm Macdonald, W. S. Morrison, Lord Zetland, and W. Elliot.
135. NC 22/24 A, diaries. The entry for 19 February 1938, in which Chamberlain gives his view of the declining relationship between himself and Eden, is the first entry since May 1937.
136. NC 1/17/8, letter from Lady Chamberlain, 22 February 1938.
137. HCD. vol. 332, col. 62, 22 February 1938.
138. CAB 23/92, 2 March 1938.
139. FO 371/22637 W2265/83/41, minutes, 24–25 February 1938.
140. FO 371/22638 W2827/83/41, Phipps, 2 March 1938.
141. PHPP 1/21, Phipps to Halifax, 3 November 1938. This gives a retrospective account given to Phipps by the Foreign Minister, then Georges Bonnet. Also PHPP 1/20, Phipps to Halifax, 27 March 1938.
142. PHPP 2/10, correspondence with Orme Sargent, 17 March 1938.
143. *Ibid.*
144. D. N. Pritt, *The Fall of the French Republic* (London: Muller, 1941) p. 103; Alexander Werth, *The Twilight of France* (London: Hamish Hamilton, 1942) pp. 171–4.
145. PHPP 1/20, 27 March, Phipps to Halifax.
146. *Ibid.*, 19 and 25 April 1938, Phipps to Halifax.
147. Ciano, 19 April 1938, p. 104.
148. FO 371/21630 C3497/317/18, memorandum by Laurence Collier, 23 March 1938, with Foreign Office minutes.
149. FO 371/21591 C3687/13/17, record of Anglo-French conversations.
150. PHPP 1/20, Phipps to Halifax, 16 June 1938.
151. FO 371/22438 R4840/899/22. See Ciano, p. 116.
152. Harold Nicolson, *Diaries and letters, 1930–1939*, Nigel Nicolson (ed.), (London: Collins, 1966) p. 343.
153. Cadogan, *op. cit.*, p. 79.

154. CAB 23/94, 15 June 1938.
155. PHPP 1/20, Phipps to Halifax, 16 June 1938.
156. Cadogan, *op. cit.*, p. 83, 16 June 1938.
157. NC 18/1/1057, 25 June 1938, Chamberlain to his sister Hilda.
158. CAB 23/94, 5 July 1938.
159. FO 371/22606 W4055; FO 371/22612 W11578. See also below, ch. 6.
160. CAB 23/92, 30 March 1938; FO 371/22628 W10527/29/41.
161. NC 8/26/3.
162. Franco was not against all forms of interference. His representative in London, the Duke of Alba, told Mounsey that Franco would eventually want to borrow money, and was inviting a party of Labour MPs to visit his territory with a view to future policy (FO 371/22661 W13957/83/41).
163. FO 371/22661 W14261/86/41.
164. FO 371/22656 W14998/83/41.
165. Dolores Ibarruri, *La Lucha* (Moscow, 1968) pp. 354–8. See also Dolores Ibarruri, *They Shall Not Pass* (New York: International Publishers, 1976); De Bayac, *op. cit.*, p. 383.
166. FO 371/24140 W955.
167. FO 371/24140 W1073, 17 January 1939.
168. John Coulson, the Third Secretary, had taken over from Evelyn Shuckburgh in September 1937 (FO 371/24140 W1073).
169. Ilya Ehrenburg, *Eve of War, 1933–41*, (London: Macgibbon & Kee, 1963) p. 239.
170. De Bayac, *op. cit.*, p. 386.
171. FO 371/22654 W13261/83/41, Air Ministry and War Office estimates of Italian air and land personnel in Spain, 4 October 1938.
172. CAB 23/96, 26 October 1938. Spain retained a place on almost every Cabinet agenda until British recognition of Franco in February 1939.
173. CAB 23/96, 21 December 1938.
174. Ciano, *op. cit.*, p. 8, diary entry for 9 January 1939.
175. Maisky, *op. cit.*, p. 125.
176. FO 371/24115 W1027.
177. CAB 23/97; FO 371/24119 W6639.

NOTES TO CHAPTER 6

1. See below pp. 193 and 213–14. For first-hand accounts of Anglo-Spanish relations see Sir Robert Hodgson, *op. cit.*; Sir Maurice Peterson, *Both Sides of the Curtain* (London: Constable, 1959); and Viscount Templewood, *Ambassador on Special Mission* (London: Collins, 1946).
2. Santiago Casares Quiroga, Prime Minister of the Republic, May–July 1936 (FO 371/21384 W6021/1/41).
3. FO 371/20538 W11228/62/41.
4. GD 181, 2 January 1937.
5. Thomas, *op. cit.*, p. 346.
6. FO 371/20532 W8949/62/41.
7. FO 371/20534 W9248/62/41.

8. Pablo de Azcárate, *op. cit.*, pp. 23–4.
9. *Ibid.*
10. A good general guide to the question of recognition can be found in J. G. Starke, *An Introduction to International Law* (London: Butterworth, 1958) pp. 105–32.
11. In this case, W. E. Hall, *A Treatise on International Law* (Oxford: Clarendon Press, 1924); John Westlake, *International Law, part I–Peace* (Cambridge University Press, 1904); W. B. Laurence (ed.), *Wheaton's Elements of International Law*, (Boston: 1863) Little, Brown & Co.
12. FO 371/20529 W8234/62/41, 10 August 1936.
13. Hall, *op. cit.*
14. After 24 July the rebel generals formed a military *junta* at Burgos. President of the *junta* until Franco was pronounced Head of State for Nationalist Spain on 1 October 1936, was general Megaul Calsanellas Ferrer (Thomas, *op. cit.*, pp. 238 and 365).
15. See above, p. 107.
16. The legal definition of neutrality was not always understood. See Duff Cooper's remark to the House of Commons on 22 July 1937: 'For myself I see little difference between the two words' (i.e. non-intervention and neutrality).
17. FO 371/21359, fol. 174.
18. CAB 23/86, 4 November 1936.
19. CAB 23/86, 11 November 1936.
20. GDs 123 and 124.
21. The Conde de Albiz, Legal Adviser to the British Embassy, worked closely with Chilton, and had strong family ties with Britain. See Hodgson, *op. cit.*, p. 80.
22. William Eric Beckeitt, second Legal Adviser, and described by Donald Macleem, then a clerk in the Western and League Department as 'to some degree pro-Republican' (letter to writer, 20 November 1975).
23. FO 371/21384 W3192/100/41, minute on dispatch from Hendaye, 12 February 1937.
24. FO 371/21352, 7 April 1937.
25. Thomas, *op. cit.*, pp. 795–6.
26. GD 506, Dr Ernst Woerman to the German Foreign Ministry, 20 January 1938.
27. CAB 23/88.
28. Sir Robert Hodgson (1874–1956), previously Chargé d'Affaires in Moscow.
29. FO 371/21384 W3192/100/41.
30. On 9 February 1937 one witness remarked that there was only a small attendance at Question Time and 'he had seldom seen a more lifeless House' (BBC Written Archives, PQ News, Acc. No. 4788).
31. CAB 23/87, 17 March 1937.
32. CAB 23/88, 24 March 1937.
33. FO 371/21287, fol. 47, and FO 371/21288, fol. 207, 25 March 1937.
34. CAB 23/88, 7 April 1937.
35. FO 371/21296 W12902/1/41, memorandum prepared in the Foreign Office for the Imperial Conference.
36. CAB 27/626, Foreign Policy Committee paper, 28 June 1937.

37. FO 371/2136 W11182/7/41, Maj. Tuckar, War Office 7 June 1937. See also Tables 19 and 20.
38. FO 371/21298 W14857, memorandum and minutes, 21 July 1937.
39. FO 371/21298 W14962, and FO 371/21299 W15803, 17 August 1937.
40. FO 371/21401 W19783/9260/41.
41. FO 371/21401 W18118/9260/41. See also statement for meeting of ministers, 2 September 1937 (CP 207/37).
42. FO 371/21402 W20486/9260/41.
43. Hodgson, *op. cit.*, p. 79. In a table drawn up in the Foreign Office showing countries granting recognition, Britain was listed as affording *de facto* recognition, not as a country which had appointed a Commercial Agent. See table 22, p. 193.
44. K. W. Watkins, *op. cit.*, p. 68.
45. Hodgson, *loc. cit.*
46. *Ibid.*, p. 85.
47. FO 371/22699 W15442.
48. Traina, *op. cit.*, *passim*.
49. Keith Middlemas, *Diplomacy of Illusion* (London: Weidenfeld & Nicolson, 1972) pp. 21–2.
50. FO 371/20537 W10314/62/41, minutes and draft reply to letter from Lord Cecil of Chelwood, 28 August–10 September 1936.
51. FO 371/21254 W10746/5994/98. In the event Spain remained a member of the League until 1941.
52. Viscount Cecil, *A Great Experiment* (London: Cape, 1941) p. 282.
53. FO 371/21345 W18101, 18291, 18292, 18343/7/41, minutes, 27 September–2 October 1937.
54. Quoted by Feiling, *op. cit.*, p. 324.
55. Notably by Herbert Southworth, *La Destruction de Guernica* (Paris: Ruedo Iberico, 1975).
56. FO 849/1, twenty-first meeting, 6 May 1937.
57. FO 371/21332 W8576/7/ and FO 371/21337 W11879/G.
58. NC 18/1/1057, letter from Chamberlain to his sister Hilda, 25 June 1938.
59. FO 371/22653 W12505/83/41. Letter to the Government from the Parliamentary Committee for Spain signed by fourteen MPs, 12 September 1938.
60. Letter to the writer from Mr George Strauss, 11 March 1975.
61. FO 371/20532 W8885/62/41.
62. CAB 23/88, 23 March 1937.
63. William Bowman, *History of The Times*, vol. IV, part ii, 1921–1948 (London: Times Publishing Co., 1952) pp. 906–7.
64. See, for example, the Hickleton Papers, Churchill College (henceforth Hickleton), (microfilm) A4 410/3.2, Henderson to Halifax, 2 December 1937; or PHPP 2/18, Vansittart to Phipps, 26 May 1937: 'If necessary I will speak to the Chancellor and he will speak to Geoffrey Dawson [Editor of *The Times*].'
65. Hickleton, *loc. cit.*
66. Bowman, *op. cit.*, *passim*.
67. Robert Rhodes James (ed.), *Chips: The Diaries of Sir Henry Channon* (London: Weidenfeld & Nicolson, 1967) p. 79; Keith Middlemas and John Barnes,

Baldwin (London: Weidenfeld & Nicolson, 1969) p. 987.

68. FO 371/21318 W290/7/41, January 1937.
69. PHPPS 1/9/, p. 47, Phipps to Eden, 28 December 1937.
70. NC 8/21/8, June 1938, report to the Prime Minister by Sir Joseph Ball, Head of the Conservative Research Department, on 'What we are up against'.
71. *Ibid.*
72. FO 371/20530 W8461/62/41. Lord Halifax objected strongly and in person to an article by Lord Strabolgi, formerly of the Admiralty War Staff, which appeared in the *Daily Herald* on 10 August 1936 and referred to the British Government's 'malevolent neutrality'. This did not prevent the same author writing another article for the *Herald* entitled 'Our Admiralty are all at sea about Spain' (on 9 October 1936).
73. Rose Macaulay, letter to *The Listener*, 17 February 1937.
74. NC/21/8.
75. FO 371/20523 W6758/62/41, 30 July 1936.
76. CAB 23/88, 24 March 1937.
77. NC 8/21/8.
78. *Ibid.*
79. Colin Seymour-Ure, *The Press, Politics and the Public* (London: Methuen, 1968) p. 29. See also F. Gannon, *The British Press and Nazi Germany* (London: Oxford University Press, Oxford 1971) for an excellent survey of the British press of the period.
80. Tony Adgate, 'British Newsreel and the Spanish Civil War' in *History*, vol. 58,
81. no. 192, February 1973.
    Ibid.
82. David C. Lukowitz, 'British Pacifists and Appeasement: The Peace Pledge Union', *Journal of Contemporary History*, vol. 9, no. 1, January 1974.
83. FO 371/20534 W9331/62/41.
84. Hugh Dalton, *Memoirs, 1931–1945: The Fateful Years* (London: Muller, 1957) pp. 97–101.
85. FO 371/20573 W9887/9549/41, 28 August 1936.
86. C. R. Attlee, *As It Happened* (London: Heinemann, 1954).
87. CAB 23/88, 24 March 1937.
88. *Ibid.*
89. CAB 23/86, 16 December 1936.
90. FO 371/21352, 7 April 1937.
91. On 16 May 1937 Largo Caballero resigned and was succeeded by Juan Négrin, a compromise candidate who was able to command the support of the communists.
92. FO 371/22659 W7163/86/41, 31 May 1938.
93. FO 371/22628 W10407/29/41, 28 July 1938.
94. FO 371/22646, 22650, 22653, 22656, War Office reports. Aid continued to cross the French border but the difficulties in trans-shipment for the Russians were now immense.
95. FO 371/22624 W5550/29/41, Leche, 30 April 1938. The Nationalists had already issued their war aims.
96. FO 371/22627 W8723/29/41, Foreign Office memorandum and minutes, 27 June–11 July 1938.
97. FO 371/22628 W10407. Leche reported that the Republicans were 'fighting

gallantly' and that Valencia was unlikely to fall in the immediate future.
98. FO 371/22650 W9841/83/41, Phipps, 20 July 1938.
99. FO 371/22607 W4378.
100. *Ibid.*, Leche, Caldetas (the temporary British Legation near Barcelona), 25 March 1938.
101. FO 371/22661 W14261/86/41, Chetwode to Halifax, 17 October 1938, complaining of an article in the *Sunday Pictorial*.
102. FO 371/22661 W13298/86/41, Chetwode to Halifax, 27 September 1938.
103. *Ibid.*, report and minutes.
104. FO 371/22631 W14601, Caldetas, 31 October 1938.
105. *Ibid.*
106. Even Von Stohrer, German Ambassador to Nationalist Spain, acknowledged, as early as January 1938, that a 'pronounced evolution' had taken place in Republican Spain, and that the risk of a communist state was now much more remote than it had been (FO 371/22659 W1445/86/41, conversation between Hodgson and Von Stohrer, 28 January 1938).
107. FO 371/22631 W16041/29/41, 25 November 1938.
108. FO 371/22661, Leche, 10 October 1938.
109. Cattell, *op. cit.*, p. 124.
110. FO 371/22656 W14795/86/4, 2 November 1938.
111. FO 371/22629, fol. 212, Hodgson, quoting Hillgarth, Burgos, 24 August 1938.
112. FO 371/22661 W14261/86/41, 17 October. The *Sunday Pictorial* was especially castigated by Hodgson. See above, p. 201.
113. See also Hodgson, *op. cit.*, pp. 129–30. Some small successes were later claimed by Chetwode. See Arnold Toynbee, *Survey of International Affairs*, 1938, vol. 1 (London, 1948) pp. 392–3.
114. FO 371/22614 W15290/5/41, W15476 and W15026, Chetwode, 31 October 1938.
115. FO 371/22631 W16041/29/41, Barcelona, 25 November 1938.
116. FO 371/22631 W14955/29/41, 5 November 1938.
117. FO 371/22631 W14601/5/41, 31 October 1938, Stevenson.
118. FO 371/22662, fols. 178–80, report of conversation between British Air Attaché and the American Naval Air Attaché in Paris, 5 December 1938. General Miaja, in command at Madrid, was also later reported to have held an international passport for some months (FO 371/24129 W6704).
119. FO 371/24114 W623/5/41, memorandum by Roberts with Foreign Office minutes, 2–5 January 1939.
120. CAB 23/97, 18 January 1939; see also CP 8(39). This was apparently a reference to a memorandum by Sir Robert Vansittart (see below, pp. 211–12).
121. FO 371/2415 W1471/5/41, 27 January 1939.
122. FO 371/24126 W1081/8/41, 15 January 1939.
123. FO 371/2415 W1752/5/41, Hodgson on leave in England, discussion and minutes, 2–6 February.
124. See below, p. 211–12.
125. FO 371/24126 W1990/8/41, report by Major Mahoney, 31 January 1939; minute by Vansittart, 13 February 1939.
126. FO 371/24126 W1991/8/41, 3 February 1939, and FO 371/24127 W2559, 1–

8 February 1939, received in Foreign Office 13 February 1939.

127. *Ibid.*
128. *Ibid.*
129. FO 371/24127 W2577/8/41, message from Franco, 4 February 1939.
130. CAB 23/97, 15 February 1939.
131. FO 371/24127 W2559, Foreign Office minute, 18 February 1939.
132. FO 371/24147 W2741/8/41.
133. FO 371/24148 W3226/374/41.
134. CAB 23/97, 15 February 1937.
135. *Ibid.*
136. FO 371/24127 W3178/8/41, O'Malley, 11 February 1939, St. Jean-de-Luz.
137. Azcárate, *op. cit.*, p. 128.
138. FO 371/24139 W3222/8/41, HMS *Devonshire*, 21 February 1939.
139. Azcárate, p. 128; Thomas, *op. cit.*, ch. 50.
140. FO 371/24147 W1581/8/41, O'Malley, 27 January 1939.
141. The complex events and activities involving Segismundo Casado are related in his book, *The Last Days of Madrid* (London: Peter Davies, 1939). See also Robert Colodny, *The Struggle for Madrid* (New York, 1958). It has been suggested that Casado was paid by British Intelligence to hasten the end of the war. See Pierre Broué and Emile Témine, *The Revolution and the War in Spain* (London: Faber, 1970) p. 572. However, until such time, if ever, as any relevant papers are released, it is impossible to comment categorically, except to say that the Foreign Office appears to have been unaware of any debt to Col. Casado. In March 1939 he approached the British Government for their assistance in an intermediary capacity, but without success. The comment was made then that it was 'quite pointless to put any pressure on the Spanish (Nationalist) Government to accept terms' (FO 371/24148 W4675/374/41, 20 March 1939). It cannot, of course, be assumed that the Western and League Department would necessarily have been aware of the full scope of British Intelligence activities in Spain. Certainly the British Government, which had always paid lip-service to the concept of a negotiated peace, sought a compromise solution very energetically from the end of 1938. But by March Britain had recognised Franco, so there was no further merit from the British point of view in a negotiated settlement.
142. CAB 23/97, 22 February 1939.
143. *Ibid.*
144. FO 371/24115 W1722/5/41, Lord Plymouth, 19 January 1939.
145. FO 371/24115 W1300/5/41.
146. FO 371/24116 W3667, 3903/5/41.
147. See n. 1, p. 256.
148. Thomas, *op. cit.*, p. 949.
149. CAB 23/93, 23 March 1938.
150. FO 371/2415 W1405/5/41, January 1939. The Republican Government moved from Valencia to Barcelona in the autumn of 1937, but left for Genova in January 1939.
151. FO 371/22627 W8723/29/41, Foreign Office memorandum dated 27 June 1938, in which Vansittart confessed to being 'filled with disquiet' at British policy in Spain.
152. FO 371/2415 W973/5/41, Vansittart to Halifax, 16 January 1939.

153. See above, p. 137.
154. Basil Liddell Hart, *The Defence of Britain* (London: Faber, 1939) p. 59.
155. HCD, vol. 326, cols. 838, 1024, 1499, 1791–2, 1824–6, 1829–30, 12–19 July 1938; vol. 350, col. 1037–8.
156. Appendix F lists instances of Mussolini's public congratulations to Franco.
157. FO 371/22650 W9399/83/41; CP 163(38), 7 July 1938. This speech was drawn to Foreign Office attention after publication in the *News Chronicle* on 12 July 1938.
158. *Ibid.*, minutes.
159. Sir Maurice Peterson, British Ambassador to Spain, 1939–40, *op. cit.*
160. Viscount Templewood, *Ambassador on Special Mission, op. cit.*, (London: Collins, 1946).
161. CAB 24/280.
162. *Ibid.* See appendix G for full text.
163. Geneviève Tabouis, *op. cit.*, p. 173. Her articles for *L'Oeuvre* were invariably filed by the Foreign Office. See also Pertinax in *Echo de Paris*, 31 July 1936 (FO 371/20525 W7453/62/41).
164. In a letter to me of 17 January 1977, Sir Walter St. Clair Roberts wrote: 'With the benefit of hindsight I believe that as from the German invasion of Poland a Spain without an alliance with Hitler would be [sic] in the best interests of the Western Allies . . .'
165. See above, p. 191; and Harold Macmillan, *op. cit.*, p. 474.
166. As late as November 1938 the Assistant Military Attaché at Burgos, Maj. Edmund Mahoney, assessed a victory in the field for the Nationalists as unlikely. He believed the Republicans could hold out indefinitely provided their supply of war material was not reduced (FO 371/22631 W14897/41, 9 November, 1938).

NOTES TO APPENDICES

1. Based on Foreign Office List, 1937.
2. FO 371/20538 W11275/62/41.
3. FO 371/21384.
4. CAB 62/5.
5. Based on FO 849/30.
6. FO 22658, fol. 295.
7. CAB 286, fols 91–7.

Bibliography

A. DOCUMENTS

Selected documents from British Government archives available in the Public Record Office

Cabinet Conclusions 1936–39	CAB 23
Cabinet Committees 1936–39	CAB 27
Committee of Imperial Defence	CAB 2
Chiefs of Staff Sub-committee	CAB 53
Cabinet Office Memoranda	CAB 24
Prime Minister	Prem/1
General Correspondence of the Foreign Office	FO 371
Non-Intervention Committee	FO 849
Non-Intervention Committee Memoranda	CAB 62
Admiralty files	ADM

Private collections

Birmingham University Library:	
The Neville Chamberlain Papers	NC
Churchill College, Cambridge:	
The Hickleton Papers (Lord Halifax) on microfilm	
The Eric Phipps Papers	PHPP
Lord Vansittart's Papers	VNST
Cambridge University Library:	
The Baldwin Papers	
The Templewood Papers (Samuel Hoare)	
Corpus Christi College, Oxford:	
The Hemming Papers (Francis Hemming)	

Other archives:

The BBC Written Archives Centre, Caversham, Berks.
Companies House, London.
The Press Library, Royal Institute of International Affairs, London. (Some material from this library is being rehoused at the London School of Economics.)

Published documentary sources:

Documents Diplomatiques Français, *1932–39*, 2ᵉ série (1936–39), tomes I–IX.
Documents on German Foreign Policy, 1918–45, series D, vol. III.
Evénements Survenues en France, 1933–45, *Les Témoignages*, vol. I.
League of Nations Trade Statistics, 1935–45 (London: HMSO).
Parliamentary Debates (House of Commons) HCD.

B. BOOKS

Primary Sources

Álvarez del Vayo, Julio, *Freedom's Battle* (London: Heinemann, 1940).
Attlee, Clement R., *As It Happened* (London: Heinemann, 1954).
Avon, the Earl of, *The Eden Memoirs: Facing the Dictators* (London: Cassell, 1962); *The Reckoning* (Cassell, 1965).
Azcárate y Flores, Pablo, *Mi Embajada en Londres Durante La Guerra Civil Española* (Barcelona: Ariel, 1976).
Bernanos, Georges, *A Diary of My Times* (London: Boriswood, 1938).
Blum, Léon, *L'Oeuvre de Léon Blum, 1934–1937*, vol. IV, part 1 (Paris: Albin Michel, 1954–7).
Bolín, Luis, *Spain: The Vital Years* (London: Cassell, 1967).
Bonnet, Georges, *Quai d'Orsay* (London: Times Publishing Co. and Anthony Gibbs & Phillips, 1965).
Bowers, Claude, *My Mission to Spain* (London: Gollancz, 1954).
Butler, Lord, *The Art of the Possible* (London: Hamish Hamilton, 1971).
Casado, Segismundo, *The Last Days of Madrid* (London: Peter Davies, 1939).

Cervera Valderrama, Juan, *Memorias de Guerra, 1936–1939* (Madrid: Editora Nacional, 1968).

Chamberlain, Neville, *The Struggle for Peace* (London: Hutchinson, 1939).

Chatfield, Lord, *The Navy and Defence: The Autobiography of Admiral of the Fleet Lord Chatfield*, vol. 2, *It Might Happen Again* (London: Heinemann, 1942).

Churchill, Winston S., *The Second World War*, vol. 1, *The Gathering Storm* (London: Reprint Society, 1951).

Cot, Pierre, *The Triumph of Treason* (Chicago and New York: Riff Davis, 1944).

Davies, John Langdon, *Behind the Spanish Barricades* (London: Secker & Warburg, 1936).

Dilkes, David (ed.), *The Diaries of Sir Alexander Cadogan, 1938–1945* (London: Cassell, 1971).

Dodd, William E. (ed.), *Ambassador Dodd's Diary, 1933–1938* (London: Gollancz, 1944).

Ehrenburg, Ilya, *Eve of War, 1933–1941* (London: MacGibbon & Kee, 1963).

Galland, A., *The First and the Last* (London: Methuen, 1955).

Gurney, Jason, *Crusade in Spain* (London: Faber, 1974).

Halifax, Viscount, *Speeches on Foreign Policy* (London: Oxford University Press, 1940).

Halifax, Viscount, *The Fullness of Days* (London: Collins, 1957).

Harvey, John (ed.), *The Diplomatic Diaries of Oliver Harvey, 1937–1940* (London: Collins, 1970).

Henderson, Sir Nevile, *The Failure of a Mission* (London: Hodder & Stoughton, 1940).

Hodgson, Sir Robert, *Spain Resurgent* (London: Hutchinson, 1953).

Ibarruri, Dolores, *They Shall Not Pass* (New York: International Publishers, 1976).

James, Robert Rhodes (ed.), *Chips: The Diaries of Sir Henry Channon* (London: Weidenfeld & Nicolson, 1967).

James, Vice-Admiral Sir William, *The Sky Was Always Blue* (London: Methuen, 1951).

Jones, Thomas (ed.), *Diary with Letters, 1931–1954* (London: Oxford University Press, 1954).

Kirkpatrick, Sir Ivone, *The Inner Circle* (London: Macmillan, 1959).

Krivitsky, W. G., *I Was Stalin's Agent* (London: Hamish Hamilton, 1939).

Lawford, Valentine, *Bound for Diplomacy* (London: Murray, 1963).

Macmillan, Harold, *The Winds of Change, 1914–1939* (London: Macmillan, 1966).

Maisky, Ivan, *Who Helped Hitler?* (London: Hutchinson, 1964).

Maisky, Ivan, *Spanish Notebooks* (London: Hutchinson, 1966).

Minney, R. J. (ed.), *The Private Papers of Hore Belisha* (London: Collins, 1960).

Moch, Jules, *Rencontres avec Léon Blum* (Paris: Plon, 1970).

Muggeridge, Malcolm (ed.), *Ciano's Diary, 1937–1938* (London: Methuen, 1952).

Muggeridge, Malcolm (ed.), *Ciano's Diary, 1939–1943* (London: Heinemann, 1947).

Nicolson, Harold, *Diaries and Letters, 1930–1939*, Nigel Nicolson (ed.) (London: Collins, 1966).

O'Malley, Owen St. Clair, *The Phantom Caravan* (London: Murray, 1954).

Orwell, George, *Homage to Catalonia* (Penguin, 1971).

Peterson, Sir Maurice, *Both Sides of the Curtain* (London: Constable, 1950).

Poncet, André François-, *Souvenirs d'une ambassade à Berlin* (Paris: Flammarion, 1946).

Romilly, Esmond, *Boadilla* (London: Macdonald, 1971).

Rowse, A. L., *All Souls and Appeasement* (London: Macmillan, 1961).

Rust, William, *Britons in Spain* (London: Lawrence & Wishart, 1939).

Salazar, Oliveira, *Doctrine and Action* (London: Faber, 1939).

Schmidt, Paul, *I Was Hitler's Interpreter* (London: Heinemann, 1951).

Schacht, Hjalmar, *Account Settled* (London: Weidenfeld & Nicolson, 1949).

Simon, Lord, *Retrospect* (London: Hutchinson, 1952).

Spender, Stephen, *World Within World* (London: Hamish Hamilton, 1951).

Sperber, Murray (ed.), *And I Remember Spain* (London: Hart-Davis and MacGibbon, 1974).

Steer, G. L., *The Tree of Gernika* (London: Hodder & Stoughton, 1938).

Templewood, Viscount, *Ambassador on Special Mission* (London: Collins, 1946).

Templewood, Viscount, *Nine Troubled Years* (London: Collins, 1954).

Thompson, Sir Geoffrey, *Front Line Diplomat* (London: Hutchinson, 1959).
Toynbee, Philip (ed.), *The Distant Drum* (London: Sidgwick & Jackson, 1976).
Vansittart, Lord, *Lessons of My Life* (London: Hutchinson, 1943).
Vansittart, Lord, *The Mist Procession* (London: Hutchinson, 1958).
Wintringham, Tom, *Spanish Captain* (London: Faber, 1939).
Zay, Jean, *Carnets Secrets* (Paris: Philippe Henriot, 1942).

Secondary Sources

Alcofar Nassaes, José Luis, *Las Fuerzas Navales en La Guerra Civil Espanola*, (Barcelona: Dopesa, 1971).
Ashton-Gwatkin, Frank, *The British Foreign Service* (Syracuse University Press, 1954).
Atholl, Duchess of, *Searchlight on Spain* (Penguin Special, 1938).
Avery, David, *Not on Queen Victoria's Birthday: The History of the Rio Tinto Company* (London: Collins, 1974).
Barcia, Augusto, *La Politica de No-interventión* (Buenos Aires: Bartolomé, Mitre, 1942).
Barea, Arturo, *The Forging of a Rebel* (London: Davis-Poynter, 1972).
Barnes, John, and Middlemas, Keith, *Baldwin: A Biography* (London: Weidenfeld & Nicolson, 1969).
Benavides, Leandro, *La Politica Economica en la II Republica* (Madrid: Guadiana, 1972).
Birkenhead, Earl of, *Halifax: The Life of Lord Halifax* (London: Hamish Hamilton, 1965).
Bonnefous, Edouard, *Histoire politique de la Troisième République* (Paris: Presses Universitaires de France, 1965).
Bourdin, Janine (ed.), *Léon Blum, Chef de Gouvernement* (Paris: Armand Colin, 1967).
Brenan, Gerald, *The Spanish Labyrinth* (Cambridge University Press, 1969).
Brissaud, André, *Canaris* (London: Weidenfeld & Nicolson, 1973).
Brome, Vincent, *The International Brigades, Spain 1936–1939* (London: Heinemann, 1965).
Broué, Pierre, and Témine, Émile, *The Revolution and the War in Spain*, (London: Faber, 1970).
Butler, David, and Sloman, Anne, *British Political Facts* (London: Macmillan, 1975).

Bullock, Alan, *Hitler – A Study in Tyranny* (Pelican, 1971).

Carr, Raymond, *Spain 1808–1939* (London: Oxford University Press, 1966).

Carr, Raymond (ed.), *The Republic and the Civil War in Spain* (London: Macmillan, 1971).

Castells, Andreu, *Las Brigadas Internacionales de la Guerra de Espana* (Barcelona: Ariel, 1974).

Cattell, David, *Communism and the Spanish Civil War* (University of California, 1955).

Cattell, David, *Soviet Diplomacy and the Spanish Civil War* (University of California, 1957).

Cecil, Viscount, *A Great Experiment* (London: Cape, 1941).

Checkland, S. G., *The Mines of Tharsis* (London: Allen & Unwin, 1967).

Chomsky, Noam, *American Power and the New Mandarins* (New York: Random House, 1969).

Churchill, Randolph, *The Rise and Fall of Sir Anthony Eden* (London: MacGibbon & Kee, 1959).

Cole, Herbert, *Laval: An Autobiography* (London: Heinemann, 1963).

Colton, Joel, *Léon Blum: A Humanist in Politics* (New York: Knopf, 1966).

Colvin, Ian, *Vansittart in Office: The Origins of World War II* (London: Gollancz, 1965).

Cook, Chris, and Sked, A. (eds.), *Crisis and Controversy: Essays in Honour of A. J. P. Taylor* (London: Macmillan, 1976).

Cooper, Alfred Duff, *Old Men Forget* (London: Hart-Davis, 1953).

Coverdale, John, *Italian Intervention in the Spanish Civil War* (Princeton University Press, 1975).

Cowling, Maurice, *The Impact of Hitler* (Cambridge University Press, 1975).

Craig, Gordon, and Gilbert, Felix (eds.), *The Diplomats, 1919–1939* (New York: Atheneum, 1965).

Crozier, Brian, *Franco: A Biographical History* (London: Eyre & Spottiswoode, 1967).

Dell, Robert, *The Geneva Racket, 1920–1939* (London: Hale, 1941).

Delperrie de Bayac, Jacques, *Les Brigades internationales* (Paris: Fayard, 1968).

Deutscher, Isaac, *Stalin: A Political Biography* (Pelican, 1960).

Edwards, Kenneth, *The Grey Diplomatists* (London: Rich & Cowan, 1938).

Esch, Patricia van der, *Prelude to War: The International Repercussions of the Spanish Civil War* (The Hague, 1951). Martinus Nijhoff

Feiling, Keith, *Life of Neville Chamberlain* (London: Macmillan, 1970).

Feis, Herbert, *The Spanish Story* (New York: Norton, 1966).

Foot, Michael, *Aneurin Bevan*, part 1 (London: MacGibbon & Kee, 1962).

Frankel, J., *International Relations* (London: Oxford University Press, 1969).

Géraud, André, pseud. 'Pertinax', *The Grave Diggers of France* (New York: Fertig, 1968).

Gannon, F., *The British Press and Nazi Germany* (London: Oxford University Press, 1971).

Gilbert, Martin, and Gott, Richard, *The Appeasers* (London: Weidenfeld & Nicolson, 1967).

Graves, Robert, and Hodge, Alan, *The Long Weekend: A Social History of Great Britain, 1918–1939* (London: Faber, 1950).

Guttsman, W. L., *The British Political Elite* (London: MacGibbon & Kee, 1965).

Hall, W. E., *A Treatise on International Law* (Oxford: Clarendon Press, 1924).

Hamilton, Alastair, *The Appeal of Fascism* (London: Blond, 1971).

Harper, Glenn, *German Economic Policy in Spain* (The Hague: Mouton, 1967).

Hart, Basil Liddell, *The Defence of Britain* (London: Faber, 1939).

Haxey, Simon, *Tory MP* (London: Gollancz, 1939).

Hills, George, *The Rock of Contention* (London: Hale, 1970).

Howard, Michael, *Continental Commitment* (Penguin, 1972).

Jackson, Gabriel, *The Spanish Republic and the Civil War, 1931–1939* (Princeton University Press, 1965).

Jenkins, Roy, *Government Broadcasting and the Press* (Hart-Davis and MacGibbon, 1975).

Joll, James, *The Unspoken Assumption*, London School of Economics inaugural lecture (London School of Economics, 1968).

Joll, James, *The Anarchists* (London: Methuen, 1964).

Kahn, A. E., *Great Britain in the World Economy* (New York: Columbia University Press, 1946).

Kleine-Albrandt, William, *The Policy of Simmering: a Study of British Policy during the Spanish Civil War, 1936–1939* The Hague: Martinus Nijhoff, 1962.

Knightley, Philip, Leitch, David and Page, Bruce, *Philby: The Spy*

Who Betrayed a Generation (London: Deutsch, 1968).

Knightley, Philip, *The First Casualty* (London: Deutsch, 1975).

Laurence, W. B. (ed.), *Wheaton's Elements of International Law* (Boston: Little, Brown & Co., 1863).

Loveday, Arthur, *World War in Spain* (London: Murray, 1939).

Luard, Evan (ed.), *The International Regulation of Civil Wars* (London: Thames & Hudson, 1968).

Macleod, Iain, *Neville Chamberlain* (London: Muller, 1961).

Marder, Arthur J., *From the Dardanelles to Oran: Studies of the Royal Navy in War and Peace, 1915–1940* (London: Oxford University Press, 1974).

Marwick, Arthur, *Britain in the Century of Total War* (Pelican, 1970).

McMurtrie, Francis (ed.), *Jane's Fighting Ships* (London: Sampson Low, 1936).

Medlicott, W. N., *Britain and Germany: The Search for Agreement 1930–1937*, The Creighton Lecture 1968 (The Athlone Press, 1969).

Middlemas, Keith, *Diplomacy of Illusion* (London: Weidenfeld & Nicolson, 1972).

Monroe, Elizabeth, *The Mediterranean in Politics* (London: Oxford University Press, 1938).

Mowat, C. L., *Britain Between the Wars* (London: Methuen, 1955).

Muggeridge, Malcolm, *The Thirties* (Fontana, 1971).

Namier, Lewis, *Europe in Decay, 1936–1940* (London: Macmillan, 1950).

Northedge, F. S., *Freedom and Necessity in British Foreign Relations*, London School of Economics inaugural lecture (London School of Economics, 1971).

Northedge, F. S., *The Troubled Giant* (London School of Economics, 1966).

Padelford, N. J., *International Law and Diplomacy in the Spanish Civil Strife* New York: Macmillan, 1939.

Payne, Stanley, *The Spanish Revolution* (London: Weidenfeld & Nicolson, 1970).

Peers, E. Alison, *The Spanish Tragedy* (London: Methuen, 1936).

Pertinax, *see* Géraud.

Petrie, Sir Charles, *The Chamberlain Tradition* (Right Book Club, 1938).

Pike, D. W., *Conjecture, Propaganda and Deceit in the Spanish Civil War*, (California Institute of International Studies, 1968).

Pike, D. W., *Les Français et la Guerre d'Espagne, 1936–1939* (Paris:

Presses Universitaires de France, 1975).

Pratt, Lawrence, *East of Malta, West of Suez: Britain's Mediterranean Crises, 1936–1939* (Cambridge University Press, 1975).

Pritt, D. N., *The Fall of the French Republic* (London: Muller, 1941).

Puzzo, Dante A., *Spain and the Great Powers, 1936–1939* (New York: Columbia University Press, 1962).

Raymond, John (ed.), *The Baldwin Age* (London: Eyre & Spottiswoode, 1960).

Renouvin, Pierre (Président du colloque sur Léon Blum, Chef de Gouvernement, 1936–1937), *La politique extérieure du Premier Gouvernement de Léon Blum* (Paris: Armand Colin, 1967). See Bourdin, above.

Richards, Peter G., *Parliament and Foreign Affairs* (London: Allen & Unwin, 1967).

Robertson, Esmond M. (ed.), *The Origins of the Second World War* (London: Macmillan, 1971).

Roskill, Stephen, *Hankey, Man of Secrets*, vol. III, *1931–1963* (London: Collins, 1974).

Roskill, Stephen, *Naval Policy Between the Wars, vol.* II, *1930–1939* (London: Collins, 1976).

Schwartz, Fernando, *La Internacionalizacion de la Guerra Civil Espanola* Barcelona: Ariel, 1971.

Seymour-Ure, Colin, *The Press, Politics and the Public* (London: Methuen, 1968).

Smith, Denis Mack, *Mussolini as a Military Leader* (Reading University Press, 1974).

Southworth, Herbert, *La Destruction de Guernica* (Paris: Rudeo Iberico, 1975).

Tabouis, Geneviève, *Blackmail or War* (Penguin Special, 1938).

Tamames, Ramón, *Estructura Económica de Espana* (Madrid: Gomez, 1965).

Taylor, A. J. P., *The Origins of the Second World War* (Penguin, 1971), Harper & Row N.Y. 1968.

Thomas, Hugh, *The Spanish Civil War* (Pelican, 1977).

Thomson, David, *France: Empire and Republic*, selected documents.

Thompson, Neville, *The Anti-Appeasers* (London: Oxford University Press, 1971).

Toynbee, Arnold J., *Survey of International Affairs* 1937, vol. 2; 1938, vol. 1. (London: Oxford University Press, 1938 ´and 1948 respectively).

Traina, Richard, *American Diplomacy and the Spanish Civil War* (Indiana University Press, 1968).

Trotsky, Leon, *The Spanish Revolution, 1931–1939* (New York: Pathfinder Press, 1973).

Viñas, Angel, *La Alemania Nazi y el 18 de julio* (Madrid: Alianza Universidad, 1974).

Viñas, Angel, *El Oro Español en la Guerra Civil* (Madrid: Instituto de Estudios Fiscales, Ministerio de Hacienda, 1977).

Vital, David, *The Making of British Foreign Policy* (London: Allen & Unwin, 1968).

Watkins, K. W., *Britain Divided: The effect of the Spanish Civil War on British Public Opinion* (London: Nelson, 1963).

Watt, D. C., *Personalities and Policies* (London, 1965), Longmans.

Weintraub, Stanley, *The Last Great Cause: the Intellectuals and the Spanish Civil War* (London: W. H. Allen, 1968).

Werth, Alexander, *The Twilight of France* (London: Hamish Hamilton, 1942).

Westlake, John, *International Law*, part I: *Peace* (Cambridge University Press, 1904).

Wiskemann, Elizabeth, *The Rome-Berlin Axis* (London: Oxford University Press, 1949).

C. ARTICLES

Adgate, Tony, 'British Newsreels and the Spanish Civil War', *History*, vol. 58, no. 192, February 1973.

Bartholdt, Johannes, 'Crisis 1936: The Dilemmas of British Foreign Policy', *Millenium*, 1973.

Carlton, David, 'Eden, Blum and the Origins of Non-Intervention', *Journal of Contemporary History*, vol. 6, no. 3, 1971.

Durrant, Henry, 'Public Opinion Polls and Foreign Policy', *British Journal of Sociology*, vol. 6, no. 2, 1955.

Gallagher, M. D., 'Léon Blum and the Spanish Civil War', *Journal of Contemporary History*, vol. 6, no. 3, 1971.

Gretton, Peter, 'The Nyon Conference – the naval aspect', *English Historical Review*, vol. XC, no. CCCLIV, January 1975.

Harvey, Charles, 'Politics and Pyrites during the Spanish Civil War', unpublished.

Kindersley, Richard, 'Britain's Overseas Investment in 1935 and 1936', *Economic Journal*, vol. XLVII, December 1937.

Lammers, Donald, 'Fascism, Communism and the Foreign Office, 1937–1939', *Journal of Contemporary History*, vol. 6, no. 3, 1971.

Lukowitz, David C., 'British Pacifists and Appeasement: The Peace Pledge Union', *Journal of Contemporary History*, vol. 9, no. 1, January 1974.

Maclochlan, Donald, 'The Press and the Public Opinion', *British Journal of Sociology*, vol. 6, 1955.

Pickles, William, 'Understanding Léon Blum', *Political Quarterly*, vol. 41, 1970.

Pike, D. W., 'Aspects nouveaux du rôle de l'Espagne dans la seconde Guerre mondiale', *Revue d'Histoire Moderne et Contemporaine*, tome xix, juillet/septembre 1972.

Preston, Paul, 'Spain's October Revolution and the Rightist Grasp for Power', *Journal of Contemporary History*, vol. 10, no. 4, October 1975.

Warner, Geoffrey, 'France and Non-Intervention in Spain, July and August 1936', *International Affairs*, vol. 38, no. 2, 1962.

Watt, D. C., 'Soviet Military Aid to the Spanish Revolution in the Spanish Civil War, 1936–1938', *Slavonic and East European Review*, June 1960.

Index

278 *Index*

Lindsay, Sir Ronald, 166
Lisbon, 60, 136
Lithuania, 134
Litvinov, Maxin, 146, 160–2
Llandovery Castle, British SS, 113
Llandudno, 164
Lloyd George, David, 125, 168, 175
Lloyd Thomas, Hugh, 25, 28–9, 30
Locarno, 2, 10, 44
L'Oeuvre, 17
London, 16, 43
London Treaty (1931), 103
López Oliván, Julio, 13, 18, 183
Loveday, Arthur, 7
Lunn, Col., 53

Macdonald, Malcolm, 159
McGrigor, Capt., 114
Maclean, Donald, 12
Madlon bonds, 99
Madrid, 5, 12, 35, 48, 108; government, 134, 186, 209
Maginot Line, 173
Mahoney, Maj. Edmond, 206
Maisky, Ivan, 10, 112, 143, 148–50, 159, 160, 162, 179
Majorca, 58, 110, 121, 127, 138–42, 150
Makins, R. M., 12
Malkin, Sir William, 20, 44, 112, 184–6
Manchester Guardian, 149
Manchuria, 2, 161
Margesson, David, 99
Marseilles, 144, 145
Merchant Shipping (Carriage of Munitions to Spain) Act (1936), 110, 112, 186
Mercury, 97, 98
Merry del Val, Marquis of, 183
Mexican Legation, 134
Mexico, 17, 176–7
MI5, 145
Mines Dept., 76
Minorca, 139
Mitchell Hood, J., 6, 18
Monarchy (Spanish), 90
Montana Project, 86
Monteiro, Armindo, 44
Montreux Conference, 34
Moors, 150

Moreno, Admiral Francisco, 113, 126
Morocco, (Spanish), 12, 36, 156, 213; Spanish mines, 91, 93
Morrison, W. S., 44
Morton, Maj. Desmond, 91
Moscow, 160
Mounsey, Sir George, 6, 12, 20, 21, 22–4, 27–8, 31–5, 137, 139, 173, 191, 199
Munich Agreement, 175, 202
Mussolini, Benito, 37, 108, 118–19, 137, 140, 189; and Chamberlain, 153; withdrawal from Spain, 154, 158, 164, 168, 179–80, 197, 203, 205, 214

Napier, Maj. C. S., 134, 136
Naples, 147
Nationalist Government, xii, 50, 57, 69, 119
Naval control, 31, 53–4, 57, 111, 188
Nazi Party, 110, 143
Negrín, Juan, 69, 170, 176, 195, 200, 202, 204, 207, 208, 209
Neurath, Constantin von, 58, 151
Neva, Russian SS, 133
News Chronicle, 149
New Zealand, 186, 189, 194
Non-Intervention Agreement, 3, 25, 29, 33, 35, 40–3; British trade, 76, 118; French border, 156; recognition, 185, 187, 194; volunteers, 132, 133, 147
Non-Intervention Committee, 3, 38, 40, 41, 196, 199, 202–3, 209, 215; deadlock, 96, 159, 189; withdrawal of volunteers, 133, 135, 147–8, 181
Non-Intervention Control Scheme, 49, 53–4, 59–60; end of naval patrol, 123; volunteers, 142–4, 147; withdrawal of Italy and Germany, 151
Non-intervention International Board, 55–6
Norton, C. J., 137
Nyon Agreement, 101, 102, 117–27, 131, 156, 200; Conference, 192

Ogilvie Forbes, George (later Sir), 5, 6, 8, 68, 70, 145, 182, 189